W9-CDN-300

WHY WE CAN'T SLEEP

WHY WE CAN'T SLEEP

WOMEN'S NEW MIDLIFE CRISIS

ADA CALHOUN

THORNDIKE PRESS
A part of Gale, a Cengage Company

GALE
A Cengage Company

Copyright © 2020 by Ada Calhoun.
Thorndike Press, a part of Gale, a Cengage Company.

ALL RIGHTS RESERVED
Thorndike Press® Large Print Nonfiction.
The text of this Large Print edition is unabridged.
Other aspects of the book may vary from the original edition.
Set in 16 pt. Plantin.

LIBRARY OF CONGRESS CIP DATA ON FILE.
CATALOGUING IN PUBLICATION FOR THIS BOOK
IS AVAILABLE FROM THE LIBRARY OF CONGRESS

ISBN-13: 978-1-4328-8107-8 (hardcover alk. paper)

Published in 2021 by arrangement with Grove Atlantic, Inc.

Printed in Mexico
Print Number: 01   Print Year: 2021

For the middle-aged women of America. You're not imagining it, and it's not just you.

CONTENTS

AUTHOR'S NOTE 9
INTRODUCTION 13

1: Possibilities Create Pressure 45
2: The Doldrums 89
3: The Caregiving Rack 105
4: Job Instability 134
5: Money Panic 158
6: Decision Fatigue 179
7: Single, Childless 203
8: After the Divorce 228
9: Perimenopause. 246
10: The Very Filtered Profile Picture . 276
11: New Narratives 301

APPENDIX: A MIDLIFE CRISIS
    MIXTAPE 323
BIBLIOGRAPHY 325
ACKNOWLEDGMENTS 335
ENDNOTES 341

7

AUTHOR'S NOTE

Most of the women in this book appear here by first name or anonymously. I wanted to help them feel safe speaking with candor about their marriages, their bank accounts, and their night sweats. However, because they are members of Generation X, I can reveal that quite a few are named Jenny, Amy, or Melissa.[1]

Except where relevant, I do not call attention in the book to these women's race, sexuality, or other demographic markers, though they do mirror the makeup of the country. They are single and partnered, mothers and childless, black and white and Asian and Latina, gay and straight, liberal and conservative, evangelical and atheist, and they hail from nearly every state, including Alaska.

I found them through friends, calls sent out from *O Magazine*'s social media accounts, experts in a variety of fields, and

9

online message boards, as well as at professional conferences, playgrounds, doctors' waiting rooms, churches, and bars.

They live in the country, the city, and the suburbs. They work, don't work, did work, will work, and have careers that include photographer, priest, tech executive, lawyer, doctor, teacher, and telephone company manager. They range in dress size from 0 to 28+. Some are having an okay time of middle age; many are struggling in one way or another. Some feel on the verge of, as one said, "blowing it all up."

I did limit my reporting in two ways: first by age, of course. Second: by class. Very poor women in this country bear burdens that are beyond the scope of a book this size. Very rich women have plenty of reality TV shows about them already. I focused on women who, by virtue of being middle class, grew up with reasonable expectations of opportunity and success.

Each chapter opens with a keynote quote. These were lines spoken to me by eleven different women whom I found representative of many others. In this polarized era, I found it reassuring, if also a little depressing, to discover how much we have in common at this age. Regardless of politics, race, and region, American Generation X women share a host of cultural touchstones — from the theme songs for shows like *The Facts of Life* — "When the world never seems / to be living up to your dreams!" — to memories of where we were when the *Challenger* exploded. And we share a daunting set of similar circumstances.

It was an honor to conduct these interviews, which often turned emotional as women discussed their fears and regrets. One woman started crying the moment I asked if I could speak with her about her experience of midlife. I was afraid I'd said something wrong. Was she mad that I'd implied she was middle-aged? No, the tears came from shock, because she'd been feeling so invisible. She said, "No one ever asks about me."

INTRODUCTION

> You come to this place, midlife. You don't know how you got here, but suddenly you're staring fifty in the face. When you turn and look back down the years, you glimpse the ghosts of other lives you might have led. All your houses are haunted by the person you might have been.
> — Hilary Mantel, *Giving Up the Ghost*

One woman I know had everything she'd ever wanted — a loving partner, two children, a career she cared about, even the freedom to make her own schedule — but she still couldn't shake a feeling of profound despair. She spent months getting a baby-sitter for her toddler daughter in the middle of the day, using the time to go alone to noon movies, where she sat in the dark and cried.

A former coworker told me that her impressive LinkedIn profile was misleading. In

13

truth, she was underemployed and for years since her last layoff had been taking one low-paying gig after another. She's unmarried, never had kids, and while that part is okay with her, she has started dreading her upcoming fiftieth birthday, having realized that she will probably never own her own home and has saved nowhere near enough for retirement.

A neighbor with a small army of adorable young children was doing part-time work she enjoyed. Her kids' father was a friendly, hardworking man. She was baffled by the rage she had come to feel toward him. She'd begun to imagine that divorced she might have a better shot at happiness. "I'd leave," she said to me one day when I asked how things were going, "if I had more money."

Another woman told me she had started to fear that she would die alone. Just like her married friends, she'd gotten a good education and had a good job, had made a nice home and was staying in shape. But somehow she'd never found a partner or had children. She woke up in the middle of the night wondering if she should have married her college boyfriend, if she should freeze her eggs, if she should have a baby alone, if she should do more or less online dating, and just how much more she could take of her friends' sons and daughters smiling on social media before she threw her laptop out the window.

An acquaintance told me she'd been having a rough time, working at three jobs as a single mother since her husband left her. Determined to cheer up her family, she planned a weekend trip. After a long week, she started packing at 10:00 p.m., figuring she could catch a few hours of sleep before their 5:00 a.m. departure. She asked her eleven-year-old son to start gathering his stuff. He didn't move. She asked again. Nothing.

"If you don't help," she told him, "I'm going to smash your iPad."

He still didn't move.

As if possessed, she grabbed a hammer and whacked the iPad to pieces.

When she told me this, I thought of how many parents I know who have fantasized or threatened this very thing, and here she had actually done it. I laughed.

"Yeah, my friends think it's a hilarious story, too," she said. "But in reality, it was dark and awful." Her first thought as she stood over the broken glass: "I have to find a good therapist . . . right . . . now."

Since turning forty a couple of years ago, I've been obsessed with women my age and their — our — struggles with money, relationships, work, and existential despair.

Looking for more women to talk to for this book, I called my friend Tara, a successful reporter a few years older than me who grew up in Kansas City. Divorced about a decade ago, she has three mostly grown children and lives on a quiet, leafy street in Washington, DC, with her boyfriend. They recently adopted a rescue dog.

"Hey," I said, happy to have caught her on a rare break from her demanding job. "Do you know anyone having a midlife crisis I could talk to?"

The phone was silent.

Finally, she said, "I'm trying to think of any woman I know who's not."

Today's middle-aged women belong to Generation X and the end of the Baby Boom, which lasted from 1946 to 1964. The Gen X birth years are identified by the Pew Research Center as 1965 to 1980.[1] The name — or anti-name — was popularized by Douglas Coupland's 1991 novel *Generation X: Tales for an Accelerated Culture.* Prior to that, it was the name of an excellent 1970s British punk band featuring Billy

Idol. The band itself was named after a 1964 book containing interviews with British teenagers — on the cover: "What's behind the rebellious anger of Britain's untamed youth? Here — in their own words — is how they really feel about Drugs, Drink, God, Sex, Class, Color and Kicks."

The term "Generation X" came to signify a hazy, as-yet-to-be-determined identity. Over time, that lack of a clear identity became the story. No one knew quite what was up with us, and so we were deemed unknowable. For a while, some experts tried dubbing us "13th Gen," because we were the thirteenth generation post–founding fathers.[2] But after some "Who *Is* Generation X?" cover stories in the 1990s, the culture more or less shrugged and turned away.

In the words of the Pew Research Center, Generation X is "America's neglected 'middle child' . . . a low-slung, straight-line bridge between two noisy behemoths."[3] We are the Jan Brady of generations — overshadowed by the older Boomers (our parents, aunts, uncles) and the younger Millennials (the kids we babysat). By one count, at 55 million, we're a smaller group than Boomers (76 million) or Millennials (62 million),[4] and we will never be the largest cohort in the country. Any day now, when Millennials surpass Boomers, Gen X will still be millions smaller than either.[5] A CBSN report on the generations in January 2019 left out Gen X entirely. That same week, a *Saturday Night Live* game-show skit pitting Millennials against Boomers gave Keenan Thompson this line: "I'm Gen X. I just sit on the sidelines and watch the world burn."[6]

Gen X has arrived in middle age to almost no notice, largely unaware, itself, of being a uniquely star-crossed cohort. "Gen Xers are in 'the prime of their lives' at a particularly divisive and dangerous moment," Boomer marketing expert Faith Popcorn told me.[7] "They have been hit hard financially and dismissed culturally. They have tons of debt. They're squeezed on both sides by children and aging parents. The grim state of adulthood is hitting them hard. If they're exhausted and bewildered, they have every reason to feel that way."

A full-fledged Gen Xer, I was born in 1976. I learned to type on an IBM Selectric. When video games came around, I played *Moon Patrol* on my Atari and *Where in the World Is Carmen San-diego?* on my school's PC. As a teenager, I worked as a printer in a photo lab and wrote hyper-sincere op-eds for the school paper while wearing overalls and Revlon Blackberry lipstick. I had an ur-'90s job, too: I interned at *SPIN* magazine, back when Nirvana was on the cover. (Fact-checking a writer's story on a new singer, one "Mary J. Bilge," I was told by her publicist, "It's *Blige,* honey.")

Whether to identify as Gen X is a decision every woman must make for herself, but I believe that if, like me, you were a kid in the Reagan years, had a Koosh ball, or know what sound a dial-up modem makes, you count.

Generation X women tend to marry in our late twenties, thirties, forties, or not at all; to have our first children in our thirties or forties, or never. We're the first women raised from birth hearing the tired cliché "having it all"[8] — then discovering as adults that it is very hard to have even some of it. That holds true regardless of whether a Generation X woman has a family or not.[9]

Since the 1990s, when the older members of Gen X began having families, we've been pitted against one another by a tedious propaganda campaign about the "mommy wars." This fake debate conceals the truth: that our choices are only part of the story. Context is the other piece, and the context for Gen X women is this: we were an experiment in crafting a higher-achieving, more fulfilled, more well-rounded version of the American woman. In midlife many of us find that the experiment is largely a failure.

We thought we could have both thriving careers and rich home lives and make more and achieve more than our parents, but most of us have gained little if any advantage. Economist Isabel V. Sawhill, of the Brookings Institution, told me that a typical forty-year-old woman in America now makes $36,000 a year working full-time. After child care, rent, food, and taxes, that leaves only about $1,000 for everything else.[10] Even women who make much more may feel uneasy about their financial future, stunned by how hard it is just getting through the week, or disappointed by how few opportunities seem to come their way.

We diminish our whole generation when we dismiss these women's complaints as unreasonable griping. Societal, historical, and economic trends have conspired to make many women's passage into middle age a crucible of anxieties — and to make us envy one another rather than realize we are all in the same leaky boat. I hope this book will help us hear women's concerns not as whining but as a corrective to the misleading rhetoric extolling an American dream that has not come within reach for

20

us — and likely will not for our children.

Some might argue that American Generation X women have it easy compared with women in other countries or of other generations. Boomers and Millennials may claim their own, perhaps even worse, cases.

"No, *my* generation was the first who were told they could have it all!" one Boomer woman said when presented with this book's premise.

The concept did emerge in the Boomers' generation, but it wasn't until Gen X arrived that it was a mainstream expectation. Boomers deserve full credit for blazing trails while facing unchecked sexism and macroaggression and for trying to raise children without giving up their own dreams. But Gen Xers entered life with "having it all" not as a bright new option but as a mandatory social condition.

"I'm supposed to have it all, too!" a Millennial woman said. "We have it just as bad!"

Millennials, certainly, have reached adulthood with crushing student loan debt, unprecedented social and economic inequality, poisonous political polarization, and a rapidly changing world with many industries in flux. But, by the time Millennials were entering the workforce, the illusion of infinite possibility had finally come under broad attack, giving way to more realistic expectations.

With all due respect to our elders and juniors, when it came to the "having it all" virus we all caught, Gen X was infected with a particularly virulent strain.

That said, Boomers and Millennials, sadly, are likely to find a lot to relate to in this book. I hope that younger Millennials will absorb useful cautionary tales and that Boomers will not be too dismayed by how far we have not come.

Put simply: having more options has not necessarily led to greater happiness or satisfaction. "By many objective measures, the lives of women in the United States have improved over the past thirty-five years," wrote the authors of an analysis of General Social Survey data a decade ago, as Generation X entered middle age. "Yet we show that measures of subjective well-being indicate that women's happiness has declined both absolutely and relative to men."[11]

This observation is often cited as proof that second-wave feminism was foolish — that if women had only stayed in the home they would be happier. How reductive that is. The truth is that we've never really tried what those feminists proposed. Yes, women went into the workforce, but without any significant change to gender roles at home, to paid-leave laws, to anything that would make the shift feasible. If you make a new law but don't enforce or fund it, do you get to call the law misguided?

In 2017, another major study found that the two biggest stressors for women were work and children, with a compounding effect on those having both.[12] We bear financial responsibilities that men had in the old days while still saddled with traditional caregiving duties. We generally incur this double whammy precisely while hitting peak stress in both our careers and child-raising — in our forties, at an age when most of our mothers and grandmothers were already empty nesters.

One in four middle-aged American women is on antidepressants.[13] Nearly 60 percent of those born between 1965 and 1979 describe themselves as stressed — thirteen points higher than Millennials.[14] Three in four women born in 1965–1977 "feel anxious about their finances."[15]

For a while, I thought only corporate strivers were having a hard time managing. Then I started hearing the same angst in the voices of women with all variations of work and home life. I was shocked when a friend whom I'd never seen rattled by anything told me that in her forties she'd become so consumed by caring for her two little kids, full-time job, side hustles, marriage, and ailing father that she worried constantly about money and couldn't remember the last time she'd slept well.

As I've spoken to women around the country, I've marveled at how similarly they talk about their lives:

Over a diner breakfast, a successful single woman in Texas told me she thought she'd have a husband and kids by now. She asked, "What did I do wrong?"

While her baby slept on her chest, a married mother of three in Oregon said she thought she'd have a career by now. "What did I do wrong?" she asked.

While scientific study of aging has increased in the past decade, the research still often skips middle age.[16] Where research is done on the middle years, the focus is typically on men. The rare middle-aged-woman book usually addresses Boomers' work disappointment or marital disillusionment[17] or tries to make light of physical signs of aging, with emphasis on our necks.

The term "midlife crisis"[18] is usually attributed to psychoanalyst Elliott Jaques, who used it in a 1965 journal article exploring how the creative expression of male artists — Dante, Goethe, Beethoven, Dickens — often changes in quality and content when they pass the age of thirty-five. "Working through the midlife crisis," he writes, "calls for a reworking through infantile depression, but with mature insight into death."[19]

In the 1970s, developmental psychologist Daniel Levinson claimed that about 80 percent of the men he studied experienced "tumultuous struggles within the self and with the external world" in midlife.[20] "Every aspect of their lives comes into question," he wrote. "And they are horrified by much that is revealed." They may find that they've given up creative dreams or sacrificed their values for a stable income — a theme taken up in countless hits in popular fiction and cinema, from the 1955 novel *The Man in the Gray Flannel Suit* to the 1996 movie *Jerry Maguire.*

As rendered in popular culture, the stereotypical male midlife crisis involves busting stuff up — mostly marriages but also careers, norms, reputations. Panic may commence when a man starts losing his hair, resulting in a frenzy to unearth college vinyl. Treatment: regular application of younger women and brightly colored motor vehicles.

There have been any number of movies and books about such men — some even played by actors who are not Michael Douglas. The Woody Allen–*American Beauty*–*Sideways* industrial complex has given us dramas in which women provide a reliably boring backdrop — the shrill wife, the tedious aunt, the sad sister — to men's life-affirming hunger for the passionate life, which materializes with suspicious frequency in the shape of a teenage girl.

A middle-aged woman's midlife crisis does, I know, pose a dramaturgical problem. In my observation — and as many experts I've spoken with have affirmed — women's crises tend to be quieter than men's. Sometimes a woman will try something spectacular — a big affair, a new career, a "she shed" in the backyard — but more often she sneaks her suffering in around the edges of caretaking and work.

From the outside, no one may notice anything amiss. Women might drain a bottle of wine while watching TV alone, use CBD edibles to decompress, or cry every afternoon in the pickup lane at school. Or, in the middle of the night, they might lie wide awake, eyes fixed on the ceiling. There has yet to be a blockbuster movie centered on a woman staring out her car's windshield and sighing.

So I understand why some people consider "crisis" too extreme a word for high-functioning women experiencing what can look like merely malaise or a funk or a rough patch. When I appeared with prominent academic Susan Krauss Whitbourne on a panel this year, she said that there was no scientific evidence for a predictable breakdown in midlife and that calling midlife stress a "midlife crisis" was "an excuse for bad behavior.

"If you're depressed in midlife," she said, "there may be many reasons for this, the least of which is your 'age.' "[21] And yet, even Whitbourne granted that Generation X is a particularly morose bunch and that women of this generation were "very stressed out."

I do take her point. And can we really say women are in "crisis" if, despite how they feel inside, they're able to crank out well-structured PowerPoint presentations and arrange elaborate gift baskets for teachers on the last day of school?

My friend's sister, Jenny, a mother of three employed in the STEM field before a recent layoff due to federal budget cuts, said she didn't think she'd had a midlife crisis. Then she politely added: "Or does the tanking of my marriage, bankruptcy, foreclosure, and a move to LA after twenty-six years in Seattle following my aneurysm constitute a midlife crisis? If so, you can interview me."

When I asked my friend Aimee, who lives in Baltimore, if she was having a midlife crisis, she said no. Then she said, "Wait, like a 'What the hell have I done with my life and who am I?' sort of freak-out? I am definitely having one of those."

While that's probably an apt description of what many of the more than two hundred women I talked to for this book are undergoing, I still prefer the term "midlife crisis." I like it because it makes what's happening sound like the big deal I believe it to be. In my experience, Gen X women spend lots of time minimizing the importance of their uncomfortable or confusing feelings. They often tell me that they are embarrassed to even bring them up. Some of the unhappiest women I spoke with, no matter how depressed or exhausted they were, apologized for "whining." Almost every one of them also described herself as "lucky."

And that's true enough. We are fortunate in so many ways. America today, in the global scheme of things, offers us far more opportunity than our grandmothers or mothers had. Although many women are trying to make it on minimum-wage jobs (and have a crisis not specific to middle age), the overall wage gap is closing. Men do more at home. There's more pushback against sexism. Insert your "reason why we don't deserve to feel lousy" here. The complaints of well-educated middle- and upper-middle-class women are easy to disparage — as a temporary setback, a fixable hormonal imbalance, or #FirstWorldProblems.

Fine. Let's agree that Generation X women shouldn't feel bad.[22]

So why do we?

When I started working on this project, I knew I felt lousy, but I didn't yet fully understand why. I just knew that I was having a terrible, horrible, no-good, very bad June. Cue the 1984 Bananarama hit "Cruel Summer."[23]

I said, often, that I was very lucky and had no right to complain.

I'd been with my husband for seventeen years. Our eleven-year-old son had been accepted into a great public middle school. My twenty-three-year-old stepson was looking at physical therapy grad programs.

Workwise, I felt better than ever. I'd just

published a new book and it had run the table on press coverage — the *Today Show*! The *Washington Post*! No less than *Star* called it a Hot Book.

From the outside and on social media, I knew my life looked enviable.

So why was I miserable? That summer I woke up every day at 4:00 a.m., plagued with self-doubt and anxiety. Lying there, I thought of all the things I really should do or absolutely should not have done until either I'd cycled through my full list of regrets or it was time to get up.

Before even opening my eyes, I would see a number: $20,000. That's how much credit card debt we had. I walked around under a cloud of worry. That spring, thinking we had money coming in, we'd taken a family vacation to the Grand Canyon and done some home repairs. Three freelance gigs that were supposed to keep us comfortable until the fall and pay off our credit card debt had evaporated. One boss let me go right after I delivered what I'd thought was a completed project. Another replaced me with someone else. A third went AWOL. And now it was summer, the worst time to find work. We had only a month's worth of cash on hand and it was disappearing fast.

After nearly a decade of freelancing, I

began applying for job-jobs. When I'd left the full-time workforce following a layoff in 2009, I'd been making six figures, plus full benefits. Now I was looking for anything that would give me a steady paycheck and — dare to dream — insurance. Health insurance for my family costs us $1,186 a month. We have the cheapest "bronze" plan, with a deductible of several thousand dollars a year. (And, again, I'm lucky; a third to half of middle-aged people in this country go without necessary health care because of cost.)[24]

I'd always told myself that returning to a full-time job was my "fallback plan."

Oh, fine! I imagined saying to the corporate world. *You can have me!*

Only, now that I was willing to fall back, no one was there to catch me.

As I frantically applied for jobs and fellowships, I felt like I was living in the children's book *Are You My Mother?* I sent out dozens of résumés and was called in for two interviews. One was for a teaching job paying $600 for a six-week class. I took it, even though, between the time I spent prepping for the class and the time I spent marking papers, this worked out to less per hour than I'd made as an office manager when I was a college student.

31

The other interview was for a full-time job paying far less than the one I'd held fifteen years earlier. It would be a huge demotion, working for a company that seemed not very stable. But what the hell, right? I knew the industry was in a bad place, and a job's a job. The interview went well. On the way home, I wrestled with my hopes and dreams. I decided that I would go ahead and accept, overqualified though I was, shaky though the workplace seemed.

I didn't even get a callback.

I resolved to broaden my search, explore all my options.

Options. We still have them in midlife, but they can start to seem so abstract. Yes, I could go to graduate school and get a doctorate, but where would I find the tuition? I could switch careers — therapist? Zamboni driver? — but at this stage of life, do I really want to start from the bottom, surrounded by twenty-year-olds? If I went on an *Eat, Pray, Love* walkabout, who would pick up the kid from school?

"Every decision you make in life sends you off down a path that could turn out to be a wrong one," writes the British musician Viv Albertine in her memoir of midlife. "A couple of careless decisions somewhere along the line, that's all it takes to waste years — but then you can't creep along being so cautious that you don't have adventures. It's difficult to get the balance right."[25]

"Difficult" is an understatement. How do you know when it's time to give up a dream? How do you know if you're like one of those success stories, the type who never surrendered in spite of everyone telling them they were deluding themselves, or if you're a sap who needs to stop kidding herself, be realistic, and grow up already?

As my family enjoyed the summer, I brooded. I was sure that my career was over, mortally embarrassed to be in debt, and I couldn't stop agonizing about what to do. My thoughts were dark:

> If only I'd never gone freelance.
> If only we'd stockpiled cash for a rainy
>   day.
> If only my husband were a day trader.
> We were dumb to take that vacation.

Each morning, I looked in the mirror and saw a very tired middle-aged person — no longer young, no longer vibrant. I was forty-one, but didn't look, to myself, two years older than thirty-nine; I looked a century older. There were deep wrinkles around my

33

eyes. My skin was ashen. The skin under my arms was loose. I'd been hearing "In middle age, you're more likely to gain weight around the middle of the body" for a while; and now I knew what the magazines were talking about. I had widened, and I did not like it.

Some of this was vanity, but I also felt disoriented: *Whose body was this?*

Oh, and my very first mammogram showed an "irregularity." Two ultrasounds, a biopsy, more than $1,000 in co-pays, and weeks of dread later, it proved to be nothing. But the experience felt like the first rattle of a car ready to be traded in.

And the periods! Sometimes they'd be two months apart, sometimes two weeks. Sometimes light. Sometimes so heavy I'd bleed through a tampon, a pad, and jeans. The cramps were apocalyptic. I found myself emotionally erratic, too, in a way that seemed out of proportion to the money and work pressure. I'd slam drawers, so irritated I could hardly look at my husband. A day or two a month, I would cry so hard it was as if someone had died.

I went to the gynecologist, who said nothing was physically wrong with me. She prescribed Serenol, Swedish flower pollen delivered via online subscription at $40 a

34

month for my mood, and evening primrose oil for breast aches, and she encouraged me to take a multivitamin with calcium and vitamin D. If none of that worked, she said, we could try antidepressants — something I resisted because while on them a decade earlier I'd lost my sex drive, gained twenty pounds, and didn't want to write.

The supplements did not seem to be helping, though I took them every day and tried to convince myself that they were effective. Meanwhile, I followed every bit of reasonable advice the books and internet offered for someone hoping to feel better on a budget. I went for long walks outside in nature, took the stairs instead of the elevator, drank lots of water, cut back on alcohol and caffeine, ate vegetables, wore sunscreen, packed my lunches, planked.

I woke up every morning and showered and took care of my kid and went to the dentist and bought groceries and listened to my husband talk about his day and helped the neighbor girl with her high school applications and plucked my eyebrows. I read the books about how midlife was an opportunity in disguise. I watched TED talks and listened to advice shows.

"So," my husband said, sounding distressed. "You're a podcast person now?"

After doing everything I was supposed to do, I felt a little better, maybe? But there was still the money fear and the feeling that my career was over and the bone tiredness.

There were flickers of joy, particularly when friends came over. One night a friend texted me: "I need an OUTING."

"Want a beer?" I wrote back.

"YES," she replied.

Minutes later, she was at my place, telling me about the fight she'd just had with her husband and how much pressure she felt being the primary breadwinner, her own ambitions often delayed to make way for her family's needs. She told me that everyone at her job was younger and that after many years of being happy with how she looked, she'd started googling things like "noninvasive procedures."

"I haven't shot anything into my face — yet," she said. "I'm still wondering if it's better to go no-makeup-don't-care or lots-of-makeup-making-an-effort."

She thought spending money to look younger might pay off in the long run, because it could keep her from being pushed out by the Millennials angling for her job. The topper: she concluded she couldn't afford to have anything done.

What I didn't know that summer is that

historic forces have been at work in the lives of Generation X women:

We were born into a bleak economy and grew up during a boom in crime, abuse, and divorce. We were raised "pre-specialness," which meant not only no participation trophies but also that we were shielded far less than children today from the uglier sides of life.

We started our job hunts in the early 1990s recession, which was followed by a "jobless recovery."[26] If you were born later into Generation X, you might have entered the workforce around the 1999ish stock market peak, but then the tech bubble started to burst, landing you in the 2001 recession. Yes, the economy began to recover, and by the mid-2000s you might have taken advantage of easy-to-get mortgages, but then in 2008 the sky fell.

Now, in middle age, Gen X has more debt than any other generation[27] — a whopping 82 percent more than Boomers and about $37,000 more than the national consumer average.[28]

Compared with other generations, we also have less saved — and women have less than men. At the same time, we face a much higher cost of living than Boomers did at our age, particularly for essentials like housing.[29]

Generation X marks the end of the American dream of ever-increasing prosperity. We are downwardly mobile, with declining job stability. It used to be that each generation could expect to do better than their parents. New research confirms that Generation X won't.

Many of us have delayed marriage and children into our thirties and forties.[30] This means that we are likely to find ourselves taking care of parents in decline at the same time that we are caring for little children — and, by the way, being urged to ask for raises and lean in at work.

This stress is compounded by the hormonal chaos and associated mood swings of the years leading up to menopause. In a cruel twist, the symptoms of hormonal fluctuation are exacerbated by stress, while the symptoms in turn raise stress levels.

Meanwhile, we are bombarded with catastrophic breaking news alerts, social media's curated images of others' success, and nonstop work obligations — not to mention phone calls, texts, and email. Workers in upper management today spend an average of seventy-two hours a week making themselves available to work.[31]

Our lives can begin to feel like the latter seconds of a game of Tetris, where the descending pieces pile up faster and faster.

Worse, at this hectic age, we have to make many of the toughest decisions of our lives: *Is it time to give up on starting my own business? Is it time to switch careers? Should I get married? Should I get divorced? Am I done having kids? Will I ever have kids? Where should the kids go to school? Do I put my parent with Alzheimer's into a nursing home, and, if so, who's going to pay for it? When it comes to realizing my dreams, is it too late?*

Being beset with these hard questions while dealing with all of the pressures of midlife is like coming upon an emergency situation for which you're untrained. Your performance is unlikely to be maximally efficient.

In this, Gen Xers are ill-served by our default cynicism.

When we saw the 1989 film *Say Anything* in our youth, kickboxing romantic hero Lloyd Dobler's dinner-table speech, something many Gen Xers can recite verbatim, may have seemed profound: "I don't want to sell anything bought or processed, or buy anything sold or processed, or process anything sold, bought, or processed, or repair anything sold, bought, or processed." This proposed wisdom has not aged well.

Dobler's "unifying philosophy was adorable and original and so crazy it might work in 1989," a friend said to me the other day, "but now that guy is sitting on your futon playing Grand Theft Auto in a Pavement T-shirt."

The year I was born, Gail Sheehy published the mega best-seller *Passages,* which took seriously both men's and women's midlife reckoning with their mortality and described predictable phases of life in the manner of the terrible twos, with tags including "Trying 20s" and "Forlorn 40s."

It was a new spin on the influential psychologist Erik Erikson's work with what he described as eight psychosocial life stages. He said that infancy is about the tension between trust and mistrust. If you complete that phase successfully, you achieve the basic virtue of hope. Your adolescent years are a crisis of identity versus role confusion. Ages eighteen to forty are about intimacy versus isolation. At issue from ages forty to sixty-five, according to Erikson, is avoiding stagnation, with the goal being an investment in society that leads to "generativity," shaping a legacy and having a lasting impact on the world.

According to Sheehy, the years between thirty-five and forty-five are the "Deadline Decade," during which people might feel they are running out of time. She argued that Erikson's writing on the stages of growth applied only to men: "If the struggle for men in midlife comes down to having to defeat stagnation through generativity, I submit that the comparable task for women is to transcend dependency through self-declaration."[32]

When Sheehy wrote a new introduction to *Passages* in 2006, she acknowledged that Gen X women were a whole new ballgame: "There are still broad, general stages of adulthood, and predictable passages between them. But the timetable has stretched by at least ten years, and counting. Age norms for major life events have become highly elastic. Since there is no longer a standard life cycle, people are left to customize their own."[33] Women of this generation, she said, are living "cyclical lives that demand they start over again and again."

Gen X women had sky-high expectations for themselves. The contrast between our "you can be anything" indoctrination and the stark realities encountered in midlife — when you might, despite your best efforts, not be able to find a partner or get pregnant or save for retirement or own your own home or find a job with benefits — has made us feel like failures at the exact moment when we most require courage. It takes our bodies longer to recover from a night of drinking and it takes our spirits longer to bounce back from rejection. We may wind up asking questions like the one my friend posed to me the other night: "Do you think my life is ever going to be good again?"

"You may or may not run out of money," another woman said. "But you will definitely run out of time."

As dark as all this may sound, I promise that there is cause for hope.

When I told someone recently that I was working on this book, he said, "That must be depressing, talking to hundreds of women about how miserable they are."

Actually, I've found it the opposite. The project has made me feel less alone, and it has given me clarity about my life and my friends' lives. I see now, finally, a way out of our crisis. It begins with facing up to our lives as they really are, letting go of the expectations we had for ourselves growing up, and finishes with finding a viable support system and realizing that this stage of life doesn't last forever. The truth is, when you look at what we were up against as a generation, we are doing better than we had any reason to expect.

1
POSSIBILITIES CREATE PRESSURE

"If you said you wanted to be a nurse, everyone would say, 'Why not a doctor?' "

When Kelly was a little girl growing up in the 1970s, she believed that girls could do anything. The daughter of blue-collar parents in the northern New Jersey suburbs, Kelly was the first in her immediate family to finish college.

Kelly and her friends played a game called Mary Tyler Moore, inspired by the 1970s TV show. They would play-act being spunky, independent women living in the city on their own. Rather than pretending to be a cowgirl or a princess, Kelly would be "this young, working single woman who was out to conquer everything." She loved the theme song: "You're going to make it after *allllll!*" And she loved the cap toss. And she loved the way that Mary found her tribe at work.

Kelly went through school in the first flush of Title IX, the federal law passed in 1972 that said boys and girls must be treated equally when it came to federally funded educational programs and activities. No longer could schools legally discriminate when it came to financial assistance, recruitment, admissions, or athletics.[1] The playing field would be more level, and girls, everyone predicted, would flourish.

The thwarted ambitions of Kelly's own mother raised the stakes: "She was living through my life. There was always the fear: what if she was disappointed?"

This was happening all over the country. First-wave feminists had fought for the right to vote at the turn of the nineteenth century. Second-wave feminists who'd been fighting for women's rights starting in the early 1960s were now raising their daughters to receive the torch and to reach new levels of success: becoming doctors, not nurses; professors, not grade-school teachers; CEOs, not secretaries. If our grandparents worked the land and our parents toiled in middle management, we would get the corner office — and, of course, have a family, a nice house, and a social life. Echoing in our ears was the second-wave mother's mantra: "Girls can grow up to be anything

46

— even president!"

One midwestern woman I know wanted to go to school locally, but her own mother, who hadn't been allowed to go away to school herself, insisted her daughter leave her home state for college. The family got a second mortgage to pay the out-of-state tuition. "I spent all spring and then thirteen hours in a car driving there trying to figure out how to say I didn't want to go," the woman, now in her late forties, recalled. "My poor mother. The minute we started unpacking — which she was so excited about — I burst into tears."

"A lot of the media at that time," Kelly told me, "said, 'You can bring home the bacon, and fry it up . . .' " Kelly hummed the notorious commercial for Enjoli perfume[2] that many of us still keep in our psychic filing cabinet along with "Mikey likes it!"

In the 1980 Enjoli ad, set to the 1962 hit "I'm a Woman,"[3] a blonde woman sings that she can bring home the bacon and fry it up in a pan — and never let you forget you're a man. In the course of one day — during which her perfume, we are assured, never fades — she wears a business suit in which to make money, a collared shirt and pants in which to cook, and a cocktail dress and sultry pout in which to seduce. Tagline: "The eight-hour perfume for your twenty-four-hour woman."

So successful is the woman in the ad that while she is reading a book to off-camera children, an off-camera man's voice says, "Tonight *I'm* gonna cook for the kids." She responds with a coy, pleasantly surprised smile. I guess on this one special day she gets to be a twenty-three-hour woman.

Kelly, like many young girls watching that ad, saw the actress going from office to kitchen to bedroom not as an absurd, regressive fantasy directed at men to make them buy their wives Enjoli perfume but as a blueprint for a full life. *Looks doable,* thought many young women. *I'll go to work and come home and make dinner and be sexy the whole time, just the way I doubled up on AP classes while serving as captain of the volleyball team and editor of the yearbook and teasing my bangs with just the right amount of hair spray.*

When Geraldine Ferraro ran for vice president in 1984, Kelly was enthusiastic but not surprised — because of course women were smashing glass ceilings. It was only a matter of time, she thought, before women ran companies and eventually the country, too.

The opening montage of 1987's *Baby Boom* showed shoulder-padded women proudly marching into corporate offices. In the film *Working Girl* (1988), Melanie Griffith's character says to Harrison Ford's: "I've got a head for business and a bod' for sin. Is there anything wrong with that?"[4] (Flustered, he says no.)

Kelly and her friends dreamed big, and they went on to higher education. Supplied with both heads and bods, they assumed that in addition to conquering the business world they would one day acquire their own Harrison Fords.

Post–*Mary Tyler Moore Show,* the TV show *Murphy Brown,* starring a sardonic Candice Bergen, became Kelly's lodestar. When Brown became a single mother in the 1992 season 4 finale, while holding down a powerful newsroom job, Kelly again got the message. Women could have a life rich in both love and achievement. All you needed to make it all work was a good work ethic, supportive friends, and maybe a wacky house painter-turned-nanny named Eldin to watch your baby while you worked.

This was the plan. But once Kelly became an adult, reality intervened. While at college in Washington, DC, she started noticing that the promised land was not quite as easy to reach as she'd been told it would be. One of the main problems in making dreams come true? They cost money.

Halfway through college, Kelly realized she would need a master's degree to achieve what she wanted to in the field of psychology. Her parents wouldn't pay for more school. She was already accumulating a lot of debt from her undergraduate degree and was "terrified," she said, of ending up broke and having to move back home. She resolved to get a job and pay off what she owed. Later, she would find a way to get her advanced degree and make a career change.

She couldn't. Kelly graduated into a bad economy and had a hard time finding any job. After a long search, she wound up settling for an administrative position with scant opportunity for growth. As soon as she was able to switch, she moved to the insurance industry, then the field of human resources. She worked long hours and felt rather less than fulfilled, but it was steady work. Still, the grad school money never materialized.

A few years of dating later, she married at twenty-eight. She had her first daughter at thirty-one, at which point she stopped working full-time. She had another baby two years later, and planned to return to work once both children were in school. Two years before that could happen, though, when her younger child was three, the family was in a car wreck. Her daughter suffered a traumatic brain injury. There was a lot of caregiving to do, and there was never a question of Kelly's husband staying home.

Many women told me their careers were derailed by family responsibilities or medical problems — whether their own or a family member's. For our generation, the odds of having a child diagnosed with an intellectual disability or a developmental delay have increased. The number of teenagers thought to have attention deficit disorders went up by 43 percent between 2003 and 2011.[5] Autism spectrum disorder diagnoses surged from ten per ten thousand children in the year 2000 to fifty per ten thousand by 2010.

Even parents of children without this sort of difficulty can struggle to find good support. One single mother told me she returned from a business trip and discovered that her babysitter had neglected her baby; he had developed a severe rash. She didn't want to travel for work after that, and a few months later she was laid off for this lack of commitment.

"Plenty of women saw themselves in Dan Quayle's description of Murphy as 'a character who supposedly epitomizes today's intelligent, highly paid, professional woman,'" wrote Caryn James in 1992 in the New York Times.[6] "They were able to think, 'Murphy Brown, c'est moi,' until it occurred to them to ask, 'Where's Eldin?'"

That could be a bumper sticker for our generation: "Where's Eldin?"

Kelly had another child, who is now ten. She has never returned to work.

"I haven't worked full-time for almost twenty-two years," said Kelly, sounding embarrassed. Now that she no longer has young children at home and her injured daughter is stable, she knows she could go back, and she knows she probably has at least fifteen or twenty years left before retirement. But who will hire her? She's been out of the business world long enough that she no longer has viable connections, and she didn't love the HR industry in the first place.

"How do you go back, and what do you do, and is it going to be satisfying?" she said. "I also worry that I'm going to be too old. I have a sister-in-law who's two years older than I am. She's had a career, but she got laid off. It was really bad. She's had a really hard time finding permanent employment. And she feels it's her age, so she took the year she graduated off her résumé."

Kelly fantasizes about doing something creative. She and her husband have partially written a book about their experience raising a disabled child, though they haven't made much headway on edits or trying to get it published.

She says she's lucky to have the chance to think about these things, not to have to go to an office every day and support the family. Yet deep down, she considers her husband the luckier one. He gets to be off on his own all day. He has downtime during which he can go out to lunch or daydream. She feels she can never catch up to her own thoughts, because her more routine obligations — doctor appointments and driving the kids around, filling out forms and cleaning and cooking — never let up. "There are times," she says, "when I get *resentful*."[7]

Kelly's oldest daughter, when she was about eleven or twelve, said to Kelly one day while they were driving in the car: "No offense, but I don't want to be a stay-at-home mom."

Kelly replied: "I'm not offended. I want you to do whatever makes you happy. And if you want to have a job and be a mom, that's fine. If you don't want to be a mom, that's fine. If you don't want to get married, that's fine. Whatever you want to make you happy, that's all I want for you: to be healthy and happy."

She's given her daughter the gift of lower expectations, but she still can't permit herself the same. Every day, Kelly wakes up feeling that she should be looking for a job, writing a book, being more productive. And every day she worries that even if everyone rallied in support of her dreams now, it would be too late.

Deborah Luepnitz, a Boomer psychotherapist practicing in Philadelphia, said, "What I see in my Gen X patients is total exhaustion. They feel guilty for complaining, because it's wonderful to have had choices that our mothers didn't have, but choices don't make life easier. Possibilities create pressure."

We kept hearing again and again that we could be anything we wanted to be. We had supportive mothers insisting we would accomplish more than they had. Title IX made sure our after-school classes were as good as the boys'. We saw women on television who had families and fun careers. So, if we happened to fail, why was that? The only thing left to blame was ourselves.

One day in an email after we'd met for lunch, my friend Caroline Miller, a Boomer who started in journalism as a newspaper reporter in 1976 and went on to be editor in chief of *Seventeen* and *New York* magazine, said, "It seems unfair that the wave I got to ride through my forties, not just the economic boom but the exhilaration of finding our way as 'liberated' women, isn't there anymore. Exceeding expectations was so much easier when there basically were no expectations. Whatever you managed to do was more of a win. It's as if the idea of stress hadn't been invented yet when I was your age."

If I had to pick an onset date for Generation X stress, I'd put it in the mid-1970s. Nostalgic tributes to the '70s and '80s usually ignore the fact that in many ways it was a rough time to be a kid. Crime spiked. The economy tanked. There was an "infinite tolerance" policy when it came to bullying and a conviction that kids should fight their own battles.

One Gen X friend from New Jersey recalls her high school guidance counselor telling her that she had been "raised wrong" and was going nowhere. Another friend tells me her counselor had a public meltdown in their Philly school's lunchroom — yelling at the kids that none of them would amount to anything.

When I hear stories like that, it makes me glad that my own school administrators were largely AWOL. My friend Asia had what for the time was an extended conversation with our principal. This was their exchange:

"Asia, why did you punch that boy?"

"Because he was picking on little Eric Lee."

"Oh," the principal said. "That's okay then. Good job standing up for your friend. When you go out there, tell everyone I yelled at you."

That was a good part of the laissez-faire approach to children back then: the freedom. A bad part: without adult protection, we were more vulnerable to harassment.

At my middle school, the boys made a sport out of snapping girls' bras in the hallway. Plenty of times that happened in front of teachers, and no one ever did anything about it.

Armed with the catchphrase "Stranger danger!" — and perhaps a key sticking out from between clenched fingers on especially menacing blocks — we roamed free. We were known as latchkey kids, and we were given independence early, even though at lunch every day, we were confronted with other children's photos on our milk cartons, accompanied by the caption: missing. The image of Etan Patz, who lived not far from me in New York City and had vanished in 1979 at the age of six, spread nationwide. Adults told us that he'd probably been kidnapped and murdered (many years later, this was proved to have been true). Back then, nothing was sugarcoated — except our food.

As a little girl growing up in the outskirts of Springfield, Illinois, in the 1980s, Valarie loved riding her bike, playing in the corn and soybean fields across the street, climbing trees in the sparse woods, watching the three TV channels on a giant wood-console-encased TV set, and reading Stephen King books.

Gen X childhoods were lived in a haze of secondhand smoke, including in restaurants and on planes. We played without realizing what peril we were in. Some of Valarie's fondest memories of her childhood are of riding in the back of a pickup truck, biking with no helmet, and lying out in the sun with no sunscreen. (One woman I know said another name for Gen X could be "the Coppertone Generation.")

"My parents would leave me in the car all the time," said Valarie. "Can you imagine leaving a kid in the car now? Stores literally have signs reminding you to check and make sure you didn't leave your child."

When Valarie was ten, her father left her mother. She says she believes it was, in part, because her mother was overweight in spite of endless dieting with Sweet n' Low and Tab — which Valarie thinks led to her own battles with food.

Financially, divorce devastated many Gen X children and their mothers.[8] When a couple divorced in the 1980s, children almost always went to live with their mother, and a child's household income dropped dramatically — according to one study, by an average of 42 percent.[9] While some female-led households eventually came back strong, many never recovered anything like their former wealth.[10]

Meanwhile, the country faced stagflation, Watergate, gas station lines, steel mills closing, and President Jimmy Carter wearing a sweater on TV, encouraging austerity.[11]

"Rampant divorce, a wobbly economy, soaring crime rates, and swinging-singles culture," wrote Jean M. Twenge in *Generation Me,*[12] "made the 1970s a difficult time to be a kid." Children of divorce might become mini confessors for their parents' anxieties and dating problems — treated not so much as kids but as small people who could hear and see with adult ears and eyes.

The emergence of Russia in the post-2016 headlines has given many members of Generation X flashbacks to the aggressively anti-Russian entertainment of our childhoods. In 1983's *War Games,* a teen hacker played by Matthew Broderick has to save the planet from a thermonuclear war that he inadvertently started when he broke into a military computer. That same year, 100 million people tuned in to watch the ABC TV movie *The Day After,* in which a nuclear war between the Soviet Union and the United States leaves millions dead and society in ruins.[13] In 1984's *Red Dawn,* Russian and Cuban soldiers invade a Colorado town and start killing or reeducating the townspeople. A small group of young people — played by, among others, Patrick Swayze, Charlie Sheen, Lea Thompson, and Jennifer Grey — mount a brutal armed resistance.

One Gen X woman told me that as a little girl she wrote to President Ronald Reagan to beg him to avert nuclear war. By return mail she received, in place of reassurance, an age-inappropriate packet of detailed information about the nuclear threat.

Until 1991, it was a major theme of our newscasts and our entertainment that with no warning we could all be incinerated. The partial meltdown at the Three Mile Island reactor in Pennsylvania in 1979 and the Chernobyl nuclear power plant explosion in 1986 helped make nuclear destruction feel plausible. Psychological studies in the 1980s found that the threat of nuclear war led to high anxiety in children. The silver lining, according to one journal article, was that we didn't stew for long, because: "cynicism and apathy set in rapidly."[14]

That, and we came to assume that the very survival of the planet was iffy.

"Every night," Valarie told me, "I would send out a whispered request to the universe that the apocalypse wouldn't happen. Sometimes I tried reverse psychology." Convinced that the universe would deny her what she said she wanted, she would murmur, lying there in the dark, "I hope the world gets blown up."

When it came to TV and movies, the problem was not just that a lot of it was terrifying but also that we consumed so *much* of it. I started watching TV when I got home from school and kept at it until bedtime. For me those years are a blur of *Inspector*

Gadget, The Price Is Right, Head of the Class, MacGyver, Cheers, Family Ties, Family Feud, Knight Rider, Night Court, The Jeffersons, Laverne and Shirley, Small Wonder, The Woody Woodpecker Show, and *Benson* — with a bit of *Reading Rainbow* thrown in for culture. The saddest day of the week was Sunday, when the only things broadcasting were football, church shows, and news.

According to the Gen X "mind-set list," "The higher their parents' educational level, the more likely they were to come home at 4 p.m. to an empty house — except for the microwave and MTV."[15] When it launched on August 1, 1981, with "Video Killed the Radio Star" by the Buggles, MTV would become always-on, must-see TV for those in middle or high school at the time. Friends of mine who grew up outside major urban centers in places where MTV wasn't widely available (in one place I know of, the town banned it as satanic), VHS tapes of *120 Minutes* were passed around like notes about where to meet after school.

This was before the age of DVR and Netflix, so much of what we saw was advertising. Research from 2017 found that 83 percent of Gen X — more than any other generation — trust ads they see on TV.[16] Gen X has been described as both repulsed by materialism and deeply materialistic, and there may be something to that. Those of us whose formative years were the 1980s were steeped in a bath of greed and gluttony: the yuppies' BMW and Armani fetishes, sports car posters, *Wall Street*. We may have rebelled against it later by buying secondhand clothes, but we're inculcated, deep down, with wanting a lot of *stuff*.

I wonder, again, whether our acquisitiveness is not a sign of bad character so much as the inevitable result of a *Clockwork Orange*–style conditioning campaign. Every second of the day, no matter what else was going on, my brain was looping: "It's Slinky! It's Slinky! For fun, it's a wonderful toy! It's Slinky! It's Slinky! It's fun for a girl and a boy!"[17] I will never, ever forget that chocolate is scrunchous when it crunches, that Mentos is the "fresh maker," and that only I can prevent forest fires. Until I die, my bologna will bear the first name O-S-C-A-R.

If you raise children in a culture of economic precariousness while showing them a thousand commercials a week for Sit N' Spin, Big Wheel, Garanimals, and Hungry Hungry Hippos — not to mention product placements, as in 1982's *E.T.* (Reese's Pieces) and, self-consciously, with a slew of products in 1992's *Wayne's World* — can you blame them for feeling, years later, a deep sense of pleasure in the aisles of a big-box store or a cavalier attitude toward chucking hardcover books, face serums, and children's pajamas into their Amazon Prime cart?

The messages we received from the fire-hose spray of advertising, news, and entertainment could be weird and confusing, particularly with regard to sex and drugs.

When many of the Boomers were teen-agers, they had Woodstock and the British Invasion. But for Gen X, there was no consequence-free indulgence.

While late Boomers enjoyed an air of permission around booze and, in many places, a drinking age of eighteen — which could mean fourteen in a small town where a friendly barkeep would give you a rum and Coke if you showed up with an older sibling — for most Gen Xers there was never an illusion that drinking could be purely a fun recreational activity. Mothers Against Drunk Driving (MADD) formed in 1980. Drug Abuse Resistance Education (DARE) was founded in 1983. In 1984, the National Minimum Drinking Age Act en-couraged states to adopt a uniform mini-mum drinking age of twenty-one. IDs

63

became harder to forge. Drunk driving laws became stricter. Younger Gen Xers were the "clean-up crew for parties we were too young to attend," Kevin Gilbert sang in the 1995 song "Goodness Gracious."[18]

When the Pill was introduced in the early 1960s, sex for anything other than procreation became far less scary — until the AIDS crisis hit, twenty or so years later. Older members of Generation X were adults by the time they knew about AIDS, which meant they faced a retroactive rather than an anticipatory panic. For younger Gen Xers, AIDS destroyed any hope of sexual liberty without danger, just in time for us to become sexually active. In 1987, the World Health Organization launched its campaign to curb the disease's spread. By 1993, there would be more than 2.5 million AIDS cases globally. My school's sex ed in the early 1990s featured graphic photographs of STD rashes. My friends and I carried condoms in our backpacks and were convinced that if we didn't use them we would die.

Younger Gen Xers received an anti–sex ed lesson from Anita Hill's 1991 "Coke can" testimony about Clarence Thomas's sexual harassment (complete with patronizing questions from senators about whether she was "a scorned woman") — and, of course, from *The Starr Report.* Published in 1998, the document described in prurient detail President Clinton's sexual encounters with Monica Lewinsky, with cold-shower lines like "Ms. Lewinsky turned over the dress that proved to bear traces of the President's semen."[19] Evidently, when sexual activity wasn't killing you, it was threatening the political stability of the most powerful country in the world.

I learned about underwear as outerwear from Madonna's gyrations to "Like a Virgin" on TV in 1984, when I was eight,[20] and about romance from Alex P. Keaton and Ellen Reed on *Family Ties* when I was nine. Finally, at age thirteen, I gathered from *Dirty Dancing* that I should only be so lucky, when I turned seventeen, to meet a twenty-five-year-old dance instructor who would school me in both sex and the merengue.

As a bookish pre-internet adolescent, I found an ancient book at the library that told me vaginal orgasms were superior to clitoral ones. I finished the book with no clear sense of how one might achieve either. I saw ejaculate onscreen for the first time when a prisoner threw cum at Jodie Foster in *The Silence of the Lambs* (1991). My

65

other information on the subject came from Cynthia Heimel's satirical *Sex Tips for Girls,* which said you should swallow sperm, because spitting it out is "not considered sporting."[21]

"Remember when it was a fun thing for kids to go see a dirty movie?" my friend Rebecca said recently as we checked Common Sense Media to see if a certain PG-13 film would be okay for our middle schoolers. "You'd say you wanted to go to *Porky's* and they'd say, 'Oh, *okay,*' as if they were giving you an extra piece of candy."

In the 1990s, third-wave feminism filled in some sex-educational gaps. Many Gen X women gradually embraced sex positivity as a way to counteract the anxiety instilled in us by AIDS. There was *Sassy* magazine, and there were often photocopied, stapled zines by women at record stores and bookstores. Writers and artists like Susie Bright, Annie Sprinkle, bell hooks, and members of the Riot Grrrl movement offered more interesting approaches to sex in all its risk and promise. Liz Phair's vital 1993 album, *Exile in Guyville,* was a refreshing and relevant combination of sexual enthusiasm and romantic disillusionment.

In 1994, *Esquire* described leaders of the third-wave movement as "Do Me" feminists.

The title: "Yes." It was followed by: "That's the message from a new generation of women thinkers, who are embracing sex (and men!) . . . But can they save the penis from the grassy field of American history?"[22] Because of course that's the aim of feminism: to save the endangered penis.

"Girl Power" — a Riot Grrrl mantra — was co-opted by the Spice Girls as a demand for the right to wear miniskirts and crop tops while singing about female friendship. In 1993, *Saturday Night Live* mocked the Sexual Offense Prevention Policy of Antioch College — a program that was created in the wake of sexual violence on campus and designed to create a culture of explicit consent. In a vicious game show skit called "Is It Date Rape?" one of the contestants, played by Shannen Doherty, was a girl with a hyphenated last name who was majoring in victimization studies and won the game by calling almost every scenario date rape.[23]

That same year, my high school English literature teacher screened *The Accused,* which had come out a few years earlier, for our class. In the film, Jodie Foster's character is raped on a pool table while other men in the bar cheer. Partway through the scene, a girl in my class turned pale and ran out of the room.

67

Mötley Crüe made it clear how they wanted us with songs like "She Goes Down," "Slice of Your Pie," and "Girls Girls Girls." We might have slow-danced to Poison's "Every Rose Has Its Thorn" in middle school, but then we listened to their other songs, like "I Want Action," in which Bret Michaels vows not to give up until the girl gives in. If she's not willing, he will "take her and make her." The original cover of Guns N' Roses' 1987 album, *Appetite for Destruction,* featured a cartoon of a ravished woman and what appeared to be her *robot rapist.*

Those bands seemed indifferent to women who were not there to sleep with them — and sometimes they snubbed even those who were. In the video for the romantic ballad "Patience," baby-faced Axl sways and sings while Slash, holding a large snake on a hotel bed — this was not a subtle era — ignores one lingerie-clad groupie after another.[24]

Gen X girls grew up aware that we were vulnerable while being told that we were infinitely powerful. Meanwhile, Gen X boys and girls both learned early that whatever hurts we suffered, we would need to soothe ourselves.

■ ■ ■ ■

On January 28, 1986, an announcement came over the crackly loudspeaker system of my school. Usually, the intercom was reserved for either the Pledge of Allegiance or the cryptic proclamation "The eagle has landed," which we eventually learned meant that the teachers' paychecks were ready to be picked up in the office. But on this day, the office had, for us, far more exciting news: the intercom lady told us, the pride in her voice evident through the static, that it was finally time for the *Challenger* launch.

My fifth-grade science teacher, Mrs. Morledge, wheeled a big boxy TV into her classroom as we settled in to watch the space shuttle take off.

In that year, the oldest Gen Xers were college-age and the youngest ones were not long out of diapers. Those of us in the white-hot generational center were in our formative childhood years. I was ten.

NASA was trying to get kids more excited about space, and the hype was intense, with lessons planned around the launch and daily briefings both from our teachers and on the news. Rumor had it that a substitute teacher at our school had been "in the running" for the program. (I have reason to believe that this same tale circulated at nearly every elementary school in America.)

There had been talks, we knew, about shooting Big Bird into space. That plan was scrapped. The man behind Big Bird, Caroll Spinney, said it may have had something to do with the capsule's compactness and the fact that Big Bird was more than eight feet tall.[25]

Instead, a cheerful and enthusiastic New Hampshire teacher named Christa McAuliffe, winner of the NASA Teacher in Space Project, would be the first civilian to take part in a space mission. We had all seen innumerable pictures of her. We knew she had two little kids at home, one of whom was about my age.

The launch had been delayed several times, but this was the real thing. On our TV screen, we saw the live video of the Kennedy Space Center.[26] T minus fifteen seconds . . . We counted down from ten . . . "And liftoff!"

We cheered. For a minute or so, we watched the *Challenger* climb into the sky.

And then, while the announcer commented on the delays that had preceded the launch, the screen lit up.

The boosters forked in two directions. In

between, where the rocket should have been, we saw only a trail of smoke that looked a little like a bunched straw "snake" expanded rapidly by a drop of liquid. Where was the shuttle?

The announcer stopped talking. We stared at the screen, waiting for an explanation of what we were seeing. Seconds ticked by.

No, really: Where was the shuttle? Had it zapped into warp speed?

We looked at our teacher. We looked at the TV. We looked at one another.

Twenty-five seconds passed before the announcer said anything. Twenty-five seconds in which millions of kids across America stared at their classroom TVs, slowly beginning to wonder if that kind, happy teacher had really just died in a fireball — if her own children had, with us, witnessed her violent death.

The anchor returned to say, in far too casual a voice: "Looks like a couple of the solid rocket boosters, uh, blew away from the side of the shuttle, in an explosion."

Long pause. Another voice: "Flight controllers here looking very carefully at the situation. Obviously, a major malfunction."

A major malfunction.

That woman — that *mom* — whom they'd taught us to love and root for, had just been

71

blown up, along with other people whose faces we'd come to know. The grown-ups had made us watch. And now they were using weird language like "major malfunction." Twenty-five seconds of silence. And silence after that, too. I don't remember what Mrs. Morledge said, if anything, except that it was time for lunch.

My son's New York City public school, after what feels like every major news event or school shooting anywhere in the country, has a group discussion. The school counselor is available for questions. The dance teacher has them *dance* about it.

Gen X mothers, too, are all about processing when it comes to their own kids. Here is a message I received from a Kansas City woman I was scheduled to interview: "Hi, Ada, hoping we can reschedule our talk today. Our dog was run over by a school bus yesterday. My daughter saw it happen right in front of our house. All pretty traumatic. I've got the kids home from school today and we are hunkering down. I would really love to be interviewed for your book. I just want to be in the right headspace and that is not today."

There was little "hunkering down" with family in the 1970s and '80s. Back then, it was not seen as the adults' job to help children understand and process their fears, disappointments, and sorrows. Fitness buffs did calisthenics, not yoga. Teachers in many states spanked students.[27]

I checked in recently with some former elementary school classmates to ask if there had been an assembly or something after the *Challenger* disaster. They, too, remembered little but silence. One said that when the explosion happened on the TV in his classroom, his second-grade teacher started crying, turned off the TV, and distracted the class with an activity. Another remembers his teacher saying to first-grade students who hadn't heard the news yet, "By the way, the shuttle exploded," and then laughing nervously.

Our generation is mocked for helicopter parenting our children. We hear that we don't let them fail enough, that our swaddling them in protective gear has left them unprepared for life. This may be true. But, if so, it may well stem from traumas like that morning of January 28, 1986.

For some of us, the message of that day became: *This is what happens when you care sincerely about something.* Absent parental or administrative guidance, we tried to make sense of the *Challenger* on our own. Within weeks, the catastrophe became fodder for

73

sick jokes. I remember a kid on the playground flicking a lit match skyward.

"What's that?" he asked.

"I don't know, what?" I said.

"The *Challenger.*"

It wasn't funny, but at least it related to what we'd seen. Not knowing how to handle the horror, we found ways to pretend we didn't mind so much. It would become a penchant of ours, and a style: self-soothing through dark humor. Garbage Pail Kids. *Mad* magazine. *Gremlins.* (Only now does a telling detail of that kid's *Challenger* joke occur to me: he was *playing with matches at school.*)

We came by our defense mechanisms honestly. The murder rate reached a new nationwide high in 1974 and continued to break new records until the early 1990s.[28] The number of substantiated child sexual abuse claims rose steadily from 1977 through 1992. This may have had more to do with the rise in reporting thanks to the 1977 Protection of Children Against Sexual Exploitation Act and the expansion of Child Protective Services.[29] Or it may be a sign that more children were being abused. Nearly every Gen X woman I know has a story of being groped, flashed, sexually assaulted, or outright raped.[30]

When it came to race, too, we couldn't fail to notice a disconnect between what we were hearing and what we saw. Local Jim Crow laws were superseded by the Civil Rights Act of 1964, so Gen X grew up in the wake of desegregation. Black History Month was first recognized in 1976 by Gerald Ford. But, looking around, we saw racial injustice everywhere. In the 1980s and '90s, the news was dominated by stories like those of the Central Park Five, Rodney King, and Amadou Diallo.

For members of Generation X, once again, there was a stark contrast between what we were taught (racism was defeated by the Freedom Riders) and what we witnessed (rampant racism in society, racial tension in our schools). Yet again, there was no reckoning with the distance between our parents' ideals and our reality.

With the Berlin Wall's breaching in 1989 and the end of the USSR in 1991, the prospect of World War III seemed to vanish overnight. Our Boomer parents, who more even than we do own the Cold War as a cultural touchstone, celebrated. My father was in Germany around this time and made a pilgrimage to chip a piece of the wall away to bring home as a souvenir.

Why didn't Gen X rejoice, relieved of

childhood fears? Maybe it's because we didn't fully appreciate the historical context. Maybe it's because by then we were automatically suspicious of any supposedly good news. Or maybe it's because we'd been made to worry for so long that anytime we were told we didn't have to worry anymore, we didn't know how to stop. Instead of reveling, we doubled down on world-weariness.

When we hit voting age, Gen X was labeled "the most politically disengaged in American history," with "unprecedented levels of absenteeism" at the ballot box.[31] Rock the Vote, fronted by stars like Queen Latifah, was meant to get Gen Xers to register, but in 1996, the youth vote hit its lowest point since eighteen-year-olds won the right in 1971.[32]

There were a few Gen X–specific groups fighting for change, like Lead or Leave and its sister organization, Third Millennium. The latter, founded in 1993, fought to address the poor prospects of Generation X and future generations, a result of what they saw as Boomers' destruction of the planet. The group circulated a manifesto that began: "Like Wile E. Coyote waiting for a twenty-ton Acme anvil to fall on his head, our generation labors in the expanding shadow of monstrous national debt."[33] The group might be best known for its 1994 survey showing that a higher percentage of young adults believed in UFOs than that Social Security would still exist when they retired. None of the Gen X groups appear to have amassed many followers or wielded much influence. In 1996, an NPR story declared, "Lead or Leave Has Left."[34]

In 2000, some Gen Xers attended protests as the group of bipartisan cynics "Billionaires for Bush (or Gore)." At the Republican and Democratic conventions that year, the group dressed up in rich-people drag and chanted, "Bush . . . Gore . . . Bush . . . Gore . . . We don't care who you vote for. We've already bought them."[35]

"The institutions that had been the foundation of middle-class democracy, from public schools and secure jobs to flourishing newspapers and functioning legislatures, were set on the course of a long decline," wrote George Packer in his 2013 book, *The Unwinding.* He cited 1978 — a median Gen X birth year — as the approximate turning point in America's character.[36]

From 1995 to 1997, the health care organization Kaiser Permanente conducted one of the largest-ever investigations into the effect of childhood abuse and neglect on health and well-being later in life: the CDC–Kaiser Permanente Adverse Childhood Experiences (ACE) Study. At their annual physical exams, more than 17,000 subjects filled out questionnaires asking which, if any, "adverse childhood experiences," or ACEs, they had experienced — for example, physical abuse, emotional neglect, or domestic violence.[37]

When the researchers looked at the patients' ACE scores alongside their medical records, they discovered something shocking: the higher the ACE score, the higher the risk for physical and emotional problems in adulthood, including depression and autoimmune disorders.

No studies to date compare ACEs between the generations. It's impossible to say whether childhood trauma was more acute for Gen X.[38] (And frankly it feels a little creepy to engage in a competition about who was more neglected and abused.) Still, I find compelling the idea that some of our problems now may be connected with the damage we incurred back then.

When I reached out to a community of ACE experts, several said that some connection between high rates of childhood stress and high rates of midlife psychological and physical issues made sense. Kimberly Konkel, a childhood-trauma expert in the field of public health, told me that Generation X may well be the "least-parented" generation — more than other generations, left to fend for itself without clear rules, community support, or adult supervision.[39] She believes the stress that resulted could be connected to some of our struggles now: "Our suicide rates, liver cancer death rates, et cetera, indicate that something is significantly wrong with the generation. I think we might find that Gen X has higher rates of reactive-attachment." Reactive attachment disorder — also known by the ironic acronym RAD — involves trouble forming loving relationships as a result of not having had basic needs for caring and affection met.

Today, suicide rates are soaring among middle-aged women.[40] For women ages forty-five to fifty-four, it is now the seventh most frequent cause of death, ahead of diabetes, influenza, and pneumonia; for white women in that age group, it's number five.[41] Again, there is no proof of a connection here, but I find it interesting that women are more likely than men to have had four or more adverse childhood experiences.[42] With a score of four or higher, you are 460 percent more prone to depression and 1,220 percent more likely to attempt suicide than someone with a score of zero.[43]

In *A Generation Alone,* about Generation X's spiritual life, authors William Mahedy and Janet Bernardi employ "aloneness" as "the term that best describes the emotional, attitudinal and spiritual space Generation X occupies . . . In aloneness, one's life is filled with nothing but the clutter and busyness of activity and, all too often, the painful memories of one's own past."[44]

Women in particular seem to gravitate to the clutter and the busyness. We work so hard because we have to, for money, and very likely because we're scared.

The background static of danger in the 1970s and 1980s took its toll. We went on high alert, convinced that with enough hard work and creativity, we could keep ourselves safe from predators and diseases and other threats — could even keep the whole world safe, with the right mental effort. In midlife, we must reconcile the two primary messages of our childhood: One: "Reach for the stars." Two: "You're on your own."

Marketers have taken notice. One report on selling to us features this strategic analysis: "Life has not been stable. Gen Xers were the children of divorce and dual incomes, and were latchkey kids who grew up by themselves. Selling point: Convince them that your organization is reliable and will simplify rather than complicate their lives."[45]

Perhaps the era's insecurity is why so many Gen X girls obsessed over *Little House on the Prairie.* It was so unlike most 1970s childhoods, with the big, loving family uniting to cope with hardship.

That show's father, played by Michael Landon, was a stoic, nurturing voice. In my memory, there was only one man on television more calming, more trustworthy: Mister Rogers.

When tragedy struck, Mister Rogers advised children, "look for the helpers."[46] At the 1969 Senate hearing about public television he said his show aimed to teach children that "feelings are mentionable and manageable."[47] He never condescended. He leveled with us but without saying too much. He didn't frame things in the clunky, overearnest manner of ABC After-school Specials. That series ran from 1972 through 1997 and brought us such contrived, melodramatic classics as *Don't Touch,* about molestation; and *A Desperate Exit,* about suicide.

Mister Rogers, by contrast, advised parents to have clear, honest conversations with children when bad things happened: "When children bring up something frightening, it's helpful right away to ask them what they know about it . . . What children probably need to hear most from us adults is that they can talk with us about anything, and that we will do all we can to keep them safe, in any scary time."[48]

Mister Rogers was a welcome antidote to the rest of our lives back then. I wonder if that's why we are fascinated with him now. The 2018 biography *The Good Neighbor: The Life and Work of Fred Rogers* hit the *New York Times* bestseller list. The documentary *Won't You Be My Neighbor?* was a sleeper hit in the summer of 2018, when it was announced that preproduction had begun on *A Beautiful Day in the Neighborhood,* with national treasure Tom Hanks to play Mister Rogers.

Valarie, who as a child fretted about nuclear annihilation, is now forty-four. She has been trying to do a "look for the helpers" reexamination of her life — counting her blessings, identifying her strengths. Still, she has been crying a lot. She's not quite sure why. She likes her neighborhood in Anchorage, where she returned after completing a BA and an

MFA. She recently adopted a dog that she dotes on.[49] She works as a grant writer and bought her own house in an up-and-coming historic neighborhood. She has good friends. So why is she finding it all so hard?

Is it the clinical depression she's been battling the past twenty years? Is it that she gave up her early creative dreams? Is it that she's approaching menopause and her hormones are all over the place? Is it the responsibility of caring for her ailing mother? The stresses of her job? The work she has to do on her house? The fact that she'll still be paying off student loans at age sixty-five? Is it that she's been diagnosed with a thyroid disorder? Because she's gained weight? Is it that she envies the friends she sees on Instagram who are able to afford trips and eating out? Or is it simply that she's older and nothing feels quite the way she'd hoped it would? These thoughts swirl in her head as she drives to and from work and as she looks out her office window on dark winter afternoons in Alaska.

"I'm forty-four," Valarie says. "And I feel like, *What did I do? Have I made any impact?* I certainly haven't done everything that I thought I was going to do when I was a kid. [Mind-over-matter advice book] *The Secret* aside, I don't think that I'm going to be able to make some of those things happen before I die. I'm trying to come to terms with the fact that we can't all make that huge impact, and of course we can't get all the dreams that we want."

The problem feels not so much psychological as existential. "I've pretty much given up on anybody, other than my friends, ever knowing my name," she told me. She feels invisible, but she doesn't talk about it a lot because she doesn't want to be seen as an ingrate. "Because we're women, we're always going to be seen as complaining. We can't say anything that has a negative tone to it without being told that we should just appreciate how good things are. So we do what we can. Dye our hair. Try a winged eyeliner. Try to be present, then feel that inevitable letdown when people look right past you."

She's trying to look on the positive side, to see her parents' divorce and her lifelong financial struggles as something that ultimately gave her strength and resilience.

"We were raised with more uncertainty than generations now are, but at the same time we were also tasked with taking care of ourselves. So we knew what would and wouldn't kill us. We understood consequences more than children these days, with everything in Bubble Wrap . . . Women in their forties now have it a lot better than women in their forties in 1903. Technology has made our lives a lot easier. We don't quite look like the Crypt Keeper anymore when we hit forty."

She sounds like someone trying to talk herself into feeling fine about being in her forties, when the truth is that she feels anything but fine.

There's a phrase I can't get out of my head. At a regular poker game I play in, whenever there's a junky hand showing in seven-card stud, the dealer says, upon turning over the latest lousy card: "No visible means of support."

It's a term used in vagrancy statutes and a silly thing to say during a game. But that is exactly what's in the cards laid out before so many Gen X women: anxiety, family and work responsibilities, and a sense that time is running out. There could be good cards on the way, but with so many bad cards showing, they might not be good enough.

Valarie bought a house with her own money. She has a job helping people. She's a loyal daughter.

Kelly, too, has much to be proud of: she's raised three children, including one with a brain injury. She has a successful marriage.

And yet both women — raised with unrealistic expectations and running up against countless obstacles — see only what isn't there. They were taking care of family but didn't have a career. Or they had a career but never found a partner. They hadn't lost enough weight, they hadn't saved enough for retirement, they hadn't made a significant impact on the world.

It should be plenty to raise children or to have a career — or, frankly, just not to become a serial killer. Yet somehow for this generation of women, the belief that girls could do anything morphed into a directive that they must do everything.

One Gen X woman told me that the motto of the elite women's college she attended was: "Educating women of promise for lives of distinction." Ever since, she's wondered if she was living up to the promise, if her life is sufficiently distinct.

In a TED talk on vulnerability, Brené Brown, professor of social work at the University of Houston, describes the message we were given as little girls and its effect on us: "For women, shame is: do it all. Do it perfectly. And never let them see you sweat. I don't know how much perfume that [Enjoli] commercial sold, but I guarantee you it moved a lot of antidepressants and antianxiety meds."[50]

In any era, "not-enough-ness" is a challenge for women, says Bryn Chafin,[51] a therapist with Brookwood Center for Psychotherapy in Atlanta.

" 'Middle child' is an extremely poignant metaphor," Chafin said of Gen X. "You can get lost and don't have a lot of support." Chafin said many women in midlife are "worried all the time." Gen X triggers might be family of origin, society at large, social media, politics, and aging. The result: judgment, guilt, and shame.

"When women feel shame," said Chafin, referencing Brené Brown's work on "shame shields," "they often either overfunction, shrink back, or lash out." Those who overfunction may become type A, anxious women who are always trying to fit it all in and usually "with a tinge of self-judgment that they are failing to do everything well. It becomes a vicious cycle, where they work harder to escape the shame and then they fail and feel more shame, and so on."

Chafin has these women ask themselves questions designed to give them a sense of freedom from obligation: "Can you do anything to change this situation? Can you look at it a different way? Can you accept it for how it is? And just let it go?"

One of the goals she encourages women to pursue is what's known as "radical acceptance" — finding a way to take life as it is, not as you thought it would be. "It's one of the hardest things," Chafin says, "to radically accept what's in front of you."

2
THE DOLDRUMS

"The milestones we have ahead of us we can picture. I guess that's why people call it downhill."

"In my twenties, life was so vibrant," said Holly. "Every minute required your full attention. Now, I think, *Wait a second. Everything just slowed down.* My kids don't need me as much. Life doesn't feel as exciting as it did. That feeling — where is it?" She hit her own thigh for emphasis. "I need that feeling back."

I'd gathered a small panel of Gen X women at a lively hotel bar overlooking Nashville, Tennessee: Holly, wearing jeans and a blazer, is an education reporter I'd met a dozen years earlier. Her sister, Annie, wearing Converse and dark lipstick, had just cashed out of a start-up she'd been working at for fifteen years. Their friend Melissa, in a gray turtleneck sweater, her brown hair tied up, works for a church in Tennessee. They are all in their midforties and have several children among them — children they started having between the ages of thirty and forty.

When they arrived, all tasteful makeup and enthusiasm for appetizers, the three women struck me as consummately pulled together. "Look, we made it out of the house!" one said triumphantly, and everyone laughed. Midway through an $11 glass of wine, the laughter stopped. Holly said she felt numb. She'd been doing the same job for a long time, been married to the same man for a long time, and her life had become a parade of duty and routine. There was no affair, no sports car, no blowing up her life — just the terse, desperate gesture of hitting her own leg.

A year or so before, Melissa, too, found herself feeling stuck. She'd done everything "right": breastfed her babies, paid her taxes, taken care of people in the community all day and her family all night. And then looked around at her life thinking, "Is this my reward?"

She caught herself spiraling: *I don't want to do this job anymore. I don't want to be a mom anymore. Definitely don't want to be a wife anymore. I want to run for the hills.*

Holly chimed in: "I remember hearing my own mom say those words in our house. She was coming so unglued that she opened the door and said, 'I'm going to Mexico, and I'm not coming back!' She slammed the door and took off in the car."

"Did she go to Mexico?" I asked.

"No," said Holly.

"Of course not," said Annie. "She went to the grocery store by herself."

"Don't forget how to have fun!" an older woman once told me when I was in high school and busy with school and several jobs. "If you forget how to have fun, it becomes really hard to remember."

I didn't quite understand what she meant then, but now I do.

When our Boomer mothers were middle-aged, they, too, weathered the hormonal swings around menopause. The pressures of this stage of life, coinciding as they do with difficult physical changes, are enough to make anyone storm out of the house or snap at people or fantasize about having less responsibility. Feeling that our life is robbed of joy is a mainstay of middle age for most people at some point or other. But there is something in Holly's quietly saying that she just wants to feel something that illustrates how, for Generation X, our obsession with doing it all — and doing it all well — can add a layer of shame and loneliness. In so many women's stories I heard variations on: *We were supposed to have solved this by now.*

"I need to create some more surprises for myself in my life," one Midwest woman told me. "Because now I can plot out how it's all going to go, and I hate that. *Who will I marry? How many kids will I have?* All those milestones, gone. I've done it. Now it's just seeing my kids off to college and traveling with my husband, if we can ever afford it. I don't mean to sound so grim, really. I do love my life, but what comes with excitement is hope, right? I remember what it was like when you first met a guy, and it was so electric, and I'm never going to have that again."

From more than one woman I heard variations on what one said to me the other day through tears: "Don't get me wrong: I chose my life. I just never thought I'd feel this *average.*"

If these women chose their lives, then what exactly happened? How did choices made freely turn so stale? How could women who wanted the challenging job and the financial independence, plus the full home life, still relate to Betty Friedan's *The Feminine Mystique?* Why do they want to run away just as much as their mothers did, and why do they, too, often end up seeking emotional shelter alone at the supermarket?

At the Nashville bar, conversation turned to feeling unappreciated at home and work.

"That's the other part of the midlife crisis thing," said Melissa. "Nobody, when you're forty-five, is telling you you're awesome. Nobody. Your kids aren't going to say thank you and validate you and appreciate you. Work relationships are just not that; they care about your output."

Annie, who dated enthusiastically as a young woman, chimed in: "And if you're used to getting attention from men all the time, then that just kind of goes away in your forties."

"I remember having my first baby," said Melissa, "and thinking, *I love myself. I just rocked this baby. I got it out of my body. I made a human. I made its* femur. I remember lying in bed with this baby thinking, *I love you, but I also love me. I'm awesome.*"

Now, though, that same child heads off to school in the morning and doesn't even turn around to see Melissa waving good-bye. He does not thank her for getting him transferred out of the class where the teacher kept yelling at him or for helping with his Rosa Parks school project. He doesn't notice the packed snacks and full water bottle or the fresh sheets on his bed. He doesn't see that the clothes that no longer fit have been replaced with clothes that do. One of the great ironies of middle-age torpor and invisibility is that they often hit just as our children are in or approaching the most change-filled, attention-getting, self-involved years of their lives.

As Melissa talked, I was reminded of the time I was up on my computer until 2:00 a.m. to make a deadline and woke up at 6:00 a.m. to take my son to school. I found him in tears because the tooth fairy hadn't come. While he was brushing his teeth, I "found" a bill behind his bed that the tooth fairy must have dropped, but my son did not fall for it. This beautiful, gentle child, whom I birthed, looked at me through narrowed eyes and handed me back the money with a note that read "TO [sic] LATE."

Everyone at that table in Nashville had a story of something seemingly small that illustrated how no matter what she did, it never seemed to be enough for others — even others who loved her. Everyone also had stories about moments that made her feel completely unsupported.

Annie had a good one: She was working hard at her start-up and had two small children at home when her husband's fortieth birthday came around. She gave him a ski trip to Utah. She usually took care of most of the household bills and logistics, but her husband had one assignment, she said: the electric bill.

"Uh-oh," said the women at the table.

"So, my nanny calls me at work," Annie said, "and says, 'Hey.' It was nineteen degrees outside. She said, 'Hey, something weird just happened. The electricity went out.' And I thought, *I know what happened.* So I called Todd, and he was on the fucking slopes with his dudes. He said, 'Oh my God, okay, okay, hold on. I'm going to call right now. I'm going to call and pay it right now.' Well guess what? When they shut it off, you can't pay it over the phone. You have to go to the utility place. So I had to leave work."

For Annie, that moment symbolized how her husband seemed not to have her back. It made her angry, and it turned her into a drill sergeant. When he returned home from the ski trip, she greeted him with a list of jobs that needed doing. "Choose five and you'll do them," she said. "You do them well, and you do them on time." (Whenever

I hear anyone describe a middle-aged woman as a shrew or a nag, I wonder what sort of ski-slope phone call may have figured in the situation.)

Annie and her husband went to therapy, and Annie says there the male therapist tried to explain to her that her husband's brain was just wired differently. It was the old *Men Are from Mars, Women Are from Venus* (1992) school, but with a veneer of evolutionary psychology: "[The therapist] was saying: 'Todd, because he's male, his brain is wired as *I've got to hunt and I've got to kill!* So Todd is very singularly focused. And the way your brain has been wired, Annie, is that you are in the hut.'"

"Oh, you're in the hut, all right," said Holly.

The therapist told her: "The children are crying and the food has to be prepared. And the grandmother is in the hut with you. So you're thinking about all these relationships. And you're anticipating Todd coming back with the kill. Todd's singular focus is to hunt and kill. But that benefits the family."

Annie said she tried to go with it, to meet the therapist halfway. "I feel like in this analogy, the electric bill is the deer?" she recalled saying to him. "And the hunter would be paying the electric bill. So if he is

96

a hunter, he is a *bad hunter.*"

To Annie, the therapist's theory sounded like: "You're so fortunate to have this other kind of brain wiring, Annie! It means you get to do *everything.*"

Melissa, too, went to see a psychotherapist. She went because she'd found herself obsessing over little things and seeing them as symbolic of massive problems in her marriage. For example: *"The bed's not made. I've asked him to make it. Why can't he just make it? Why doesn't he love me enough to make the bed?"*

When Melissa's mother turned forty, it was with an empty nest and "Lordy, Lordy, Look Who's 40!" partyware. When Melissa was forty she was pregnant — and taking care of her ailing father, plus three children, and working full-time.

Ultimately, Melissa hit rock bottom on the fifteenth anniversary of September 11. She'd seen the tragedy firsthand because she was living near the Twin Towers. A friend had lost his life there. On the 2016 anniversary, she was spending the day reflecting on what had happened and what she'd seen. She started crying and found she couldn't stop.

Going through her head were how many things had changed that day — not only for the country, but for her: "September tenth, everything was different. The whole world was different. I wasn't afraid. I didn't have a career. I didn't have a husband. I didn't have kids. Everything about me was different."

She followed her therapist's advice and took time off to sort through all these feelings: "I spent five days at an intensive program. I kickboxed and screamed in the woods and walked a labyrinth and wrote a letter to my fifteen-year-old self and talked to my mom." She realizes, she says, how self-helpy it all sounds, but she threw every cliché she could think of at the problem and found a lot of it actually did help.

She changed jobs, stopped drinking for a while, switched from coffee to tea. She also stopped expecting her husband to change: "Fifteen years I waited for him to bring home dinner," she said. Now she's reconciled to the knowledge that he will never, ever bring home dinner.

Oh, and one more thing helped her feel more alive: she bought a new car.

There's no more iconic midlife-crisis fix than swapping the family wheels for something sporty.

"I turned in the minivan," Melissa said triumphantly.

"What did you get instead?" I asked.

A Ferrari, I thought she would say. A Ford Mustang. A Dodge Viper. A convertible.

There was a pause as every woman at the table waited to hear about the hot new car.

"A Prius," said Melissa.

"Not a Cadillac?" asked Annie, deflated.

"No," said Melissa.

There was silence, and then Annie said what we were all thinking.

"I'm sorry I have to say it," said Annie. "A Prius is not a midlife-crisis car."

"It's also ten years old," said Melissa. "But it might be the nicest car I ever get."

Annie recently sought help for the doldrums, too, via an unholy number of ballet exercise classes and a few doctor visits: "Physically, I hadn't been feeling well. I knew there was something hormonal going on. I went to a couple of different doctors to talk about it. My gynecologist told me: 'Oh, well, if you're having heavy periods, let's do a hysterectomy.' I said, 'Hey, let's put the brakes on, because we haven't talked about anything else.' " (Her doctor is not the only one rushing to surgery. One study estimated, based on their numbers, that 18 percent of hysterectomies performed annually in the United States for benign conditions may have been unnecessary.)[1]

"Then a specialist finally got the answers because he did the right blood work. In my first consultation with him, he said, 'The medical community does not pay enough attention to women in their forties.' He's probably in his late sixties. He's been doing this for a long time. He said, 'What happens to you in your forties, as a woman, will determine how long you live, will determine how happy you are for the next forty years. Your body is changing so dramatically. The hormone shifts that you're going through are not insignificant. And they have so many downstream health effects.' "

When Annie's test results came in, the doctor told her: "You have zero testosterone in your body. No wonder you have no energy, don't want to have sex, and feel tired and listless all the time." Hormone therapy — something many women of this age (for reasons that will be made clear in chapter 9) associate with a higher risk of cancer — has resurrected her energy and libido.

I've heard stories of other low-energy, low-libido women being steered, by women's magazines or nonspecialists, toward role-playing games, sexier outfits, or sex toys (as ever, more things to plan and shop for). Trying to look or act "sexy" in middle age can be a tough needle to thread. One woman told me that when she hit forty she felt the world was telling her: "Hand over your miniskirt. Step into this Eileen Fisher sack." If you don't comply, one woman told me, you run the risk of being mocked as "mutton dressed as lamb."

After long periods of dating during our single years (during which members of Gen X tally an average of ten sexual partners),[2] we may feel frustrated by the relative calm of a monogamous partnership. Or, if we missed out back then, we may go for it now.

"I spent my forties sleeping with men I didn't get to sleep with in my twenties," one woman told me. The only problem: she was married. Her husband caught her in an affair and didn't trust her for years afterward. Not only did she put her marriage in peril, but she also wound up being stalked for years by her affair partner's wife.

My friend says she knows why she did it. She felt her sexual potency waning. She wanted to feel alive again — just like Holly hitting her leg. And, in the short term, it worked. My friend went out and found some aliveness, all right. But at a price. It's the catch-22 of midlife restlessness: that trip alone to the supermarket may make you feel dead inside, but going to Mexico could spell disaster.

A forty-two-year-old software engineer in Asheville, North Carolina, told me she grew miserable enough about a lack of passion that she did go ahead and blow it up.

"A couple of years ago," Diana said, "I was getting ready to turn forty. My life was very comfortable and pleasant and safe. I was in a long-term relationship and everything was fine. It was also unsatisfying, empty, and lonely. And then some things happened. I had a couple of friends die unexpectedly. I don't know if that got me thinking; it wasn't conscious. I just look back on it now and I can see that it was kind of a trigger. I started realizing that I was so afraid of everything. I kept hearing the word 'fear' come up in my conversations all the time."

Diana broke up "a very nice, pleasant relationship with a really wonderful person. And I hurt him. I took up with a more unsafe relationship because it was full of passion I had never felt before." She also started riding motorcycles and took a pole-dancing class. She made new friends with each hobby.

So, did it work? Did she get over her malaise?

"I don't really necessarily feel like it was the right thing," she said. "Or a 'good' thing or a beneficial thing, even, but I feel like it's all been necessary. I would say the breakup is still causing me some pain, and I'm plagued with second thoughts and doubts about the decisions I've made. But the other stuff, the pole fitness, the motorcycle, every other aspect of my life, I'm so grateful for. I've let go of so much of the fear that I had holding me back from an enjoyable, passion-fueled life. I wouldn't change that at all."

Wind was whipping up outside the Nashville bar, and darkness had fallen. Inside, somewhere between Beyoncé's "Love on Top" and Sia's "Cheap Thrills," the music had grown very loud. A young woman came in and sat at a nearby table. She was wearing a short, tight, brightly colored dress and very high heels. It was hard not to stare as she shimmied and flirted. She was glowing.

"You'll never feel *that* way again," said Annie to us, gesturing toward the girl.

"I don't *want* to feel that way," said Holly.

"When I was that age," said Annie, "I was living in New York City and I weighed, like, a buck ten. I bought wild clothes. I thought I lived in *Sex and the City,* you know?" Her takeaway from that show: "Women can have sex and nothing's going to happen. You're just having fun. Now, she says: "I have moments where I'm driving my minivan, and I drop my kids off at school and I'll remember something from back then, and I'll go, *ooh.*"

"Cringing?" asked Holly.

Annie shrugged. Just remembering. "And I keep going in the minivan."

"Just a little faster," said Holly.

As we spoke, our eyes kept darting over to the young woman, who was growing drunker and louder and more electric. She'd become the sun of the room; all activity was revolving around her. She was swaying now, eyes closed, full of life, full of energy, full of the future, blind to the four older women gazing at her from a table in the corner.

I thought of the memento mori optical illusion "All Is Vanity," published in *Life* magazine in 1902. A young woman stares into a vanity mirror. Looked at another way, the image becomes a skull. *That's our table,* I thought: *the reminder of what comes next, when the tiny dress doesn't fit, when you can't have five vodka sodas and feel fine the next day.*

Our table declined the offer of a third glass of wine. We put on our jackets and hugged good-bye and left the bar. Behind us, the young woman's night was just beginning.

3
THE CAREGIVING RACK

"It felt as though if I got up and did one thing, then I was failing with all the other things. Because there was absolutely no way to get through the checklist. No matter what I did that day, I was going to be a failure."

Taking my son to school the other morning, I overheard a woman apologetically say, "Mommy literally has no hands."

I raised my eyebrows at my son. *Literally?*

When I looked over, I saw the woman. She looked very tired, and she was holding multiple tote bags, a plastic container filled with little trains, a sippy cup, and her young son's hand.

My hands were full, too, I realized: my laptop and books, my gym clothes, my son's after-school bag.

The Boomers and oldest Gen Xers were the first to be described as a "sandwich" generation — squeezed by the need to care for children and aging parents and perhaps also grandparents — simultaneously.[1] But the pressure on younger Gen Xers when it comes to caregiving is especially intense. The sandwich metaphor feels far too tame. I prefer to think of it as being on a rack, wrists and ankles tied to opposite ends, with the two pulls ever strengthening.

Our generation's delay in childbearing means that many of us find ourselves either struggling with fertility or raising little kids in our forties — at the very moment when our parents may need help, too.[2]

This increase in the quantity of care that we must provide coincides, awkwardly, with social agitation for enhanced *quality* of care.

In her book *All Joy and No Fun,* Jennifer Senior explains how "children went from being our employees to our bosses."[3] Gone are the days when children were routinely relied upon to do major chores around the house or on the farm, to fetch a family's groceries. Today, parents are far more likely to see their children's needs and desires as paramount, their own and their spouse's as secondary.

"The new trappings of intensive parenting are largely fixtures of white, upper-middle-class American culture," Claire Cain Miller

106

wrote in the *New York Times* in 2018. "But researchers say the expectations have permeated all corners of society, whether or not parents can achieve them."[4]

Since our own childhoods, the time parents spend caring for their children's basic needs has risen dramatically. According to the Pew Research Center,[5] in 1965 mothers spent nine hours a week on paid work and ten hours on child care. In 2016, mothers spent twenty-five hours on paid work and *fourteen* on child care. Something has to give, and it's usually women's leisure time or sleep. Even so, of mothers with full-time jobs, 43 percent still lament spending too little time with their children.

Meanwhile, social support for parents has dropped. Childless friends and neighbors offer less help than in the past, though there are many more of them, relatively speaking: the proportion doing any child care at all was down to about 3.7 percent in 2016 (from 4.5 percent in 2004).[6] According to a study that examined the longitudinal data of men and women from their late twenties to their midfifties, work is good for our mental health *except when there are young children at home.* When the children get older, psychological benefits of work return. But in that work-and-small-children phase, mothers suffer. Men in the same circumstances show no such effect from the stages of parenthood.[7]

I asked Chrystal Evans Hurst, forty-five, of Dallas, the author of *She's Still There* and a mother of five, if one moment summed up midlife for her. She described a recent morning when she felt unable to get out of bed because the second she did, she'd be behind on her to-do list. She lay there, frozen.

Generation X women keep many lists: grocery lists, chore lists, deadline lists, schools-to-apply-to lists, holiday-card lists. Some are on paper and some on smartphones or sticky notes or whiteboards, but they can also seem to loop on a scroll behind the women's eyes.

If our generation has been told for decades that we have so much freedom, so many choices, such opportunities, the question women with young children face is: how free are we to reach for the stars in midlife if we have someone else depending on us? Especially when our concept of good parenting involves so much more brain space and such higher costs than it did for our mothers and grandmothers? *And* when we expect ourselves to be excellent, highly engaged parents while also being excellent, highly engaged employees?

Generation X is downwardly mobile as living costs climb, but we're working hard to give our children advantages we didn't have. According to the USDA's "Cost of Raising a Child" report, families with incomes over $107,400 will now spend $454,770, adjusted for inflation, to raise a baby born in 2015 to the age of seventeen.[8] One friend of mine told me the other day: "I grew up an 'at-risk youth.' My Barbie clothes were all made of scraps of leftover fabric. My daughter goes to French immersion school."

Some of the stress on parents we can chalk up to an objectively more competitive educational landscape. I applied to exactly one high school. I took my SATs hungover and still got scholarships. Now, I have friends who can't get their kids into the public elementary school across the street from their apartment because too many parents want their kids to go there. I know young people who have 4.0 GPAs and long résumés with clubs and sports and service hours who struggle with college admissions. According to a 2019 *Wall Street Journal* article, last year all but one Ivy League school accepted less than 10 percent of applicants.[9]

But there's a new internal calculus, too. Once, when pressed about having another baby, I said that we couldn't afford it. This was an absurd answer. I know people who have successfully raised more children on less money. It still felt true because so many nonnecessities seem necessary to me: books, camps, after-school programs, travel — above all, the freedom to give them my attention.

According to a 2015 Gallup poll, no less than 56 percent of working mothers would prefer to stay home.[10] That is a huge number, but I can't imagine anyone who has worked with a baby at home — including the 39 percent of dissenters — being shocked by it.

The question of whether we'd rather be home with our new baby or not usually is academic. Few families today can get by on one income; and few employers will grant employees significant time off.

When I had my baby, I didn't let myself ask the question of what I wanted to do, because I had no real choice. I was the breadwinner in an expensive city. I did want a career and it had been made clear to me that my bosses were being very generous giving me six weeks of leave and a day or two a week of working at home, plus freedom to pump in the company restroom.

And I was lucky. I received more concessions than other women I know did after they gave birth. On my return to the office, I splurged on the Medela Pump in Style with Metro Bag in pastel blue. It looked like overnight luggage, so whenever I picked it up and headed to the staff bathrooms, my deputy wisecracked, "Another weekend in the country?"

Our parents' generation, on the whole, did not struggle with exactly the same pressures. If our mothers worked, they often held jobs in which they could clock in and clock out. They weren't getting pinged from 7:00 a.m. to midnight every day.

Expectations of parental attention, too, were lower. If a 1970s mother had to work or go out, there was no shame in leaving school-age kids home alone, watching TV.

One Gen X woman tells me that her Boomer mother comes to visit and is mystified. "Why do you *play* with them?" her mother asks. "We never played with you."

That is a common sort of exchange between Gen X parents and their elders.

When it comes to parenting, X has as a generation probably done too much. And I am not basing this only on a Gen X Facebook post that I saw recently: "Toddler

111

game suggestion: Play archaeologist! Give her a dry paintbrush, and lie down on the couch. Tell her you are a dinosaur fossil, and she has to gently and painstakingly excavate you."

In the Boomer-parenting year of 1975, Marguerite Kelly and Elia Parsons published the wildly popular book *The Mother's Almanac,* seeking to "deescalate the idea that you have to be an expert to raise a child."

Gen X has been issued the opposite message. Many of the parenting books now in vogue encourage new parents to breastfeed for at least a year and not to sleep-train — two things that usually entail sleep deprivation for mothers. Subject to fierce internal pressure to give our children advantages we never had, we are the perfect consumers of baby swings, Gymboree classes, and $200 wooden balance bikes for toddlers — whether or not we can afford them.

Millennials who don't have kids yet may find this debate perplexing: *Who's right, the hands-off Boomers or the hands-on Gen Xers?* They may have an opportunity here to see how Gen X parents have overcorrected for their own childhoods and to take a sensible middle path. I dearly hope they remember how frazzled we were and will vow never, ever to make their own baby food.

It's still too early to say for sure, but it looks as though Millennials might be swinging the pendulum back toward a more relaxed mode of parenting. One 2013 marketing study found that most Millennial parents see the value of unstructured playtime and think of themselves not as helicopter parents but as drones — near enough to swoop in when needed but otherwise content to linger in the clouds.[11] In a Pew Research Center study, more than half of Millennial mothers surveyed said they thought they were doing a very good job as parents.[12]

Perhaps they'll excel, too, at being partnered while raising little kids. In his 2017 book, *The All-or-Nothing Marriage,* psychologist Eli J. Finkel points to research which found that, compared with 1975, spouses were spending far less time alone together — fewer date nights, less seeing friends — but doing almost three times as much shared parenting.[13] Maybe that's why Gen X parents often complain that midlife marriage can feel like running a daycare center with someone you used to date.[14]

Even some advocates of lower parenting standards sound judgmental: An article in

Live Science, "Why Supermoms Should Chill," is one example.[15] Lead sentence: "Trying to have it all could be bad for your mental health." In my experience, there is only one thing worse for a woman's mental health than trying to be a superhero, and that is being told to "chill" — especially since any efforts to do so incur swift blow-back.

When a lawyer I met in New York had her first baby, her traditional African mother told her she had to stay in the house for three months. After a few weeks she was getting stir-crazy, so she called her doctor for a second opinion. The doctor said: "You can take her out. Just don't have her around a lot of people, and make sure you wash your hands."

A new store had opened nearby, so this lawyer took her baby there.

"First of all, that's just sad," she said. "That's my big outing: 'Let's go to Target!' And while we're there my daughter starts screaming. Not crying but wailing as if something was wrong. I was in the beauty aisle and a bunch of people started hounding me: 'How young is that baby?' 'Why is she even out of the house?'

"I go up to the register, pull out my credit card, and everything goes flying. And *I* start crying. For real. My daughter's screaming. I'm screaming. Everything's everywhere . . . One person said, 'I know how you feel. It's okay. Here's your wallet. She's fine. Congratulations on your baby.' "

That was the only person this new mother encountered that day who she felt wasn't judging her. "It's like you're supposed to know what you're supposed to do," she said. "And we're not going to help. We're going to surround you and stare at you and worry about your baby. You don't exist here, unless we're pointing out what you're not doing."

Most of our mothers did not face this level of scrutiny. My mother cooked more than most mothers I knew, but we still ate Swanson Hungry-Man fried chicken TV dinners regularly and Entenmann's chocolate doughnuts for breakfast.

The food of the 1970s and '80s was barely food at all. Anna Pallai, of the 2018 book *70s Dinner Party* told me that a fancy salad then was often "vegetables in lime gelatin and lots of mayonnaise."[16] The most '70s party meal in Pallai's estimation? "The Sandwich Loaf: a loaf of bread cut horizontally, into which you put various fillings, like salmon, cheese, egg, chicken. The whole thing is frosted in a green- or yellow-tinted cream cheese-and-mayo spread — perhaps decorated with edible flowers."

It sounds terrible.

"Oh," she said. "It is."

Like many Gen Xers, I rode around in cars with no seat belt, was left in the back while adults went into stores, and bounced around in the beds of speeding pickups. My cousin and I routinely spent trips goofing in the back of my aunt and uncle's Volvo. While the car was moving at sixty miles an hour, we would pull down the back seats, crawl into the trunk, and then pull the seats back up after us. The trunk!

If today's social norms were applied to any of the generations of parents who preceded us, there wouldn't be enough Child Protective Services agents in the world to handle it. The stack of neglect reports would reach to the moon. That goes for all parents before us. Boomers were practically feral as children, just like us. The difference: we were far more likely to grow up in divorced homes, among neighbors we didn't know, and in places with high crime rates.

Today, our streets are safer than ever. Still: no, I have not let my son, who is now twelve, go out into the world alone as much as I did as a child. It's not rational. Independence evangelizers like Lenore Skenazy of the movement Free-Range Kids are entirely correct that we should give our kids more freedom. I have a theory about why we don't: Gen Xers helicopter over our kids because we have too-vivid memories of what happened — or could have happened — to us when our parents didn't hover. That visceral sense of danger is hard to reason with.

Still: how much more work could I have done over the past five years if I'd kicked my son out of the house when I had a deadline and told him to be back before dark? The mind boggles.

"I had no supervision when I was a kid," comedian John Mulaney said in his Netflix stand-up special. "We were free to do what we wanted. But also, with that, no one cared about kids. I grew up before children were special."[17]

So many things that seemed normal when I was young now seem bizarre. When my son was little, *Sesame Street* issued DVDs of episodes from the 1970s with a warning label: "These early *Sesame Street* episodes are intended for grown-ups and may not suit the needs of today's preschool child."[18]

I laughed. Then I watched them. Kids jump on box springs left on the sidewalk.

They run through construction sites. They roam, helmetless, through grimy neighborhoods with minimal supervision. I felt a mix of nostalgia for my childhood and horror at my son's being exposed to that alternate universe.

Gen X mothers typically do not let their kids jump on box springs. They are more likely to serve at cupcake-decoration tables, pumpkin-carving stations, face-painting booths. My son's elementary school used the scheduling site SignUp-Genius. In my head, I always heard this phrase as sarcastic: "Yeah, go ahead and sign up, *genius*. You *definitely* should spend four hours on Saturday morning supervising the sand-art activity at the Spring Garden Party instead of resting or cleaning your house, *genius*."

Once you're in the system, you can try to get out, but your school family will keep pulling you back in, like the Mafia.

From: Angela
To: Graciela, Debbie, Kavita, Laura, Jasmine, and 35 more
Subject: Lice

Hi all. Just wanted to let you know Ivy's got lice . . . Just what I need at the moment . . . So, I know we circulated some

118

tips last year . . . Listerine, Pantene, tea tree oil?? What were they????

I thought I'd let ya know so you can spend the weekend checking. They also have been playing "hair salon" at school — so no more of that! I will notify the school on Monday.

From: Jasmine

Sorry to hear this news! People have rec'd Listerine/mouthwash to dry them out or heavy conditioner/mayonnaise to suffocate them. Do either of these things along with putting a plastic bag or shower cap on for a couple of hours. Comb out with a fine-tooth lice/nit comb.

Prevention . . . Aqua Net hair spray to coat the hair. Some kids find this too stiff or uncomfortable on a daily basis. (Whatever! Like itching nonstop is comfortable?)

From: Syd

Hey guys. I only wash the kids' hair once a week and I rub oil (blend of coconut, ylang-ylang, rosemary, and anise) into their hair every day before I send them to school, which is why my kids always have greasy hair. It has been great at preventing the kids from getting reinfected. Good luck. Shaving heads will also probably nail it.

These emails are a few of the dozens in this thread — itself just one of dozens in my School email folder. Other threads include: *Gift Basket for Gala, Science Exploratorium, Wonderful Wednesday, Holiday gift for Ms. Campos, Can you help on Family Portrait Day, lost toy, enterovirus, mindfulness, playground dynamics, summer camp, babysitting help today, International Night, lockdown drill, book fair, fund-raising committee, bake sale.*

Each email will cc twenty to forty women. These women have jobs. One is a teacher. One is an event planner. One runs a restaurant. It's not as though they have tons of free time. And yet, I've noticed that men are rarely, if ever, copied. I've tried to loop my husband in on some of these chains — just so he can share in the joy, of course — but somehow his name never sticks on the list.

One year I was at a meeting where the PTA moms were trying to come up with auction items for the annual fundraiser. My usual recommendation that they offer a romantic weekend in Vermont with Mr. Matt was once again rejected, so I suggested a get-out-of-jail-free card that would entitle the winner to a full school year without a single email about anything school related.

No one found it funny.

Fair enough. If anyone who's not in that world makes a joke about PTA moms, I defend those women to the death. Because the truth is that this is how things get done, especially at public schools — how the funds get raised, how the volunteers are wrangled, how the teachers receive their gift certificates and their oversized greeting cards signed by the cast of the school musical.

To people ignorant of these threads, the labor is invisible. It is also, as anyone who even comes close to it can tell you, *exhausting.* Many hours and dollars a year go into reading these emails and then acting on their directives — sending the kid in with a bagged lunch for the museum trip, buying something for the class basket, wrapping the Secret Santa present, venmoing Angela for the principal's gift. This is an inconspicuous "mental load" that women commiserate about: the holiday gifts and grocery lists and travel plans and all the other "little things" that can eat your brain.[19]

Time-use surveys show that while Gen X men do more at home than their fathers did, it's still not enough to spare women the bulk of the work. Arlie Hochschild's 1989 book, *The Second Shift* — which showed that working women came home from the office and did a second shift as homemakers — remains timely.

According to the Pew Research Center, in 2016, fathers reported spending eight hours a week on child care. That's more than three times what fathers spent with their children in 1965. According to the Bureau of Labor Statistics, working women with children under the age of six still spend an average of 1.1 hours of each workday physically taking care of them. Men? Twenty-six minutes.[20] According to Pew, men today do ten hours a week of housework, up from four. Not enough to close the gap.[21]

Recent Pew research on two-income families showed that fathers said they shared household work and child care equally.[22] Mothers disagreed, and their "perceptions are supported by plentiful research," according to the *New York Times*.[23] According to another report, after a baby was born, women's total time working — including paid work, child care, and housework — went up twenty-one hours a week; men's climbed twelve and a half.

There is still a presumption that men are the heads of household, even when they earn less and do less. In fact, according to a 2018 report from the US Census Bureau, both men and women in a heterosexual couple tend to misrepresent — even to census takers — their incomes if the woman earns more. Women understated their income by 1.5 percent and men exaggerated theirs by 2.9 percent. The researchers who noticed this called it "manning up and womaning down."[24]

Part of the problem may be that women have moved into formerly "male" work without the reverse being true. "the jobs that many men used to do are gone or going fast," Isabel Sawhill and Richard V. Reeves, both senior fellows at the Brookings Institution, wrote in the *New York Times.*[25] "And families need two engaged parents to share the task of raising children. As painful as it may be, men need to adapt to what a modern economy and family life demand."

Instead, changing gender roles are causing a backlash. "Women who earn more than their husbands," Sawhill told me, "actually do *more* housework in an effort to compensate for their higher earnings and the psychological drama involved."

And even though women tend to say that they want men who help with the kids or do more at home, when they find such a man they may despair in the way that "Breadwinner" did in a letter to the advice podcast *Dear Sugars:* "I hate that I want a more traditional lifestyle with a husband who can provide for me. I am so ashamed of my feelings."[26]

Fantasies of an equal partnership, in which both partners do equal amounts of work, make equal amounts of money, and each cook dinner three and a half times a week, typically run up against the reality of just how grueling it is to take care of children when both parents work. Often, both parties wind up feeling underappreciated.

At the other end of the caregiving rack are Generation X's aging parents. While men are doing more these days to take care of the elderly as well as children, the main burden still falls on middle-aged women (average age: forty-nine) more than on any other group.[27]

Many of us deal with aging parents who are divorced, which often adds tension while doubling the number of homes that need cleaning and fridges that must be stocked with food.[28] Moreover, because we were born during a baby bust and are apt to have few siblings, we can count on less backup. In 2010, the ratio of possible caregivers for a person over the age of eighty was 7–1. By 2030, it's predicted to be 4–1; by 2050, just 3–1.[29]

The cost is significant, especially for women. According to a 2011 MetLife study, when a woman leaves the labor force early to care for a parent, the potential toll of lost wages and lost Social Security benefits averages $324,000 over her lifetime.[30] Six in ten caregivers become obliged to make changes at work, like taking paid or unpaid time off.[31] Family caregivers spend about $7,000 per year on out-of-pocket costs relating to caregiving; for women, that's an average of 21 percent of their income.[32]

AARP's family and caregiving expert, Amy Goyer, told me that she has lived these stats herself. For about a decade, she took care of both her ailing parents and an ill sister, while working full-time. She said she believes that, ideally, women come into their own in their forties and fifties, finding their true callings in life, but that often today: "women are too busy to even think about it."[33]

The caregiving rack is likely to stretch Millennials and Gen Z even more than Gen X. As cancer treatments progress and people live longer with chronic illness or dementia, the absence of family leave and of affordable health insurance could prove yet more debilitating for those cohorts in midlife.

There is one positive trend, for younger women: the gender gap in caregiving is narrowing, though the pattern of having children later and parents living longer persists. It didn't happen in time for Gen Xers to benefit that much, but younger men appear to be taking on more as fathers, husbands, and sons. According to a recent AARP report, Millennial men in the United States actually do 47 percent of caregiving.[34]

At the first-night party of a professional conference I attended in Miami, I fell into conversation with three women. The first woman I'd encountered as we waited for a shuttle bus to the party. She had just ended a phone call and looked perturbed.

"Are you okay?" I asked.

"Well, no," she said. Her husband had encouraged her to come to the conference. She deserved a night off away from their little kids, he'd said. Mere hours later, he had palmed the kids off on her in-laws. She wanted them home, with him watching them. Should she change her flight and go back early? She opened an airline app on her phone.

The next woman onto the bus was also frowning. Her five-year-old daughter had just bawled at her on FaceTime, telling her she should come home, and — apologies to the young lady — the exact wording was: "Why aren't you heeeerrrreeee???"

The third woman, when about to take the conference stage for a presentation, had received a text with confusing news of a playground accident involving her child. She made it through the hour, then called home to learn it wasn't a big emergency after all.

We stood at the party in our cocktail attire and high heels. Up walked a chiseled male author. We asked what book he was promoting at the conference. He told us that he had built a raft out of plastic bottles and sailed it across the Pacific.

I felt a combination of awe and envy, attraction and resentment. This guy didn't seem like someone who had babies wailing at him on FaceTime. He did not appear to be thinking about rebooking a flight to reclaim children from in-laws. He was just enjoying the warm Miami night. Did he have a family? Many of the female authors at the festival mentioned their spouses and children in their author bios; the male ones rarely did.

A waitress came over with a tray of drinks. The male author casually reached to take one. We women knocked ours back like marathoners drinking Gatorade.

America gives middle-aged women little support in their caregiving roles. While the Family and Medical Leave Act (FMLA) has been in place since 1993 — the federal law allows eligible employees of public agencies or private companies with fifty or more employees to take off up to twelve weeks for health, pregnancy, newborn, or other family caregiving needs, unpaid, without being fired — US workplaces mostly ignore the needs of working parents, 40 percent of whom aren't covered at all under FMLA.[35]

In nearly every other developed country, women have help from the government. The UK famously offers six weeks of parental leave at 90 percent pay, followed by a flat rate for another 34 weeks, but even Turkey, China, South Korea, Mexico, Indonesia, India, and Saudi Arabia permit at least seventy days at half pay.[36]

According to the American Psychological

Association, health insurance anxiety pervades the United States. Some 66 percent of American adults, at all income levels, report being stressed by the expense of health insurance.[37]

"It is by this point a commonplace that inequality is as bad as it has been in a century," writes Emily Cooke in a review of Alissa Quart's *Squeezed: Why Our Families Can't Afford America,*[38] "that every sector of the population save the richest is treading water at best." She ends her review with a note that she and her partner, both having lost jobs recently, can't see themselves having more than one child.

One of my son's best playground friends when he was a toddler was a little girl named Ella. Her Swedish mother and I spent many days together with them, negotiating the naps and snacks and activities and the odd work email popping up at the exact moment the kids were colliding on the slide.

Johanna had lived in the United States for several years, but there came a point when she and her husband, who is from Florida, hit a wall. They were working too hard with too little to show for it. So they moved to Sweden. My husband and I bought a bike and a dresser at their garage sale to remember them by.

After many years away, Johanna and Ella recently came to visit. I asked how the move had worked out. Johanna described the first month back in Europe as a revelation. It's not entirely fair to compare the complicated, vast United States with a relatively tiny, largely homogeneous country, but I think there's a lesson here.

"When we got back to Sweden," she said, "it took two weeks before Ella got into kindergarten. It was really close to where we stayed and in these pretty little red houses. It was free. And they got lunches — good lunches that she still talks about, actually."

I asked Johanna what having her child in a free, high-quality school eating free, high-quality food every day did for her as a mother.

"I could start thinking again," said Johanna. "It was amazing. I realized: here we can actually get a balance in our lives again."

Religious communities once played a significant part in American life — offering fellowship, advice, and material help, from child care to casseroles, not to mention a unifying concept of universal order and purpose. Generation X has largely rejected organized religion. As a nation, we are still in name religious (71 percent Christian), but the number of people checking "none" on religious-affiliation surveys keeps rising.[39] Americans in their twenties and thirties are less likely to regularly attend services now than at any time in recent US history.[40] Middle-aged women may opt instead for individualized practice of yoga or Buddhism.[41] Astrology is booming.[42]

In a pinch, the occult provides a narrative. Maybe it's: "You drowned in a past life, and that's why you're scared of water now." Or maybe it's: "The reason this is a hard time is that you're in a Saturn return, and that's throwing everything out of whack." What a gift to hear that your miserable week is not your fault, just a planet that will soon cycle away.

Mira Ptacin, author of *The In-Betweens: The Spiritualists, Mediums, and Legends of Camp Etna,* told me she likes having mediums on call. "I can text them anytime, day or night, and be like 'riddle me this,' " she says. "And they will provide me with some answer. The last time, one of the mediums gave me an accurate date of when my parents would sell their home. I just texted again because I've been having a weird, nagging sensation about my dad's health."[43]

Astrology and psychics offer breaks from

wondering. Wondering can be so painful. Making decisions, seeing patterns, and imagining the future can be so hard. How soothing to be told that magic is real, providing ready reasons for loss or failure.

Also: crystals don't require preauthorization. Across the country, there is an alarming shortage of mental health professionals, particularly those who take insurance.[44] A psychotherapy session might help more than a gong bath, but which is cheaper?

In 2018, I was invited to teach a memoir seminar at a creative writing conference. Teaching fiction down the hall was the novelist Min Jin Lee, who had recently won fame with her book *Pachinko.* The teachers had to give little lunchtime talks and I went to see hers. She described how she had worked on her writing for many years with very little support. Almost no one believed in her, she said. She made no money from it. The world seemed to want her to quit, to focus on her house and family, to stop trying to become a published author.

At one point, she'd gone to a writers' colony, paying $2,000 she couldn't really afford in order to do the residency, and she cried at night from missing her young son. One day, she heard a fellow writer say how

embarrassing it was that there were house-
wives who had *paid* to be there rather than
attending on fellowships.[45]

"I realized," Lee said, "it was me she was
talking about."

Today, Lee encourages others to keep doing whatever they feel called to do that isn't
taking care of other people.

"I bet when your friend is sick, you bring
over food," said Lee. "When your mother
needs to go to the doctor, you take her, even
when she doesn't ask nicely. When the
school nurse calls, you rush to pick up your
child even when you have a lot of work to
do. You know how to do this already: love
when it's difficult. It's a superpower. You
just need to use it for yourself, too."

During the Q&A, a middle-aged woman
in the audience raised her hand. "But I feel
guilty taking time away from my family to
write," she said. "I think about all the things
they need."

Lee looked the woman in the eye and said,
"But what about *you*?"

The question hung in the air.

4
JOB INSTABILITY

"I should be in the prime of my career. Not only do I feel like I don't have a career, I don't even have a job."

"I don't know that I have a formal career, not one I carefully chose and then built," said Lori, forty-one, who grew up in Pittsburgh and is now a contracts analyst in Charlotte, North Carolina. "I just sort of wandered around until I finally landed in my current job. And it's fine. It's corporate, it's safe. Predictable. But sometimes, I have these moments of clarity — usually during lengthy conference calls. This voice in my head suddenly starts shouting: *What are you doing? This is pointless and boring! Why aren't you out there doing something you love? Name one thing you love! Cheese? Okay, great. Let's get some goats and start making cheese, and we can sell it from a truck. We'll call it something clever.* And then,

I spend the rest of the conference call thinking up names for my imaginary cheese truck: *Hmm, some pun on a wheel? Fromage on a Wheel?*"[1]

So why not go ahead and become the Fromage on a Wheel lady?

"I have friends who have told me over the years, 'Just quit your job and be a baker or be a cheese maker,' " she said. "I've never had that option. Especially now. We have a child. You want to provide security and safety and health insurance. Those things overrule your own personal preferences. What if something really bad happens? Or if we lose a job?"

She shuddered.

The overall wage gap has closed somewhat — to eighty-two cents on the male dollar in 2017.[2] But the gap increases when you look at women in middle age.[3] Claudia Goldin, former president of the American Economic Association and a widely acknowledged force in the field, has pointed out that by the time college-educated women are forty years old, they earn just seventy-three cents to a man's dollar. After graduating with an MBA, women earn ninety-two cents. A decade later: fifty-seven cents.[4]

A 2018 study by the Institute for Women's Policy Research (IWPR) reported even more dire news: Looking back over a fifteen-year span, the IWPR observed that when you take into account women's breaks from full-time work, the wage gap widens to forty-nine cents to the typical men's dollar, significantly less than the eighty cents usually calculated using a single year of census data.[5] The report found that women who take just one year off make 39 percent less than women who stayed in the workforce for the full fifteen years.

Despite the prevalent gap, almost a quarter of women now manage to outearn their husbands.[6] But women are still under-represented when it comes to top-paying jobs.[7] A 2018 report by PayScale, a compensation-research firm, found that "by midcareer, men are 70 percent more likely to be in executive roles than women." In late career, the rate soars to 142 percent.[8] That's now, when many Gen X women are in mid or late career.[9]

Only *3 percent* of venture capital goes to women-run companies.[10] As of 2019, women hold just 4.8 percent of CEO positions at S&P 500 companies.[11] In fact, as you may have heard, fewer women run large companies than men named John.[12]

Gen Xers now hold roughly 37 percent of management positions in the United States and 51 percent globally.[13] But, just as Generation X ages into managerial positions, those positions are vanishing. In the past two decades, US corporate hierarchies have become flatter, with a reduction, according to the National Bureau of Economic Research, in the ranks of middle managers.[14] It seems that every day there's another report of a company's bold new plan to cut costs and increase annual savings by "streamlining" — read: having fewer people do more work.[15]

"Despite their growing influence and responsibilities at work, Gen Xers are most overlooked for promotion and have been the slowest to advance," according to consulting firm DDI's Global Leadership Forecast 2018,[16] which reported, too, that Gen X leaders are "under-recognized" and "typically expected to take on heavy workloads." The result: demoralization. A 2019 MetLife survey found that Gen X employees were notable for having "less enthusiasm for purpose in the workplace than other generations."[17]

One bright spot in the post–Great Recession world: while many industries are convulsing: jobs in science, technology, engineering, and math (STEM) are proliferating.[18] However, women held only 26 percent of STEM positions in 2011. That number was even lower for women of color: only 6 percent of STEM workers, male and female, were black. According to the 2018 Women in the Workplace report from Leanin.org and McKinsey and Company, corporate America has made almost no progress on gender diversity in the past four years.[19] Women's presence as a percentage in computer occupations has actually declined since the 1990s.[20]

When I asked Eileen Appelbaum, codirector of the Center for Economic and Policy Research, whether Gen X women's fear that they have no job stability is based on reality rather than paranoia, she said: "It's not psychological."[21] Over the last three decades, in Appelbaum's words,[22] "the structure of firms has undergone a major evolution . . . [Companies have] outsourced many of the tasks previously performed in-house or by subsidiaries."

There seems no end to ways in which the changing economy has been bad for workers who look to settle into management slots in midlife: offshore production, unions losing power, deregulation, automation.[23]

In the wake of the Great Recession, longterm unemployment hit older women harder than any other group. Headlines confirm our worst suspicions. *Harvard Business Review:* OLDER WOMEN ARE BEING FORCED OUT OF THE WORKFORCE.[24] **PBS** NewsHour: WHY WOMEN OVER 50 CAN'T FIND JOBS.[25] The *New York Times:* FOR WOMEN IN MIDLIFE, CAREER GAINS SLIP AWAY.[26]

As of this writing, unemployment has just hit a new low.[27] But age discrimination is real: A recent *New York Times*–Pro Publica investigation found that Facebook job ads were not showing up on the pages of people over a certain age, because the site let potential employees target younger demographics for their ads. When Verizon sought recruits for a financial planning and analysis unit, the ad went out to people ages twenty-five to thirty-six.[28] Older users never saw it.

A recent lawsuit against the media company Meredith highlighted the age disparity in men and women on TV news. In five years, the company removed seven female anchors with an average age of 46.8 and replaced them with younger women, whose average age was 38.1. Meanwhile, male anchors remain a decade older, on average, than their female coanchors.[29]

Many of the country's highest-profile CEOs are in their thirties and forties — so if that's your dream, you're likely to sense your window of opportunity rapidly closing. The woe trickles down: if you are in the corporate world at a time when everyone in management seems to be in their thirties, and you're in your forties and not there yet, what can you look forward to?

We expect ourselves to be further ahead, faster, even after entering the workforce at a historic disadvantage. The ominous term "downsizing" invaded American speech in a solidly Gen X birth year: 1976.[30]

"If twentysomethings entered the decade floundering in the job market, did they deserve to be labeled dazed and confused?" wrote Margot Hornblower in *Time* in 1997.[31] "They had come of age after the U.S. took what some economists call the great U-turn. Energy prices first soared in 1973, and workers' wages stagnated. Between 1979 and 1995, some forty-three million jobs were lost through corporate downsizing. Newly created jobs paid less and offered fewer benefits."

Now Gen X women find themselves competing in middle age with both younger and older workers. In 2011, the Center for Work-Life Policy called Gen X the "wrong place, wrong time" generation: "thwarted by boomers who can't afford to retire and threatened by the prospect of leap-frogging

Millennials."[32]

Gen X journalist Ann Sterzinger wrote on *Medium* that, after she got into the game, the rules changed: "We watched as the standard age for a reporter went from ten years older than we were to ten years younger in the space of five years."[33]

Gen Xers often see their bosses pursuing Millennials for any job that involves social media.[34] One woman in California told me younger employees in her office were given social-media responsibilities that she had coveted:[35] "There's an idea that because I'm fifty-two I won't know about social media. I actually know a butt load. I had to help my kids navigate it."

Hoping to advance against the odds, Gen X women read books like Sheryl Sandberg's *Lean In* or Mika Brzezinski's *Knowing Your Value* and flock to classes and seminars about corporate life. I went to one in 2018: the Catalyst Conference in New York City, a series of workshops and lectures and panels at the Hilton in midtown Manhattan, designed to inspire and support professional women. Catalyst is an advocacy group that conducts research on women and the workplace. At this conference were many well-groomed women in their forties wearing pantsuits and nodding when speakers used corporate jargon to flatter them as "intentional change-makers."

Carla Harris, vice chairman, managing director, and senior client adviser at Morgan Stanley, a thirty-year veteran of Wall Street, gave one of the keynote speeches at Catalyst. Wearing a glittery silver jacket and black pants, short hair and statement jewelry, she dispensed "Carla's pearls" of wisdom about powerful leadership. Beneath the ballroom's pink and gold ceiling lights, she described her strategies for cultivating good relationships at work. During the Q&A that followed, a woman in the audience asked a question about combating "imposter syndrome" — the lurking suspicion that you're a fraud, less able than those around you, and that you'll eventually be found out.

Rebecca Henderson, CEO of Randstad North America, one of the biggest staffing firms in the country, told me that Gen X women suffering from imposter syndrome have a tendency to "underestimate how hard US companies are working at hiring females and ensuring an equal relationship between men and women. These women have far more power than they think they do."

Henderson offers this example — one you

may have heard before: "An unemployed forty-five-year-old woman, college educated, looks at a job description and thinks, 'Oh, I think I only have about seventy percent of the skills; I won't apply.' A man looks at that same description and thinks, 'Great, I have fifty percent of the skills; I'll apply!' That happens every day."[36]

Harris seemed dismayed by the persistence of imposter syndrome, something that dogs men, too: "When I graduated from Harvard Business School thirty years ago, everyone was talking about that." Harris, a Boomer,[37] told the audience that they needed to believe in themselves. When you're told by bosses that you're worthy of a job or a promotion or a trip to a conference like this one, she said: "*Trust their judgment.* Do not stay down in the valley; there's too much room at the top of the mountain."

That same day, in one of the breakout sessions, I met a cheerful blonde woman from Texas born at the tail end of Gen X. She told me she and her husband both worked for the same big company. When their son was born seventeen months earlier, she fell into postpartum depression and was passed over for a promotion while on maternity leave. But she got back in there, did everything the Catalyst speakers were encouraging her to do, and it worked. "It took a year," she said proudly. "But I got there. I'm now leading my team."

I congratulated her and asked how she and her husband had sorted out caring for the baby.

Her face fell. I suddenly saw how tired she was. Their baby is in "very expensive daycare," she said. A lot of it. She and her husband start their day at 6:30 a.m. But the daycare facility doesn't open that early, so they had to hire a nanny, also expensive, to bridge that time. And they don't get off work until 6:00 p.m.

They can't afford the pricey Houston real estate market on only one income, so it's lucky that both of them want to work. They've cobbled together a strategy by which they spend a huge amount of money while seeing very little of their baby during the week. She seemed proud of her good work and proud of her baby and incredibly conflicted about the financial and emotional gymnastics required to have both. Some women who "have it all" may see their children awake ninety minutes or less per weekday.

This woman, like so many Gen X women, had always done everything "right." Good grades. Good job. Good work ethic. And this is where it got her: in a conference room in midtown Manhattan, taking fervent notes on how to get to the top of that mountain where she keeps hearing there is so much room for people like her.

In 1950 only 12 percent of married women with children under the age of six worked.[38] After a sharp increase, rates have leveled off since 1990, at about 76 percent.[39] Now the question is: how do you work and also do everything else, or very much of anything else?

Claudia Goldin has found that women's earnings start out being roughly equal to men's but then diverge as the women start juggling home and family. The solution to this inequity, she writes,[40] "does not (necessarily) have to involve government intervention and it need not make men more responsible in the home (although that wouldn't hurt). But it must involve changes in the labor market, especially how jobs are structured and remunerated to enhance temporal flexibility."

Goldin predicts that the gender gap in pay would be "considerably reduced" and might vanish if firms "did not have an incentive to disproportionately reward individuals who labored long hours and worked particular hours." There's a rare idea: the private sector could do something to help women — that it's not just up to us to cultivate sponsors, mentors, or advisers and to demand our place at the table.

Nearly every friend of mine in corporate America has her own tricks for dealing with harassment or condescension, annual reviews, difficult teammates. One, a divorced mother of three, overcomes her shyness and dislike of confrontation by chanting her kids' names in her head while psyching herself up to ask for an assignment or a raise. If it were just up to her, she says, she'd avoid those conversations, but her children are depending on her income, so she makes herself go into the office and advocate for herself. When it works, she feels triumphant. When it does not, she feels she's let down not only her children but also all of womankind.

Internalizing the idea that it's within your power to climb the mountain if only you believe in yourself enough and do the work has led us to the logical conclusion: if you haven't made it to the mountaintop, what's wrong with you?

In a 2018 *Harvard Business Review* summary of research,[41] behavioral scientists wrote that they "fear that *Lean In*'s main message — which emphasizes individual action as a way to address gender inequality — may lead people to view women as having played a greater role in sustaining and even causing gender inequality." The more we talk about what women should do, the study's authors said, the more women tend to be blamed for not fixing it.

The fact is, you can read a hundred books, go to ten conferences a year, take your sponsors out to a dozen coffees a month to pick their brains, but ultimately, unless you're the boss, you are not in charge of hiring yourself, giving yourself a raise, or making your workplace less toxic or more flexible.

In her book *Reset,* the diversity activist Ellen Pao says that she once tried to take the advice of *Lean In* and to claim a seat at the table. It was on a private jet flight with powerful men. She boldly joined their conversation only to discover that it was not about business but about porn stars.[42] Her conclusion: "Taking your seat at the table doesn't work so well when no one wants you there and you are vastly outnumbered."

Michelle Obama put it more bluntly on her 2018 book tour, telling a New York crowd: "That whole 'so you can have it all.' Nope, not at the same time. That's a lie.

And it's not always enough to lean in, because that shit doesn't work all the time."[43]

One major problem seems to be that, as Susan Chira wrote in the *New York Times,* research "has shown that it's harder for assertive, ambitious women to be seen as likable, and easier to conclude they lack some intangible, ill-defined quality of leadership."[44]

The "think leader, think male" mind-set is still common, according to a Catalyst study entitled "The Double-Bind Dilemma for Women in Leadership: Damned If You Do, Doomed If You Don't."[45] Women in the corporate world often are regarded as either too passive or too aggressive, too ambitious or not ambitious enough, too flighty or too off-putting. Add that to the enduring afflictions of sexual harassment, ageism, pregnancy discrimination, and run-of-the-mill lack of power.[46]

A social worker I know loved her workplace. A hardworking and engaged employee, she believed that she might be able to stay there until she retired in a decade or so. Then, without warning, the nursing home where she worked was bought by a big conglomerate. Right away, the bosses started to do things that demoralized the staff: pay cuts, less time for sitting with each patient, uncomfortable uniforms. "I loved that job," she told me while we stood on the grass under a light rain at her daughter's college graduation party. "Now it's a slog."

In an analysis of Gen X women's career paths, advertising agency J. Walter Thompson boiled the facts down into a slogan: "Never presume success."[47]

Director of the Institute for Ethical Leadership at Rutgers University and author of *The Working Life*,[48] Joanne B. Ciulla told me that one major irony of modern life is that people tend to identify with their work more than with anything else — an unfortunate inclination now, without job security.

"This is an era when life should be filled with all sorts of rewarding activities," she said. "Yet many find themselves caught up not only in long hours of work but in debt and suffering from stress, loneliness, and crumbling families."[49]

A professor for the past forty-three years, Ciulla sees Gen X women in shock from this state of affairs, because, she says, they have credited "the false illusion that all the problems had been solved.

"It used to be amazing to listen to my students," said Ciulla. "They just had very unrealistic expectations about the gender situation in the world. They'd say, 'We don't need feminists anymore. It's been solved. And feminism turns people off.' They thought we were crazy old bats."

By middle age, we can't help seeing how much inequality still exists.

"So we're definitely getting our comeuppance now," I said of Gen Xers who when they were younger dismissed Boomer feminists.

"Yeah, well," Ciulla said, sounding truly sorry for us. "It's kind of a sad comeuppance. Being a fifty-year-old woman out of a job is hard. If you're a professor, you can be old, but in most other jobs, they don't want old women. The stats hold that up. They have a much harder time getting into the workplace and lower salaries. And often they're single parents."

Is there no hope?

"I'll give you one hopeful thing," Ciulla said. "And that is the fact that more than fifty-six percent of college graduates are women. Eventually, women will start catching up, because they will be more qualified."

Many experts have told me that CEOs must commit to building a fair culture, and there must be metrics in place for judging performance in place of a gut feeling about someone being a good guy (in which case you hire an awful lot of guys). If diversity were another measure of an executive's success and were judged alongside sales, things could change quickly.[50]

One lawyer who does work on diversity and equal rights in corporate America told me she is often asked what companies should do to improve things for women and other disenfranchised groups. She has a list of recommendations. Then she told me her honest advice, rarely stated quite so directly, for any company that really wants to create equality: "You should burn this shit down and start over."

It's possible, while depressing, that corporate life is not inherently compatible with life-life. To elude problems with the modern workplace, perhaps women should opt for self-employment via entrepreneurship or the so-called gig economy.

According to Freelancers Union founder Sara Horowitz, most freelancers are women. She believes it's because "the traditional work structure just isn't working well for them . . . our lives play out in stages that don't fit well with a corporate world dominated by men. By our thirties, many women are starting families and struggling with taking time away from the office. By our forties, we're often hitting the glass ceiling in terms of pay and promotions. By our fifties and sixties, unfortunately, we're often being ignored altogether."[51]

It's tough to find good gig-economy statistics.[52] Contract workers are a diverse group, including day laborers, musicians, and consultants. But a conservative summary of the research puts the proportion of workers who are currently full-time freelancers at 11 percent.[53] Some experts predict that half the workforce will be freelance by 2020.[54]

Making your own schedule, working for yourself, "doing what you love" — especially when contemplated from an office cubicle — can seem like all upside. You become your own boss, and the sky is the limit.

Last year, I accepted an invitation to appear at a conference where I would listen to entrepreneurial attendees' spiels and give them advice on pitching their projects to the press. I would receive $250 to be there for a few hours, and I believed I would be useful. Having worked at magazines on and off since the early 1990s, I felt confident that I could give them advice on what to do and not do.

What I did not know is that a huge number of those pitching that year were aspiring life coaches. The stories I heard from many of them were ghastly: One told me she had eight family deaths and five miscarriages in one year. Another said her child was abducted. Several had survived domestic abuse or cancer. These experiences made them want to transform their lives, to help people, and so they had become empowerment speakers. They were following their passions. But it was unclear to me how these passions would result in the paying of bills.

Brooke Erin Duffy, an assistant professor of communication at Cornell University, calls the rhetoric around pursuing work you love "aspirational labor": "Aspirational labor is a mode of (mostly) uncompensated, independent work that is propelled by the much-venerated ideal of *getting paid to do what you love.*"[55] The problem: doing what you love often does not pay.

"The rise of independent work and freelancers has given us a lot of interesting narratives in entrepreneurship — the "mompreneur," the "girl boss," Duffy told me.[56] "Independent work is seen as empowering and democratic and freeing us from the traditional confines of the workplace . . . [But] independent work comes with incredible demands. You're managing a business all by yourself, and you have all the stresses and uncertainties and anxieties that come from being your own boss." Many women like the ones I met at that conference, having left corporate America for the gig economy, found themselves working twice as hard for a quarter of the money.

For those who like going to an office or having decent health insurance or who thought their hustling days were behind them, self-employment can feel like a demotion — and it can make a full-time position more elusive. One good thing, at least, about freelancing is that you don't need to worry about losing free or subsidized benefits, because you already pay for them in full yourself.

As a freelancer for the past decade, I know this from personal experience. Some years are flush; some are meager. There's no way to plan ahead. I hustle constantly. Each year, I cobble together work as an author, ghostwriter, magazine freelancer, and teacher. Every gig could be the last one. With no clear demarcation between work and home, I often end up both working all the time and continually being distracted. I have spells of envying others in my field who have proper desks rather than kitchen tables surrounded by toys, and the company of people who aren't strangers at Starbucks.

My friend Tara called me while she packed to go to Miami to cover a hurricane for her news organization. On my cell phone as I walked to pick my son up from school, I told her that another freelance gig had evaporated for me that morning. I do love my work, but I must regularly cope with not getting something that I thought I was perfect for, or with the start of a job being delayed and delayed and then vanishing, or with being let go from a project that seemed to be going well.

"You were so smart to take an office job when you did," I told my friend, who has a sure-enough place of work, actual business cards, and a 401(k). "To get out of freelancing and find some stability."

She laughed loudly. "Did you hear the first part of our call?" she said. "My boss is sending me to Florida to *die in a hurricane.*"

I hadn't spoken to Lori, the North Carolina contracts analyst who dreamed of starting a food truck, for a few months, so I called her.

"I got laid off," Lori said. "I'm trying to find a new job and I'm also trying to figure out if maybe I should be looking to do something else. But you know, that's not ideal, because there's no cash to start my cheese truck or anything.

"I was interviewing with one company for

almost as long as I've been unemployed. I had several interviews with them. Just last week we mutually decided that it wasn't going to be a good fit, because this job would have been sixty or seventy hours a week" — leaving little time for her to spend with her three-year-old son.

Speaking of him: "A lot of people have assumed that since I've been staying home I've kept my son home with me. But I can't, because you can't get into a preschool on a moment's notice. So while I'm unemployed we're still shouldering the burden of his preschool tuition."

If they pulled him out of school he'd go to the bottom of the waiting list to get back in once she found a job. So she's paying for child care she doesn't need. To cover it, she and her husband have started borrowing from their retirement savings.

"I definitely thought that I would be more financially stable than I am," Lori told me when I asked how middle age is different from what she expected. "I thought potentially we could survive on one salary, or I could pursue a dream. Or we could take two vacations a year — someplace nice, where you have to get on a plane, you know?"

She did everything she could to make that

possible. She picked a stable field. She earned a good degree. She married someone with a professional job. They waited to start a family until she was thirty-eight, so they'd be financially ready. At one point, they wanted to move to a bigger city but chose not to because it was more affordable to stay in Charlotte. And now, not only can't they swing a vacation; she feels that they can't afford to have the second child she always wanted.

"I'm grateful for what I have, but I definitely didn't think that I would be struggling in many, many ways by the time I got to forty," she said, then paused. "We did a lot of things right, you know? My husband and I. We did a lot of things right."

5
MONEY PANIC

"Money is weird, because it's a primary source of stress, and nobody's allowed to talk about it."

Gen X women undergo a bone-deep, almost hallucinatory panic about money. The worst part: it's a fear based on experience and complicated by a sense that we shouldn't be having this problem. We are some of the best-educated human beings ever and among the first adults in recent American history in worse financial shape than our parents.

The American dream is no longer dreamable for many of us. The gap between the richest 1 percent and everyone else has been increasing for the past thirty years; it widened greatly in the 1990s, as we were entering the job market.[1]

"Stagnant wages, diminishing job opportunities, and lost home values may be

158

painting a vastly different future for Gen X and Gen Y," reported the Urban Institute. "Today's political discussions often focus on preserving the wealth and benefits of older Americans and the baby boomers. Often lost in this debate is attention to younger generations whose wealth losses, or lack of long-term gains, have been even greater . . . Despite their relative youth, [Gen X and Gen Y] may not be able to make up the lost ground."[2]

"Since joining the workforce and starting to save, Generation X has endured the roller coaster of the financial markets," wrote Catherine Collinson, president of the Transamerica Center for Retirement Studies. "Gen Xers have enjoyed the irrational exuberance in the late '90s followed by the dot-com bust and post–September 11 market declines. They rode the equity markets up in the recovery through 2007 — and suffered steep declines as the markets spiraled [in 2008] into the worst recession since the Great Depression. Many lost their jobs; some lost their homes."[3]

A major report called *The Fading American Dream* — the product of research conducted by Raj Chetty's Equality of Opportunity Project at Harvard — found that rising in the US class structure is less and less possible, with middle-class families seeing the sharpest decline in opportunity. Of American men born in 1940, 95 percent could expect to earn more than their fathers. For American men born in 1980, only 41 percent can.[4]

For Generation X women, the news is worse.

"We still see that this trend holds," said Robert Fluegge, a researcher on Chetty's team.[5] "If you're looking at the income in a woman's entire family — her income and her partner's or just hers, if she has no partner — those numbers are the same." Whereas our parents together had a 90 percent chance of out-earning their parents, we have, with our partners, just a 50 percent chance of doing the same.

And if you look at just the woman's individual income against her father's? That's where it gets strange.

"Women have been entering the workforce in large numbers," said Fluegge. "More women are working white-collar jobs. They're better educated. You might expect that this [downwardly mobile] trend wouldn't hold [for them], but it does. When you're looking at the comparison between daughters' and fathers' income in the same time period, for daughters born in 1940, forty to forty-five percent will outearn their fathers. For daughters born in the 1980s, that number is down to about twenty-five percent."

One in four. That's our chance of outearning our fathers. Is that what I'm hearing?

Fluegge said yes: "Daughters are much less likely to earn more than their fathers. We've still seen a decline in the chances that daughters have despite all those other changes that women have gone through, and changes that have been made in the way that women interact with the workplace. It paints a pretty stark picture."

He went further: "It's one of the defining problems of our time, both economically and more broadly than that. Economic inequality and its effects are real and strong and something we need to understand better and address. To me, the main takeaway of this study is that changes in inequality over the past forty years have had really, really substantial effects on people's livelihoods and their conception of the American dream."

Generation X women raised by feminist Boomer mothers may feel extra shame at failing to thrive financially. When I was growing up, my mother often told me: "Always make your own money." It was not bad advice. She didn't want me to be dependent on a man. For her, money was freedom and power, and she wanted me to have as much of both as possible. The advice had an unintended side effect, though: I work hard, all the time, but when I fail to make an adequate amount of money, I feel terror. I become convinced that not only have I put my credit score or my family's budget in jeopardy, I've set back the cause of feminism and endangered my freedom. I don't just feel broke; I feel doomed.

"I call my midlife crisis Betty," said a forty-three-year-old filmmaker in Brooklyn, New York. "Betty is on me about being single and broke. Not having money reaches deep into you."

It hurts our emotional well-being, our confidence, and our sense of what's possible.

One friend of mine gave birth to her only child in her early forties. When her son was two she started to suspect something was wrong. Getting him treatment would consume much of her energy and paycheck for the better part of a decade. "It's been a lonely, weird road," she told me, "chasing the train of the special ed world. I can barely keep up. His 'case' is so time-consuming and expensive I feel like I've missed a few years of his life. I'm a bit crushed. But working hard to recover. Now he has the best doctors, staff, people dealing with him. I've kicked a lot of ass. But it's taken its toll." She recently started a new career as a real estate agent and is working hard to establish herself in that world. "It's a big stress ball," she says. "And I teach yoga! Sometimes I want to pack it all in, sell off my life, and go live in the woods. But oh — money."

In their forties, our parents' generation could expect to own a house and to have savings. In our forties, we are often still scrambling the way we did at twenty-five. According to a 2017 national survey by CareerBuilder, 78 percent of US workers live paycheck-to-paycheck; nearly three in four say they are in debt.[6]

The reasons we're in this spot are many, but I keep coming back to Generation X's almost comically bad timing. As reporter Lisa Chamberlain put it in her book about Generation X, *Slackonomics:* "The Great Middle Class Squeeze got under way just as we were becoming the middle demographic of the middle class."[7]

In *When: The Scientific Secrets of Perfect Timing,* Daniel H. Pink discusses research on Stanford MBAs that showed how the state of the stock market when they graduated influenced the career path they took.[8] In a bull market, with share prices rising and the future looking bright, students were more likely to work on Wall Street. In a bear market, when share prices were tumbling, many graduates opted instead to work for nonprofits or to consult.

Much of Gen X graduated into a weak job market. Headlines included: SCRAMBLE FOR JOBS: GRADUATING INTO A RECESSION — A SPECIAL REPORT: DEGREES AND STACKS OF RÉSUMÉS YIELD FEW JOBS FOR CLASS OF '91,[9] BLEAK JOB MARKET AWAITS CLASS OF '92,[10] and FOR '93 GRADUATES, JOB HUNTING 101 WON'T BE A BREEZE.[11] A summary of graduation-year job markets in the book *Late Bloomers* by Alexander Abrams and David Lipsky reads: "1980: okay, 1981: soft, 1982: lousy, 1983: awful, 1984: soft, 1985: okay, 1986: good, 1987: good, 1988: good, 1989: soft, 1990: awful, 1991: lousy again, 1992: lousier, 1993: worse again."[12]

The Economic Policy Institute reports that the average hourly wages paid to young college graduates hit a new low in the mid-1990s.[13] Graduating into a strong economy versus a weak one could amount to as much

164

as a 20 percent difference in wages over time.[14]

The US economy strengthened in the 1990s — but not for Gen X. While the GDP grew 91 percent, taking inflation into account, between 1981 and 2001, Gen X was hit hard by the 1987 market crash, the 1991–92 economic slowdown, and the bursting of the dot-com bubble, setting off a recession — followed six months later by the terrorist attacks of September 11.[15] According to the Bureau of Labor Statistics, the country lost more than 2.7 million jobs from March 2001 to March 2002, right when many younger Gen Xers were trying to gain a foothold.[16]

"Gen X has had quite a tough time," says Hugo Scott-Gall, of Goldman Sachs Research, who remarked that the 2001 and 2008 downturns[17] were "scarring and very important events, and they have changed the attitude towards how they save and how they invest." In plenty of cases, they do neither. More than half of Gen Xers plan to work past age sixty-five or expect not to retire at all.[18]

The lucky ones who have managed to put money away don't always leave it untouched until retirement. Forty-five percent of our generation have already withdrawn money from retirement savings, despite negative tax implications and early withdrawal penalties.[19] Across the country, fortysomethings — especially women — aren't saving anywhere near enough for a comfortable retirement.[20]

"I have a million dollars in my retirement account," a forty-nine-year-old biotech executive told me. "And I'm still worried. Our kids are going to have to take out loans for school. Then, there are the retirement calculators on the internet. All of the information is: 'Lady, you'd better save money because no one else will take charge of your financial future!' I was incredibly frugal my whole life. I've been working my ass off since I was ten years old, babysitting. And still I am stressed out about money."

A forty-five-year-old woman who runs her own dog-walking business said: "I have five, six hundred thousand dollars in retirement accounts and savings. And I have no children and I'm divorced. I own my own small business. And I feel like I'm going to be in a cardboard box when I'm seventy, on the street. I feel like any amount of money isn't enough. I know I probably, for my age, have so much more than my friends, but I still fear that every single day."

These two women are outliers in having

so much saved, but average in their shared conviction that no amount will provide true security. Listening to women talk about their finances, I keep thinking of the money-obsessed mother in the 1926 D. H. Lawrence short story "The Rocking-Horse Winner," which many of us read in high school: "The house came to be haunted by the unspoken phrase: There must be more money! There must be more money! The children could hear it all the time though nobody said it out loud."[21]

It doesn't help that we're in the second-longest economic expansion since 1854 and poised for a "correction" soon.[22] Everywhere are reminders that the market could crash at any time.[23] As I'm writing this, an emailed news summary, popping up in my inbox, features the headline, "What Will Cause the Next Recession? A Look at the 3 Most Likely Possibilities."[24]

For several years after a layoff in 2009, I'd managed to reach six figures or close as a freelancer. But I went into one year expecting to make roughly that and instead, thanks to a run of bad luck, took in just $36,000. My husband didn't have a good year, either. We had a little kid. What were we supposed to do? We closed out my IRA. It wasn't much, but it seemed like enough to tide us over until work picked up again. Then digging out of that hole took years.

A middle-class, midlife existence is just so *expensive*. According to the US Department of Labor chart entitled "Generational Spending Habits,"[25] Gen X spends more per household on housing, clothing, eating out, food at home, and "all other spending," and only a tiny bit less than Boomers on the one other category: entertainment. We lay out a lot, especially on our children.

Nearly half of Gen Xers carry a credit card balance month to month.[26] A 2009 law, the Credit Card Accountability Responsibility and Disclosure Act, put restrictions on credit card companies' efforts to sign up those under twenty-one — peddling cards from college campus tents and offering freebies for signing up, for example — that left so many Gen Xers with consumer debt by the time they were out of college.[27]

According to research compiled in 2019 by MarketWatch under the headline "All the Ways Gen X Is Financially Wrecked," compared with Millennials and Boomers, Gen X is in the worst financial shape overall.[28] According to the credit-reporting firm Experian, we have the highest average credit card debt ($7,750), average mortgage debt ($231,774), and average non-mortgage debt

($30,334).[29] Our generational average FICO score is a far from excellent 655.[30]

According to Pew, Gen Xers lost almost half of their wealth between 2007 and 2010.[31] Despite their bouncing back on that front,[32] high debt lingers, and so does a sense of fragility. National Opinion Research Center at the University of Chicago's General Social Survey reports that, most times, people forty-five to fifty-four are more likely than other age groups to say they are "pretty well satisfied" with their finances. But it's not so for Gen Xers reaching this age. Coming to what were supposed to be our top-earning years, we discovered that they no longer brought top earnings. A 2017 working paper published by the National Bureau of Economic Research reports that "the stagnation of lifetime incomes is unlikely to reverse."[33]

A *New York Times* article from that same year dubbed people born on the early end of Generation X "Generation Grumpy," because those in this cohort have entered supposedly flush times only to feel that "they are not doing as well as they might have expected."[34]

Predictably, the comments were along the indignant lines of: *"Grumpy?!?!"*

A commenter calling herself Anita from

Richmond explained that Gen X wasn't just a bunch of whiners miffed about not being millionaires: "This generation is unhappy because we are all going to be working until we die."

The media often minimizes Gen X's midlife angst. My favorite headline from this genre: DROWNING AT MIDLIFE? START SWIMMING.[35] Literally, the woman says she headed off a midlife crisis by swimming three times a week.

In the mid-2000s, mortgages were being handed out like candy. Younger Gen Xers had just entered their prime first-home-buying years and older Gen Xers who owned a home were starting to think about trading up. At last, those who'd been locked out of the American dream could think about buying property or having the home they'd always wanted.

Then came the subprime mortgage crisis. The unemployment rate went from 5 percent in December 2007 to 10 percent in October 2009.[36] In a flash, homes in big cities lost 10 to more than 30 percent of their value.[37]

Gen X "took most of the hit from the housing bust," according to a Harvard report. Home ownership rates for our demographic "have fallen further than those of any other age group."[38]

One forty-eight-year-old Connecticut woman I spoke with bought a big house with her husband in 2005 for $850,000. Theirs was one of the many that wound up underwater in the housing crisis. When she and her husband divorced, they sold the house for $715,000, losing the difference, plus everything they'd put into it — their total savings. They lived together for several years after they'd split, because they couldn't afford separate places.

Between 2000 and 2005 and since 2013, home prices have outpaced salary growth[39] — resuming a trend by which, from 1970 to 2000, the cost of buying a home rose by more than 80 percent, adjusted for inflation.[40]

A forty-two-year-old friend of mine in New Jersey told me, "I'm scared as shit. We never bought a house. And now we have two kids, so the idea of buying something is like a dream — it happens in fairy tales! You look back and you're like, 'Oh my God. What about retirement?' 'Will we ever own anything?' 'How are we putting these kids through college?' It's really, really scary."

The *Wall Street Journal* reported that Gen X "has suffered more than any other age cohort from the housing bust, according to an analysis of federal data, suggesting homeownership rates for that group could remain depressed for years to come."[41]

Since 2000, across the country the cost of renting is up, and so is the number of people trying to find cheap housing,[42] of which there is a nationwide dearth.[43]

"Lower your expenses" is good advice, but moving to a cheaper place or a cheaper part of the country can carry its own costs, beyond the rental truck. Even if you can't quite afford the place you're in, there may be no better options anywhere within commuting distance of well-paying work.[44]

The economic divide between prosperous areas and poor ones has grown exponentially in our lifetimes. "If you made the wrong choice about where to live in the mid-2000s, you could be stuck now," says Lisa Chamberlain.[45] "If you stayed in San Francisco you might be okay. If you got out of Dodge and went to Nebraska — not so much. In Cleveland you're not going to be accumulating wealth. Millennials can still reinvent themselves. But if you put down roots and had a family somewhere with a lack of opportunities, it's going to be very hard to get out and relocate into a more expensive market."

Then there is student loan debt, which

can kneecap a family for generations. Gen X graduated with plenty of debt, and it's getting worse.[46] I know people who have paid off their own student loans just in time to start paying for their children's education. The average yearly cost of a four-year public college is now 81 percent of an American woman's median annual income.[47] And our children may have even more trouble paying back student debt than we did. Millennials in their early thirties now earn 4 percent less on average than those of us born between 1966 and 1980 did at the same age.[48]

The *New York Times* editor M. H. Miller, a Millennial who graduated just after the 2008 Great Recession, recently wrote of how the seemingly insurmountable debt he took on in order to attend New York University has hamstrung him and his parents. "I've spent a great deal of time in the last decade shifting the blame for my debt," he writes. "Whose fault was it? My devoted parents, for encouraging me to attend a school they couldn't afford? The banks, which should have never lent money to people who clearly couldn't pay it back to begin with, continuously exploiting the hope of families like mine, and quick to exploit us further once that hope disappeared? Or was it my fault for not having the foresight to realize it was a mistake to spend roughly $200,000 on a school where, in order to get my degree, I kept a journal about reading Virginia Woolf?"[49]

Health care is another expense that can wipe out a family's savings, even if they have health insurance. Middle age is when conditions like type 2 diabetes are most likely to be diagnosed.[50] According to the National Institutes of Health, chronic pain disorders, like TMJ, are more common in women, and strokes happen more often to middle-aged women than to middle-aged men.[51] Our risk of getting breast cancer in our thirties is 1 in 227. In our forties: 1 in 68. In our fifties it is 1 in 42.[52]

One woman I know was diagnosed with breast cancer when her daughter was a toddler. In the years that followed, she had a biopsy, lumpectomy, double mastectomy, implants, nipple surgery. Some of her most vivid midlife memories are of lying in recovery rooms "full of women filled up with gas to their necks, moaning."

About 75 percent of autoimmune patients are women, Virginia T. Ladd, president and executive director of the American Autoimmune Related Diseases Association, told me, and autoimmune diseases overall are on the rise. The reason why such afflictions — particularly thyroid disorders like Hashimoto's disease — are booming remains mysterious. "It's most likely something in the environment, because genes do not change that fast," Ladd told me. "We've added lots of things to our environment, including the overuse of antibiotics, which may significantly change the gut, the microbiome. It's probably also influenced by how our world is compared with how it was thirty or fifty years ago."[53]

According to the Social Security Administration, the year in which the Social Security trust fund is projected to be exhausted is 2034.[54] That's right as many of us will be hitting retirement age. Roughly three-quarters of Gen Xers don't believe Social Security will provide them with full benefits when they retire.[55] If the reserve funds are depleted, that doesn't mean no more Social Security checks.[56] But it may well mean people receive just about three-quarters of what they're counting on; cuts to Social Security would hit women hardest.[57]

"Chances are, Social Security will still be around once you hit the eligibility age," writes *New York Times* finance columnist Ron Lieber. "But it probably won't provide enough money, after taxes, for all the expenses you'll face in retirement. Plus, it's possible that some of the rules will change before it's your turn to collect."[58] His guide on how to save for retirement includes the ever-popular compounding-interest chart, showing that if you sock away $5,000 a year, starting when you're twenty-two rather than ten years later, you end up with a surplus of about half a million dollars at retirement. No mention there of the payoff if you don't start until forty-two. Good. I don't want to know.

Now for financially positive morbidity: Generation X will probably become solvent one day — when they inherit their parents' wealth. According to CNBC, over the next few decades, the Baby Boomers, the biggest and richest generation in US history, will transfer $30 trillion in assets to their Generation X and Millennial offspring.[59]

"Gen-Xers are within hailing distance of their prime years," reads a 2018 Blackbaud Institute report. "Regardless of the fascination with Millennials, Gen X is poised to be the next big thing for philanthropy . . . The 'Age of X' in philanthropy may be as little as a decade away."[60]

The size of the inheritance is, of course, contingent on many factors, such as how much of their fortunes Boomers will need for long-term care. The average cost of a private room in a nursing home is $7,698 a month.[61]

There are those who argue that regardless of whether we come into money Gen X has a potentially game-changing capacity for doing good in the world. A decade ago, writer Jeff Gordinier argued in his book *X Saves the World* that Gen X's cautious attitude was just what society needed. A 2018 book by Matthew Hennessey of the *Wall Street Journal* and a 2017 article in *Vanity Fair* by Rich Cohen made similar arguments.

According to Cohen, Gen Xers are "the last Americans schooled in the old manner, the last Americans that know how to fold a newspaper, take a joke, and listen to a dirty story without losing their minds." He said that our supposed cynicism and dread amount to sanity: "We could not stand to hear the Utopian talk of the boomers as we cannot stand to hear the Utopian talk of the millennials. We know that most people are rotten to the core, but some are good, and proceed accordingly."[62]

"Unlike the millennials, we remember what life was like before the Internet invaded and conquered nearly everything," Matthew Hennessey writes. "In that memory resides the hope of our collective re-demption, the seed of renewal that could stem the rot, decay, erosion, and collapse all around us."[63]

Without a psychological overhaul, though, it could be that Gen X women will never save the world or ever feel financially secure even if they inherit a pile of money. When I ponder the last decades of our parents' lives — and then try to wrap my mind around stemming rot and decay in society — I don't feel empowered. I think: *That all sounds very expensive.*

6
DECISION FATIGUE

"I have always looked forward to my forties, thinking that's when I'm going to feel like a real woman. I think I may have felt like that for two months. And then I said, 'Oh my God, this feels horrible!'"

I first met my friend Nikita a decade ago in a New York City park when we were new mothers in our thirties and our infant sons became friends. I was not surprised to learn, given her athletic build and long, straight brown hair, that she'd been a teenage model — a Brooke Shields type from a logging community in the Pacific Northwest. In her twenties, she'd traded modeling for working as a dancer and then for teaching yoga. In her thirties, she had become a doula. Some days she'd show up to the park exhausted but relieved, having stayed up all night helping one of her clients through a birth. Then she had a second baby — a girl — herself.

Throughout those early years of baby rearing, she and I fetched each other coffee and watched each other's kids. We polished off boxes of Wheat Thins sitting on the playground bench, breaking up fights, holding dripping ice-cream cones, helping small bodies into and out of onesies and then, suddenly, 4T swim trunks and then, what seemed like a second later, size 8 snow pants. We talked and talked: about our kids' schools, about what to make for dinner, about — wait, what did the baby just put in her mouth?

Then, right when the whole early childhood thing was wrapping up for us and Nikita started to talk about going back to school, she became pregnant again. Soon after that baby — another son — was born, she found living in the city next to impossible. The costs were too high. Wrangling a stroller on the subway was no longer a delightful challenge. Her family rented out their New York place and moved back to the Northwest, though to Portland, Oregon, a more urban part of the state than where she'd lived in as a girl. They bought a house, which she renovated. Her first son is in middle school, her daughter is in elementary school, and her baby is toddling. Her husband, who's from Kansas, helps manage his family's farm and has recently joined a community of fellow comic book artists. The kids are happy. Still, when we spoke on the phone last fall, I heard an edge in Nikita's voice that hadn't been there before.

"I have nothing to complain about," she said. "But at the same time, you just feel miserable. Before now, I never had real depression, where you just don't want to get out of bed, you don't want to speak to anybody, you don't want to take a shower. It's a dark sensation."

The other day her ten-year-old daughter found a photo from when Nikita was younger and said: "That was *you*? You used to be so pretty!" Nikita recalled recently being mistaken for her baby's grandmother.

She feels in limbo, disconnected from her life. Her days are filled with responsibilities, chores, and errands. There's no narrative through line. She wonders what the point is of any of it.

"I guess that's the really sad part," she said. "I keep thinking, 'Who cares?' Obviously, I'm not talking about the kids. But all of the time and money and energy we spend working on these houses and building stuff up together and creating this complicated joint existence. I don't actually feel attached to any of it."

Middle-aged women I spoke with often second-guessed their life choices.

"I sometimes secretly wish I'd worked for Goldman Sachs right after Yale," a forty-nine-year-old executive told me. "I feel like I could have retired by now. Or at least be secure about retirement. Sometimes I'm angry about marrying someone with no assets and a mountain of debt. But I think I'm happier having a loving partner. I think. What do I worry about most? Not having money when I'm old. I'm scared about that. I spend a lot of time wishing I could be more at peace with my choices and with the life I have."

Nikita told me she has started to think of building a new career for herself, but she hesitates: "The idea of starting over and having zero experience and zero credibility doing something else is really daunting and scary. I keep telling myself, 'People do it all of the time.' " Still, she's stuck in the grind of daily obligation and can't seem to make a decision about what direction to take. And she seems not to fully trust herself.

"When all your choices have led you here to this place," another woman told me, "how can you trust yourself to make a right choice now?"

Adulthood exerts a steady pressure on us

to make decisions: which car insurance to get, where to send the kids to school, whom to marry, what job to have, whether or not to switch careers. Gen X women internalized a fatalism that one friend described to me as: "You have so many choices! Go for the most difficult one or whatever guarantees misery and hardship!" No wonder women in midlife may feel tempted to delay decisions, to hang out a little longer in an in-between state.

Personally, I have had a tortured, not entirely coherent approach to decision making and labels dating back to the 1990s. It was manifested in reluctance to commit or to join in, especially when it came to rites of passage.

In 1993, when I was a junior in high school, one of my best friends, a senior, came over to my house instead of attending his prom. We stayed up all night watching a stack of high-school-massacre horror movies on VHS — *Carrie, Prom Night 4, Massacre at Central High.*

The next year, I went to my own senior prom with a friend I'd recently started sleeping with but refused to call my boyfriend — because who needs labels? (He was totally my boyfriend.) I bought a very pink dress at a secondhand store. In a

183

parody of what we thought the prom was about, we dyed my heels, his cummerbund, even his socks pink to match.

Resistance to commitment, to picking a path, has long been a Gen X hallmark. The 1990 *Time* magazine cover story about Gen X, "Proceeding with Caution," said: "A prime characteristic of today's young adults is their desire to avoid risk, pain and rapid change."[1] A twenty-two-year-old in the article — a man now fifty, assuming he's still out there — said he didn't want a serious relationship, because "not getting hurt is a big priority with me."

Caring went out of fashion in the 1990s. Our era's sex symbols were heroin-chic figures like Kate Moss. Heartiness aroused deep suspicion. In the late 1980s, I served proudly as co-captain of my middle school's basketball team. A few years later, I played no sports. My lunch consisted of coffee, cigarettes, and maybe an orange.

Our generation had few shared heroes. The 1992 MTV Video Music Awards, hosted by Dana Carvey, demonstrated that Boomers were still in charge. Among the stars performing were Eric Clapton, Def Leppard, and Elton John. A big winner of the night, thanks to the song "Right Now," was Van Halen, a band whose members were born in the 1940s and '50s.

Gen X "got no war to name us," to quote the Replacements' song "Bastards of Young." So much of our pop culture — *The Breakfast Club* (1985), *Heathers* (1988), *Pump Up the Volume* (1990), *My So-Called Life* (1994–95), *Twin Peaks* (1990–91) — reflected an existential, what's-the-point ambivalence.

Entertainment set in sunny California — *Beverly Hills, 90210* comes to mind — provided some escapism. One of the only purely delightful movies I recall from my teenage years was 1995's *Clueless.* The enthusiasm, the money, the non-neurotic reaction to mistakes — upon sideswiping a parked car during her driving test: "Ooh! Should I write them a note?" — it all felt more exotic to me than a foreign film. It still did not counteract the gross tonnage of despair to which we were subjected.

As a tween, I had a poster of River Phoenix on my wall. As far as I was concerned, he was the handsomest man in the world, particularly in the 1988 drama *Running on Empty.* He would be dead of a drug overdose before I was out of high school. Kurt Cobain, singer of the Gen X anthem "Smells Like Teen Spirit," would also die that school year — in April 1994, right around the time

185

my prom date and I were dyeing things pink. (Appropriately enough, the song itself was ironic, named after the deodorant Teen Spirit, mocking generational anthems.)

Molly Ringwald as Samantha in *Sixteen Candles* (1984) — her birthday forgotten by her family, her panties exhibited in a boys' bathroom — was the ultimate Gen X teen girl icon. When she wasn't being sexually harassed she was being bored to death. She was *over it*.

Ringwald recently wrote a *New Yorker* article revisiting the films she made with director John Hughes. She recalled an interview she did with him for *Seventeen* magazine in which he acknowledged that those movies were designed to legitimize the angst of the Gen X teen, something the wider culture wasn't doing.

Hughes said, "My generation had to be taken seriously because we were stopping things and burning things. We were able to initiate change, because we had such vast numbers. We were part of the Baby Boom, and when we moved, everything moved with us. But now, [with Generation X] there are fewer teens, and they aren't taken as seriously as we were."[2]

Millennials are anything but ignored, and they seem to have received a sunnier message. The key Muppet for younger Millennials was the perpetually sunny Elmo. Ours were Kermit, his mouth warped by anxiety; Big Bird, who for fourteen years was accused of imagining Snuffleupagus; and Oscar the Grouch, a sociopath.

Maybe Millennials seem optimistic because they're young. But even when we were young, we *seemed* old. Younger generations may not be better off than Gen X — in certain ways, they may be *worse* off — but have a better attitude. After all, one of their earliest memories is September 11. I wonder if Millennials may benefit from witnessing our struggles and our snide remarks about the future. Could it lead them to lower their expectations for themselves? And could that make all the difference?

"We always have transition periods," says Elizabeth Earnshaw, a couples and family therapist in Philadelphia.[3] "But midlife is a period of time where you might want to make transitions but you're stuck by financial stuff .When you're sixteen and you're transitioning into adulthood, you can do whatever you want because [unless you're poverty-stricken] money isn't really holding you back or you don't care about it. When you're in your twenties, you don't care about it as much either. But when you're forty years old and you've decided you might want to go back to school or take fertility treatments or whatever, you are financially tied to so many things."

She sees Gen X women flailing in reaction, unsure what to do and missing who they were in a simpler time.

"They might not go out and buy a convertible," says Earnshaw. "But they might be buying purses behind the scenes or having affairs. They flirt, fantasizing about what it would be like to not have kids or to go live in Miami or to go back to school. They often revert to whatever life they were living before they started doing whatever's making them feel stressed. If, prior to having a marriage and kids, you were in college going out with your girlfriends every single weekend and drinking and getting dressed up, now you go out every weekend to concerts with your friends. It could be traveling. It could be collecting something. It could be exercising the way you used to. I've had a couple of people who have said that they're smoking in their bedroom out the window the way they did when they were sixteen."

"I feel like I'm dealing with the death of some dreams that I had," said Erin, a thirty-nine-year-old woman who'd recently moved back home to Kansas City with her husband and children after giving up on making it as an actress in California. "I had that attitude of 'I'm out of here, Midwest! I'm going to go to Hollywood!' And now I'm back here."

She's driving the same roads she drove as a teenager, although now she looks older and there are kid seats in the back. The radio's playing the same music, although now the Gin Blossoms are on the oldies station.

In a 2018 book called *The Happiness Curve,* Jonathan Rauch described research on a "U-curve" dip in well-being that occurs in midlife everywhere in the world, including among great apes.[4] There have been academic challenges to the U-curve thesis,[5] but according to research by economists Andrew Oswald and David Blanchflower, in the United States, women's happiness bottoms out around forty; men's, around fifty.[6] (Maybe that's another reason the female experience isn't much discussed: By the time men start fretting, women might seem unaffected because they've been through it already.)

Even if you have no negative turning point in your life — a bad illness, the death of someone close to you, or an addiction crisis

can induce the more extreme "V-curve" —
Rauch reports that midlife is at odds with
happiness. The curve doesn't mean that it is
impossible "to be very satisfied with your
life in middle age," Rauch writes, "*but it is
harder . . .* The happiness curve is like an
undertow that pulls against you in middle
age. That doesn't mean you can't row
against it."[7]

Stanford psychologist Laura Carstensen
has said in a study and a TED talk that the
increase in the human life span is good
news, because stress, worry, and anger all
decrease with age. This is known as the
"paradox of aging," because, technically,
being older is more difficult — health and
energy usually decline, for starters — but
people tend to be happier toward the end of
life than they are in their forties.[8]

That said, the U-curve, having been
observed in the past, isn't necessarily a
guarantee of future performance. What if
ours is history's first curveless generation,
surfing a diagonal line straight to the graph's
lower right-hand corner? Midlife markers
sure seem to be more complicated for us.
There is no clear timeline in Gen X adulthood.

The other day at the library, I watched an
educational film called *Midlife Crisis?*

Amid stock images of middle-aged people reading pamphlets, playing solitaire, and walking in nature, the film propounded that men of this age are prone to depression and find it hard to talk about their lives. Once the male-focused books *Life Begins at 40, The Seasons of a Man's Life,* and *Men in Midlife Crisis* had been thoroughly discussed, women were granted a moment when this text appeared on the screen: "In the average woman's 35th year: Last child goes off to school. Risk of infidelity begins. She reenters the workforce. Divorced women remarry. Some women *'Run Away.'* Childbearing option decreases."[9]

The film was made in 2000, and it shows. A woman of that age may have children in school, or she may be trying to get pregnant for the first time. She has almost certainly been working since her teens. And she is likely to be facing a host of other obligations — while possibly beginning to confront perimenopause. Though one thing does hold: the *"Run Away"* option may be tempting, especially for women married to partners having their own midlife crises.

As Nikita was out running errands one day, her phone pinged. It was Amazon saying: "Thank you for shopping with us. You ordered *More Than Two: A Practical Guide to*

Ethical Polyamory. We'll send a confirmation when your item ships."

Nikita looked at her phone. The family Amazon account was connected to her email address, but she had not ordered the book. That meant her husband had. "He'd told me before that he was interested in the idea," she said. "But seeing that book order gave me an out-of-body experience."

There's something so Gen X about that moment. Not only does the woman of the house have to decide what's for dinner and which sink to buy for the rental property — now she must also make the call on whether or not her husband is allowed to sleep around.

To a man who doesn't want to be a cheater, it can make a kind of sense. He loves his wife and decided he would act on his lust for other women only with her explicit approval. In this case, she denied permission: "I'm not going to make you feel okay about it," she told him. "On top of everything else, I don't have to soothe your guilt."

Generation X has put everything on the table, up to and including traditional boundaries around relationships. The open-marriage discussions, which went around in circles for months, made Nikita nostalgic for a time when husbands had flings on business trips. At least back then wives were spared lachrymose conversations about monogamy when they'd rather be watching television.

"There are days where I can knock it all out of the park, right?" said Nicole, a woman in Northern California with six-year-old twins. "I volunteer at the kids' school. I do my part-time work. I clean the house. I walk the dog. Five million things. And then there are days where, after doing a couple of those things, I think, *I'm just going to read my magazine.* Or I don't bother to clean the floor or I leave stuff on the counter. That's just the way it goes.

"Well, this past weekend, my husband looked around, and said, 'So, what do you do all day?' I lost it. It wasn't a polite conversation. I got really upset. I literally thought I was having a mental breakdown. I went into a room and cried so much it hurt.

"We took a break and when we talked later he apologized. I told him, 'All I heard from you is: "You don't do what you need to do and you are failing." ' *I am failing.* I couldn't go to sleep because I just went over it, over it, over it again in my head."

If Gen X women are haunted by a vague

feeling that things are terrible and might not get better, it could be the U-curve. It could be perimenopausal depression. It could be temporary, situational stress. It could be a feeling left over from childhood that the other shoe is about to drop. And it could well be the pressure of decision making.

One woman told me that it felt as though nearly everything in her life was always pending. For the past year, she'd been in counseling with her boyfriend of three years, trying to decide whether or not to break up. For at least as long, she'd been trying to decide how to grow her real estate photography business. Meanwhile, to put it bluntly, she's been waiting for her pets to die.

"I got cats when I was twenty-eight," she said. "One of them was diagnosed with diabetes in 2007. The other one was recently diagnosed with hyperthyroid and kidney disease. I feel like I have an honorary graduate degree in cat nursing. I don't want to lose my cats, but also maybe it's time for them to . . . yeah."

Women with children may face additional pressures once they start trying to be more serious about their work. One CEO told me that the number one thing that she sees holding women back in their careers is maternal guilt.

A short Retro Report documentary called *The Mommy Wars*[10] dismantled the "toxic myth" that lasted through the 1990s: that putting young children in daycare or with other caregivers while mothers worked would damage them. The result of the myth was a brainwashing campaign designed to make women feel bad. The most chilling parts of the documentary are the clips of daytime talk shows and nighttime news programs that pit working women and stay-at-home mothers against one another. Then the anchors or hosts, so many of them men, turn somberly to the camera to ask if a woman should choose her job or her children.

Has the same "your career or your life" question ever been asked of men? Despite research showing that a father's attention is one of the key factors in a child's emotional health? Not to mention, again: a working mother in 2000 spent *just as much* time interacting with her children as did a stay-at-home mother in 1975.

In the documentary, sociologist Amy Hsin points out that as far as how a child turns out, the amount of time spent interacting with a mother is a drop in the bucket compared with other factors like the child's parents having a good education, the child's school's quality, and growing up in a safe neighborhood. Those are all things that a woman with a career can help make possible.

The "Mommy Wars" uproar did drive home one truth: pretty much everyone in America would like to have more support. This wasn't much of a revelation. In 1971, Judy Syfers Brady wrote the justly famous essay "I Want a Wife": "I want a wife who will keep my house clean. A wife who will pick up after me."[11]

Economist Heather Boushey writes in *Finding Time*[12] that when women started working, America lost its "silent partner" — the traditional American wife: "She took care of all the big and small daily emergencies that might distract the American Worker from focusing 100 percent on his job while he was at work. Little Johnny got in a fight on the playground? The American Wife will be right there to talk to the school. Aunt Bea fell and broke her hip? The American Wife can spend the afternoon bringing her groceries and making her dinner. The boss is coming over for dinner? The American Wife already has the pot roast in the oven."

What I, personally, wouldn't give for my very own American Wife. She would cook my meals and clean my bathtub and make my appointments and enforce my son's screen-time limits and drop by to visit my 101-year-old grandmother at the retirement home every week. I would get so much work done. My home would be spotless. I would sleep eight hours a night — heck, maybe nine.

You can buy that sort of support, of course. But then there's a question of whether or not you're earning enough to warrant the cost. When my son was a baby, I spent an entire stage play with tears streaming down my face — not because the show was sad or because I particularly missed my child, but because the play was awful and I felt physical pain that to see it I was spending $17 an hour, plus takeout and cab fare, for the sitter.

The whole "throw money at the problem" solution is awkward also because it suggests that fixing rich or middle-class women's problems requires poor women's work: the manicurist, the takeout delivery person, the night nurse, the Uber driver, the masseuse. Talk about invisible labor.

A decade or so ago, we were told that educated women were leaving the workforce in droves to be with their children, and pundits debated the value of mothers' working versus not working. Then Heather Boushey pointed out that data wasn't actually there to suggest that women with children were opting out of the labor market in growing numbers. According to her, "The main reason for declining labor force participation rates among women over the last four years appears to be the weakness of the labor market."[13]

In other words, they didn't "opt out" so much as "surrender." If you say, "Would you prefer the fish or the chicken," but the chicken is on top of a mountain and it's raining, while the fish is right in front of you under a tent, can that meaningfully be described as a choice? Do you really get to say that the woman choosing fish opted out of chicken consumption — that she must be biologically hardwired to prefer fish?

Think pieces about Generation X teem with lists of qualities we supposedly display. For example: "Superficial, easily distracted, rootless, inscrutable, self-centered, unfocused, pathetic."[14] Or: "With caution — and on little cat feet — wary, worn before wear, fearful, and suspicious."[15] Or as *Newsweek* put it in a 1993 editorial called "The Whiny Generation": "pusillanimous purveyors of pseudo-angst."[16]

198

Generation X's "endemic, possibly pathological, sarcasm," as music critic Carl Wilson put it,[17] was immortalized in films like *Slacker* (1990), *Singles* (1992), and the Ethan Hawke canon, epitomized by his *Reality Bites* (1994) rendition of the song "I'm Nuthin" and when he tells Winona that all they need to be happy are cigarettes, coffee, and conversation. Such characters reflect a generational jadedness and sarcasm — a pose barely covering a deep vulnerability.[18]

Gen X men's fictional avatars made not caring look sexy. "It was this cool new Gen X model of masculinity," said a friend. These were guys who didn't sell out or settle or do anything they didn't want to do. They were free. "But then a lot of us in this generation actually went out and married guys like that," said my friend. "And it's cute at twenty but at forty it is *incredibly irritating.*"[19]

Another friend of mine said she was dismayed to learn that the men she desired in her twenties were not actually crafting a new model of masculinity. They just spent the 1990s on Ecstasy.[20]

The hero of the 1986 John Hughes classic *Ferris Bueller's Day Off* takes nine sick days in his senior year, because, as he says, "Life moves pretty fast. You don't stop and look around once in a while, you could miss it." He doesn't want to waste time in a class-room; he craves adventure.

As a teenager, I found Ferris's approach, up to and including his disregard for "isms," attractive. As a grown-up woman with dreams of her own and enthusiasm for several isms, I am no longer drawn to men who find responsibility and authority comical. Can you imagine coparenting with Ferris Bueller?

It would be worse still to have married Tom Cruise's character from *Risky Business,* one of the biggest hits of 1983. "More clearly than any other film of its period," writes Ginia Bellafante,[21] "*Risky Business* hinges the privileging of male mediocrity on the exploitation of female disadvantage." That film, like so many of the era, taught us that men would be rewarded with wealth and advancement if they behaved badly or were lazy.

One forty-year-old woman in the Midwest told me she married a dead ringer for Eddie Vedder: "I'm not joking," she said. "He is so passive. He's my trophy husband. He's this musician who's really laid-back and sort of a dreamer and definitely of the generation where adulting smacked him in the face. He definitely defers to me all the time

200

with all the decisions, and I'm like, What is that about? Is he afraid to make the wrong decision, so he just waits? Or is it putting the wife in the mommy position? I don't know."

According to research on decision fatigue: "An excess of choices often leads us to be less, not more, satisfied once we actually decide," as one *New York Times* story puts it.[22] "There's often that nagging feeling we could have done better." Choosing where to live and where to work and how to spend your money is daunting enough, but making such high-stakes choices at your weariest — it's like trying to have an intimate conversation in a sports bar during the Super Bowl.

I saw my friend Nikita again not long ago. She seemed more relaxed. When I asked about her marriage, she told me things were better. A few months after her husband first broached the open-marriage question, she was no longer nursing their baby and felt as though she could at least have the conversation without getting mad. But by that point, her husband was no longer interested in the idea. " 'So, you just worked through it?' she asked him. 'Meanwhile, you put me through months of processing and now you've decided, "Oh, maybe I don't really care anymore." It was just a phase?' "

That was the gist. Recalling this conversation to me, she sighed.

That decision about her marriage had been made, and some others, too. The older kids were in better schools; the youngest would be starting preschool before too long. Renovations on their new home were almost finished. Renting out the New York place brought in enough money that she didn't have to work. Still, she wants to do more with her life. She's just not sure what that is.

"My entire life, whenever I've made big changes it's been because of a moment of clarity: *Aha! This is what I'm supposed to do!*" she said. "I think whatever's supposed to come next will reveal itself. I hope it will."

7
SINGLE, CHILDLESS

"God isn't going to tell you a partner and baby are never going to show up."

"I thought I'd be married and have kids by now," said my friend Sarah Hepola, the author of *Blackout,* as we ate breakfast together at a diner in Dallas.

Sarah and I worked together in our twenties at the *Austin Chronicle.*[1] We went to see a lot of bands play, drank as if drinking was our job, and saw each other living not exactly our best lives. But we had fun. One time, inspired by the roller-skating cult-movie-musical *Xanadu,* we went skating and considered ourselves prodigies even though we fell down a thousand times.

She told me, "I see my [married] friends around me and they're struggling, but I can't help thinking that I would prefer their struggles to my struggles. They say, 'I just want to go out and have sex with some random guy,' and I think, 'Why? I want to go home and watch a movie with my husband. I want kids to wake me up at four a.m.' "

What she's describing sounds like the makings of the perfect Gen X movie: a *Freaky Friday* remake in which a married woman with children swaps lives with a single woman who has a hot dating life and a cool job.

"Because there is this increasing number of women living alone," says Sarah, "I think there is a push to tell narratives that are about their triumph. But I don't feel triumphant. Nor do I want to be some sort of reactionary, cautionary tale. That is not the truth of it either."

For a long time, her desire for children was abstract: "The decision about whether or not to have a baby has been kind of vague, free-floating." Then, at forty: "My desire to have a baby blossomed really powerfully. At forty-one, I started dating this guy in another state. There were a lot of red flags along the way that this was not going to be the relationship that I wanted it to be, but I ignored them. I needed to make it work because I felt like this was my last chance. By the time that relationship ended, I was forty-two. Then earlier this year, I was diagnosed with fibroids and I'm looking at a possible hysterectomy." She hasn't given up on finding a partner with whom she might adopt children, though she's haunted by the question: *Where is he?*

One therapist I met gave me an especially poignant term for the feeling Sarah describes: "ambiguous loss."

"When you think about women in their forties," says Kelly Maxwell Haer, executive director of the Boone Center for the Family at Pepperdine University in California, "it's a very rare person who pictured herself single. The ambiguous loss of singleness is the type where the desired partner is psychologically present in a person's mind but physically absent."

Generation X women are told incessantly that they should do — or should have done — things differently in order to get what they want. Still, however many times you make a vision board or try to magic a partner or a baby or money or success into your life, sometimes it doesn't happen. And that's not necessarily because you didn't try hard enough.

So how do you know if there's still hope?

"Ambiguous losses are a particular type of loss that is hard to define and lacks closure," says Dr. Haer. "The ambiguous loss of singleness is particularly challenging to navigate. The person could be found in five minutes. Or never. You're not going to get an email from God that says you're never going to have a partner. That hope lingers on, and it's hard to live in hope that is not met. It's not like the closure of death, where you know this person has died, and it's over, and you can go through grief and move on. Humans don't do uncertainty well."

In 1950, about 22 percent of American adults were single. That number has more than doubled, marking one of the most significant changes to American demographics in the past century. In 2016, 59.8 million households in the United States were maintained by single people — 47.6 percent.[2] Close to 40 percent of babies are now born to unmarried women.[3]

Gallup reported that, as of 2013, 16 percent of Gen Xers had never married. That's compared with 10 percent of Boomers and just 4 percent of our grandparents' generation.[4] Headline after headline on the order of RECORD SHARE OF AMERICANS HAVE NEVER MARRIED proclaims the rise of the singles.[5] This trend appears to be continuing with Millennials.[6]

Even those members of Generation X who

do marry tend to delay it. Thanks to us, the age at which Americans marry is at a new high. The median age of first marriage, which hovered between twenty and twenty-two for women and between twenty-two and twenty-six for men from 1890 to 1980, has risen to almost twenty-eight for women in 2018, and nearly thirty for men.[7]

We've also seen what the National Marriage Project calls the great crossover: since 1989, the median age of a first-time mother has been earlier than that of first marriage. That has been true for decades among the poorest women in America, but there has been a "rapid and recent" trend in that direction for middle-class women with a high school diploma or some college.[8]

There's a lot of good news here.[9]

College-educated women who wait until thirty or later to marry have higher incomes.[10] Delays in marrying have been credited with bringing down the divorce rate.[11] Thanks to the decrease in the stigma around singleness, women are better able to chart their own course. Women are no longer dependent on men the way they were in prior generations. Until the Equal Credit Opportunity Act of 1974, it could be difficult for a woman even to get a credit card in her own name. Today, single women are far more likely than single men to buy their own homes.[12]

Sociologist Eric Klinenberg, author of *Going Solo,* has said that the rise of single people in America has played a role in revitalizing cities, in part because they tend to go out and socialize more than married people do. He also sees another benefit: "In a moment like this," Klinenberg told *Smithsonian* magazine, "living alone is one way to get a kind of restorative solitude, a solitude that can be productive, because your home can be an oasis from the constant chatter and overwhelming stimulation of the digital urban existence."[13]

The downside: middle-aged women may feel ready to marry only to discover there is no one available whom they want *to* marry.

"I teach aerobics, right?" a DC friend said the other day. "And I have to load the car myself. Every week. I just have to put every piece of equipment and my boom box and all of it in the car. And all I can think is: *Am I going to have to do this myself forever? Will I never have a man to help me?*"

She's had a lot of trouble finding him. She goes to church and wants a man who does, too. She's well educated and ambitious, so she wants someone accomplished. She also wants someone roughly her age, and capable of fixing things around the house. She has now met, she thinks, every single heterosexual professional man in the Washington, DC, area who goes to church and owns a tool kit. She feels her options are far more limited than people who aren't in her shoes could imagine.

There is data to back up my friend's dismay. According to research cited in journalist Jon Birger's book *Date-onomics,* there is a nationwide "man deficit," at least among the college educated.[14] In New York City, where I live, there are 400,000 more women than men.[15] One Pew study showed that most women consider it very important for a man they might date to be employed, but for every one hundred unmarried women there are only sixty-five employed unmarried men — a dire ratio that shrinks to forty-seven when only divorced, separated, and widowed men are counted.[16]

This is bad news for Generation X women, a relatively well-educated group.[17] An awful lot of men who say they want an intellectual equal in reality tend to shy away from women who are better educated than they are or make more money than they do. In one study published in the *Personality and Social Psychology Bulletin,* men were more likely to express romantic interest in a

209

woman they had not met if she outperformed them in a test than if she did worse than they did. But in face-to-face interactions, the men were more likely to be romantically interested in the woman if she did worse on the test than if she outperformed them.[18]

Meanwhile, my aerobics-instructor friend hears all the time that she might have better luck with less boxes for the man to check. To her, this sounds like being told to settle. Single women in their forties keep getting advised to do that. Women's magazines and smug married friends accuse them of being too picky or too independent or too *something*. They're told they must not have looked hard enough.

Dating in middle age can wear down even the hardiest souls.

Romantic comedies and fairy tales have filled us with unrealistic fantasies, while Tinder has convinced us that if we keep looking long enough, we will find the one soul mate out there for us. It's a perfect storm of disappointment and frustration and transactional encounters.

"Online dating technology inflames everyone's knee-jerk judgment and pickiness," said one friend. "Swipe left on the guy with the big head, swipe left on the guy without a job — and who knows if you might have liked that guy in real life?"

Life is much more complicated at this age than it is in our twenties. One single friend of mine felt vulnerable following the death of her mother but was cheered up by a series of fun dates. Only, after hanging out with the guy a few times, she learned that he wasn't exactly divorced from his children's mother — or even separated from her.

Another friend in her midforties said she's not going online in the wake of her recent breakup: "I'd rather look through midcentury modern end tables on Etsy than scroll through men."

Still, the pressure to date more or date better can be intense. One divorced mother of two told me that she hasn't dated since her divorce a few years ago and doesn't particularly want to. But now that she's getting older, women in her family have begun to fret over her singleness. "My mother and her generation used to say, 'A woman needs a man like a fish needs a bicycle,' but now, suddenly, they're Mrs. Bennet from *Pride and Prejudice:* 'Ooh! He'd be a good catch!' "

Susan Patton, nicknamed "Princeton Mom," wrote a book in 2014 called *Marry*

Smart, encouraging women to snap up a man in college lest they turn into overeducated spinsters. "Another Valentine's Day. Another night spent ordering in sushi for one and mooning over 'Downton Abbey' reruns," she wrote in a *Wall Street Journal* opinion piece.[19] "Smarten up, ladies."

But what if you've read the advice books and done your best and in middle age you're still alone? On the TV show *UnREAL,* the bachelorette character Serena says all her friends are married, and she adds, "The weird thing is I did everything right. I did everything just like them. My friends say that I'm just too picky. That no guy is good enough. But the truth is, nobody picks me."[20]

Since the oldest Gen Xers entered their fertile years, there has been a rush to convince women that their chances to marry or have children are falling every second of every day, like a rock thrown off a cliff after college graduation. In June 1986, *Newsweek* declared via a cover story that middle-aged women were destined for spinsterhood by their having delayed marriage. A forty-year-old, white, college-educated woman, the story said, was more likely to be killed by a terrorist than to get married. Never mind that the article was based on a modest 1985 demographic study called "Marriage Patterns in the United States"[21] that made no mention of terrorist attacks. According to the abstract, one conclusion was simply: "Education is the most important correlate of decisions about the timing of first marriage." Stop the presses.

In 2002, the incendiary book *Creating a Life* by economist Sylvia Ann Hewlett asserted that 40 percent of women making $50,000 or more a year were childless at age forty-five and that fertility dropped after age twenty-seven.[22] Magazines fanned the flames with cover stories like "Baby Panic," which read: "These days, the independence that seemed so fabulous — at least to those of us who tend to use that word a lot — doesn't anymore."[23]

Offering a catharsis was Tina Fey on *Saturday Night Live*'s Weekend Update: "Sylvia's right. I definitely should have had a baby when I was twenty-seven, living in Chicago over a biker bar, pulling down a cool twelve grand a year."[24] Fey provided a counterexample, too: she gave birth to her two daughters at the ages of thirty-five and forty-one.

In 2014, the American College of Obstetricians and Gynecologists issued a statement that women's ability to have babies decreased gradually beginning around age thirty-two and then more quickly after age thirty-seven.[25] *Newsweek* recanted the "terrorist" article twenty years after publishing it. Still, bogus statistics continue to haunt the culture, striking fear into the hearts of women who want children but haven't had them yet.[26]

Many Gen X women make a conscious decision not to marry or not to move in with a partner — or not to be parents. They are able to go where they want when they want, to work as much as they want, to cultivate friendships, to give back to the community, to make their own life without interference from or obligation to anyone else. Members of the Childfree by Choice movement state a strong case for living life without kids and for offering support to those who make that choice.

One single friend of mine is a foreign correspondent. She has lived all over the world, including in Lebanon and Tunisia. When I see her every couple of years or so, she looks even more stylish as she sips wine and flips her long hair and tells me about her "lovers" and how she can see the Mediterranean Sea from her office. She's never wanted a permanent partner or a child. She is de-

lighted with her life, a walking advertise-
ment for singledom.

Another woman I know married young
and then divorced at the age of thirty. At
thirty-five, she was still single. She decided
that pursuing more than one goal at a time
wasn't going to work for her, and so she
threw herself into her career full tilt: "And
that's essentially what I've been doing the
past six years. I went to grad school. I got a
master's in public administration. And I
actively never wanted my job to be my
whole life, but I'm super happy with where
I am professionally now."

Briallen Hopper writes in the funny essay
"How to Be Single"[27] about how you should
defend your singledom, even if that means
filling your home with newspapers and feral
racoons. ("Do not rule this out just because
it's a cliché. It works.") Then, if you still
find yourself being courted by someone, she
says you should: "Send them a Havisham
GIF, either Helena Bonham Carter from
Mike Newell's 2012 version of *Great Expectations* or Gillian Anderson from the 2011
BBC version or Martita Hunt from the
1946 David Lean version. (Anne Bancroft
from the 1998 version is too hot.) If your
date tries to keep bantering or flirting, just
keep sending Havishams until they stop."

Single women may still be marginalized or stigmatized even — some say especially — when they are happy about being single. In her book *Singled Out,* social psychologist Bella DePaulo calls this "the singles treatment": "No matter how fabulously happy and successful you may be," she writes,[28] "you can still get the singles treatment. In fact, some people who dole out the treatment sometimes seem especially miffed by singles who are not whining about their singlehood or pining for coupledom."

In the 1959 Doris Day–Rock Hudson movie *Pillow Talk,* Thelma Ritter's oft-drunk character, Alma, approvingly quotes Rock Hudson's character, saying, "If there's anything worse than a woman living alone, it's a woman sayin' she likes it."

That seems to have been gospel for 1959. But many happily single women hear it even now. In a 2018 *New York Times* op-ed called "I'm in My 40s, Child-Free and Happy. Why Won't Anyone Believe Me?"[29] writer Glynnis MacNicol told the story of meeting an older man she admired at a dinner party. He told her she had a terrible life and had his leftover steak wrapped up for her to take home.

This "I'm happy/No, you're not" nonconversation isn't only patronizing. It sets women who are delighted to be alone against women who are unhappy being alone. Many women in America today are like my international vixen friend — cheerful possessors of prime real estate, embodiments of sexual freedom and independent glamour.

"My father's mother raised two kids by herself during World War II after her husband died," said a fortysomething woman who gets paid to eat at exciting restaurants all over the world. "For heaven's sake, I have it so easy. I'm living in a nice house, in a nice neighborhood. I have friends, family. I have nothing to complain about." She said she contemplated single motherhood when Angelina Jolie was on all the tabloid covers. *She has six. I could have one!* she thought back then. "But if I'd had a kid then, I couldn't do any of the things I do now."

And yet, one single woman told me that she's starting to realize that for decades to come, she might well be buying her own orange juice when she has the flu. She knows she could get a friend to do her a favor or pay someone to do it, but said that feels depressing.

A few happily single women told me they wonder if their independence may present new challenges in a later phase of life. In past generations, an unmarried woman might live in the family home as a "spinster aunt." Such women had a family role, a financial backstop, and companionship. Now huge numbers of women in this country leave their parents' house in their late teens. Then, if they don't partner up, they may live on their own for fifty or sixty years.

The gap between how many children women say they want (2.8) and how many they are likely to have (1.8) is the widest that it's been in the past forty years.[30] In May 2018, the Centers for Disease Control reported that the US birth rate is lower now than at any time since 1978. Reasons for the baby bust of the 1960s and '70s include a faltering economy and women's heightened ability to control their fertility. The Pill was approved as a contraceptive in 1960 and abortion was legalized nationwide in 1973. A recent *New York Times* survey turned up three leading reasons given today for not having a child: wanting more leisure time and personal freedom, not having a partner yet, and not being able to afford child care.[31]

"I was in grad school until my early thirties," writes Briallen Hopper, who wrote the Havisham essay,[32] "often making less than

$25,000 a year, and when I finally got a job, my student loan payments cost about as much as child care. At one point a friend with two kids teasingly referred to my student debt as my 'loan baby.' I began to imagine my loan baby as a malevolent ghost, a changeling who had pushed my real baby out of the nest before it could be born."

Sometime in our forties, most of us stop being able to have a baby. That can be a relief or it can be devastating. So many friends of mine did want children but for many reasons it never happened. They had a breakup that laid them low for crucial years of fertility, or they dated online forever without finding anyone they connected with, or they worked and worked until, when they had time for a family, there seemed to be no one left in their whole town still unattached.

One friend told me that in her twenties she believed that the ticking-fertility-clock-themed *Ally McBeal* (the 1997–2002 dramedy about a young, flighty female lawyer in Boston who wore miniskirts and fantasized about dancing babies) was an antifeminist conspiracy. She said she believed that gender was a social construct and that her body was her domain. She put a lot of effort back then into not getting pregnant, so much so that she was blindsided when she eventually wanted to get pregnant and could not.

"Having kids was the thing I wanted my whole life," says Karen, forty-two, a psychotherapist in Arizona. She pauses. "I had to turn off the Facebook feature with 'Six years ago . . . whatever.' I was torturing myself with it. If only I'd done things differently then, I'd have a baby now."

Technology has prolonged women's hope of having a biological child. IVF was introduced in 1978. In 2016, 263,577 assisted reproductive technology cycles were performed in US fertility clinics.[33] The egg-freezing boom is an even more recent phenomenon. The first live birth to a woman via frozen eggs was in 1999; by 2016, there were egg-freezing parties for employees on Wall Street, and at Apple and Facebook.

"One thing that's a little different for this generation," says Margie Lachman, professor of psychology at Brandeis University, "is there have been some medical breakthroughs around fertility. Things like storing eggs or IVF. You see movie stars having babies in their forties." Nicole Kidman and Salma Hayek had their first babies at forty-one. Halle Berry had her second child at forty-seven. Susan Sarandon had her second at forty-five. Geena Davis had her first baby at forty-six — and then twins(!) at forty-eight. Nevertheless, Lachman says, "I don't think it eases the dread."

It also doesn't always work, as a few couples I know discovered after several rough, expensive years. In 2016, just 22 percent of assisted reproductive technology procedures with the woman's own eggs resulted in a live birth.[34]

One single forty-nine-year-old woman I know who'd always wanted kids explained that she'd comforted a married friend through a miscarriage. For months afterward, her friend felt stalked by pregnant women — wherever she looked, there they were, plump and radiant. The pain was overwhelming, but then the friend became pregnant again and had a healthy baby. "I was happy for her, truly," the single woman said. "But sometimes I want her to imagine what it's like to live in that world, surrounded by glowy pregnant women. But to do it forever. And to be utterly alone while doing it."

A woman from Georgia in her late forties, Michele, told me that after fifteen years of trying to conceive or adopt she's decided to give up. Strangely, she says, one of the hardest parts of not having children has been the feeling of social isolation from her friends who are parents: "It's been very lonely," she told me. "Having that lack of connection has been really, really hard. It's a hollowness that very few in your circle understand."

I recently asked a friend of mine if she was still trying for a baby, and she said no. It was heartbreaking the way she said it, like how a doctor would tell you a loved one didn't make it. She'd been having a couple of miscarriages a year for years, and finally decided it was enough. She'd done procedures. She'd taken pills. She'd acted on everyone's advice and still her body had said no. And now she was saying no.

She could adopt, people told her. But no, again. The average cost of a domestic or an international adoption through an agency ranges from $25,000 to $50,000.[35] She and her husband didn't think they could scrape that together. They could go the far cheaper route of adopting from the foster care system, but she said she didn't feel she could handle the uncertainty that can be involved in that process when people are trying to adopt an infant rather than an older child.[36]

The reasons why women don't wind up

with the families they wanted, taken one by one, may seem random or like bad luck. But there are patterns. Women blame themselves, ignoring the fact that their decisions are not being made in a vacuum. Wanting a career you love isn't bad. Wanting to be stable financially before you have a child isn't bad. Wanting to have the right partner isn't bad. Unfortunately, sorting all these things out takes time. And women have many fewer fertile years than men, who can father children well into their fifties.

In order to have a family life and a career, women must move twice as fast to arrive at the same place. Rather than being assisted with this unlikely feat — say, via paid parental leave, accelerator programs at work, or partners willing to sideline their own careers for a few years — women are scolded, told they should have found a boyfriend in college, had a baby by twenty-seven.

In the coming decades, single Gen X women will find creative ways to navigate old age while maintaining their independence. I know quite a few women who are planning to have a "bestie row" of houses with their friends in old age or to live together *Golden Girls*–style.

"My best friend and I have been talking about it for a long time," said a forty-six-year-old Florida woman. "I have these friends that I truly love so much. I want to be with them all the time. I'm constantly texting them or talking to them on the phone or planning things together. I have this fantasy that I'm going to win the lottery and buy a building and move everybody in."

I have seen friends make one another executors of their wills and their medical proxies — with a vow to visit the hospital and tweeze stray facial hairs should the party of the first part become comatose.

Then, of course, some women wind up out of the blue getting everything they'd ever wanted.

Jo, a landscape architect, grew up in Connecticut. At forty, she found herself single and childless, though she'd very much wanted to have a family. She'd been going out with one of my husband's best friends and we all thought they were going to get married and have kids.

They moved in together, and Jo became pregnant at age thirty-nine. Then, tragically, she miscarried. To make it worse, her partner did not seem disappointed enough and didn't want to try again. The expense and effort were too much. As a lesbian couple, they had to find a sperm donor. A vial of sperm can cost hundreds of dollars, plus the cost of freezing, storing, and shipping. To have herself inseminated at the doctor's office, which provided a better chance for conception, was another $300.

Heartbroken, Jo left her partner. She entered the dating world again at age forty, feeling she had about five minutes in which to find someone and get pregnant.

This year, she got married and had a baby. So, how did she do it?

I called Jo the other day to ask her. I told her that I'd interviewed dozens of people who'd entered their forties single and childless, hoping to change that, and hers was the only success story. I congratulated her on her efficiency.

She burst out laughing. And then she told me how it had happened.

A year after the breakup, she met someone and they started dating. Eventually, she broached the subject of having a baby: "It takes a while when you're in a new relationship, to have that conversation," Jo said. "At least for me. I think I was afraid that if it didn't work out then I'm back to square one. I had considered just having a kid on my own, and I talked to my family about that. I was just terrified to pull the trigger."

But a year into the new relationship at age forty-one, Jo went to the gynecologist, who told her: "If you still want to have a kid, you really need to do it now."

"Can you just tell me how much time I have?" Jo said she asked the doctor. "What are we looking at?"

The doctor, of course, couldn't say.

And so Jo went to her girlfriend and laid all her cards on the table. She said it was her last chance to have a baby, that she would do all the work, but that she'd love to have her support.

"What did the girlfriend say?" I asked.

"She immediately dumped me," said Jo. "And so then I was like, *Here I am again, in the exact same situation. The kid thing keeps killing my relationships.*"

Only this time around, she was older. Maybe too old.

Then, two months later, Jo started dating somebody new who, as luck would have it, wanted a baby, too.

After six months of dating, they started trying.

Fortunately, Jo had just been given a raise at work, and she loved her job: "I like what I do. I believe in what I do, and I've been doing it long enough that I feel like I'm appreciated in a way that makes me feel good about it as well."

The extra money helped when they decided to try fertility treatment. In their first round of IVF, she became pregnant.

On her forty-fourth birthday, Jo gave birth to a nine-pound-eight-ounce boy; soon after, he attended his mothers' wedding. Our friend, whom Jo had broken up with those few years earlier, was there to hold the baby while the newlyweds danced.

There are plenty of happy endings, too, that don't involve children or weddings.

The other day, I checked in with my friend Sarah, who'd told me over breakfast in Dallas about her struggle to find a partner. "Recently I've tried to expand my dating pool," she told me. "To say yes to people I would normally say no to because they were too young or lived too far away. And while I'm not ready to plant a 'mission accomplished' flag around here, it's really improved my dating life. I'm having fun. Less despair. It's a very lonely place to be, waiting for someone who never materializes."

8
AFTER THE DIVORCE

"I was talking about the Christmas dinner that we always have at the other parent's house as the original family unit. Out of nowhere, my son said, 'You don't have to come.' "

My friend Hannah had just moved into a new apartment with her two children. This was the first time since she and her husband split up that at their mother's place the kids would have their own rooms. The apartment was bright and roomy, and she was thrilled to have found it.

At her housewarming party, I took a seat in the kitchen to keep her company while she cooked. On the wall hung a calendar marked with the days of the week the kids were at their dad's or at their mom's. She pulled a sheet pan out of the oven with oven mitts and set it on top of the stove. She mixed a sauce. She arranged a platter.

Children ran in and out of the kitchen and arriving friends poked their heads in to say hi.

Then two kittens wandered in.

"When did you get cats?" I asked.

She didn't answer right away.

"Wait," I said. "Are these the Christmas kittens?"

"Yes," she said, opening a bottle of wine. "I'm cat sitting for the cats my ex-husband's new girlfriend gave my children for Christmas. Yes, the Christmas my son said I didn't have to attend if it would be 'awkward' for me with Dad's new girlfriend. I told you that before, right? That my child told me I *didn't have to come to Christmas dinner.*"

She reached down and petted one of the kittens. Then she took a very long swallow of wine.

In contrast to all the education we have today about the "good divorce," "conscious uncoupling," mediation, and healthy coparenting, the standard scenario modeled for us in the 1970s and '80s was a contentious split ending with a mostly absent father and a broke mother — then maybe, a few years later, stepparents and stepsiblings.

University of Chicago sociologist Linda Waite, senior fellow at National Opinion

229

Research Center, says that Gen X was at a disadvantage from the start because of our parents' high rate of acrimonious divorce.

"If your parents are divorced," Waite told me, "you see the world in a fundamentally different way. You see the world as unstable. You see promises as not meaning anything. You have role models for how things go bad but not role models for how things go well. That left people cautious and scarred and without models for good relationships."

Our generation are the beta-tested victims of the Boomers' record-high divorce rate. We may be late to marry in part because we are terrified of divorcing, doing to the next generation what was done to ours.

The divorce rate, which peaked in 1980, recently hit a thirty-six-year low.[1] Boomers, the vast majority of whom did not experience the pain of divorce as children, could view their divorces as radical acts of freedom. Divorce is significantly more normalized for Millennials and younger people and thus far less associated with failure. But for Gen X, it may be especially terrifying.

In a *New York Times* piece entitled "The Good Divorce," Susan Gregory Thomas writes that if a Gen X woman does divorce, she will often go to great lengths to make it amicable — doing anything "to spare children the horrors of the *Kramer v. Kramer* bloodbaths of their own childhoods."[2] They are also more likely to keep plugging away at a difficult marriage, hiding their feelings from fear that rocking the boat will sink it.

One woman I know had a hard-charging breadwinner husband for twenty years. He was laid off during the recession and became depressed. Rather than return to work full-time, he became a consultant, for half his former income. "The premise of our marriage for twenty years up until that point was that he was the earner and I was the freelance-writer mom." She felt fortunate that she was able to find full-time work, given the job market, but she hated that she no longer had the latitude to pursue her dreams. Intellectually, she knew that was the kind of compromise marriage sometimes entailed: he had supported her; now she was supporting him. She still couldn't shake a feeling of resentment and anger that he had changed the rules in the middle of the game.

"I wish I could say it all came out right in the end," she said, "and that I was truly heroic. But I can't."

Kara, a forty-four-year-old in Atlanta who had two children earlier than many Gen Xers, came undone when her older daughter went away to college a couple of years ago.

"I stumbled through most of my life. I wrapped everything into being a mother and a wife and then just really didn't have an identity of my own. It's been a rocky two years."

Once, going out on a date with her husband gave her a terrifying preview of what married life would be like with an empty nest when their younger daughter went away to college too: "He was tired. I wasn't feeling well. And we didn't have anything to talk about. What are we going to do? If we're struggling now, what are we going to do when both the kids are gone?"

When my childhood friend Jenny went back to school, she didn't work for two years and so she and her husband had to stretch his salary to cover them and their two children, ages seven and nine. "I was cutting coupons and getting can-can specials," she said. "And he'd say, 'Don't worry about me, I'll get takeout.' He thought that was the right thing to do, and I was trying to explain to him that, no, that's not helping. He's ordering food in, and I'm putting water in tomato sauce to make it stretch." It was like two Americas living in one house, especially because his work took him around the country. "He's going to Napa, and I'm saying, 'We're not moving the car today, because I have just enough gas to get to school.' "

They did marriage therapy and worked it out, but it can be hard in this phase of life to see the difference between a fundamentally good marriage going through a bad patch, like hers, and a toxic marriage that should probably end.

A forty-eight-year-old marriage and family therapist who lives in Fort Lauderdale, Elizabeth Stabinski is a Florida Family Court mediator. She herself divorced recently after twenty-two years of marriage. She has three sons, ages fourteen to twenty. And because she helps people avoid divorce for a living she is now feeling, she says,[3] "very much like the shoemaker who has no shoes."

"Despite having empathy for my clients for decades," she said, "I never really realized what a crazy maker getting a divorce, even a peaceful one, can be, even for those lucky enough to have an amazing support network and a career. I walk around feeling like I am riding an emotional roller coaster most days, sometimes so excited about the prospect of my future and other times frozen in fear.

"The thoughts that race around my head the most are about growing old alone. I don't regret my divorce, but I would like a life partner. It's hard having to re-create yourself in your forties. You have days that you feel great and days where you feel like the wind has been knocked out of you. In a relationship there's an illusion that you're not alone. After a separation or a divorce, that illusion isn't there anymore."

"I've fantasized about divorce," Julie, a woman I know in New York, told me a couple of years ago. "Two of my friends are getting divorced and I've been watching one very closely. She feels that a burden has been lifted." Divorce may be contagious. In a 2009 study analyzing thirty years of marriage data, participants were 75 percent more likely to get divorced if a friend was divorced.[4]

Julie said there's no abuse in her marriage but that she and her husband have been bickering since they had kids: "From day one!" she says. "Bringing the baby home, my husband couldn't believe how much I had to breastfeed. He said, 'There must be a more efficient way to do this.' We had a terrible fight in couples' therapy last week and I almost walked out. At some point, who cares who's right or wrong? I don't care who wins."

Two years later, I went back to Julie to see

how things had gone. "My husband and I are currently separated. Actually, it's been great," she said. "It was the shock he needed to make some profound changes. And for the first time in a long time, I feel a deep love for him again. The separation is only a couple of months old, and already he seems markedly different. Lately, I've been feeling we could reconcile. Interesting — the journeys marriages go on sometimes. Also, over the summer, I had a romance, as a newly single middle-aged person, and got my heart broken as if I was twenty-five all over again. I'm fifty-three. I can't decide if this was something precious to reexperience at my age or something to be avoided."

In unmarried heterosexual relationships, according to a study by Stanford psychologist Michael J. Rosenfeld, men and women are equally likely to ask for a breakup. But that changes in marriage: roughly two-thirds of divorces in the US are initiated by women. We expect more from marriage than our ancestors did, and women expect even more from it than men do.[5]

In middle age, especially, it can become hard not to blame a partner for what we can't do in life. One way to escape the trap is to tell the story in another way. "Being able to narrate our inner experience is one of the most powerful ways we can change how we *feel*," writes the psychologist Daphne de Marneffe in her book *The Rough Patch*.[6] She sees so many women in her practice blaming their partners for what they themselves have failed to accomplish. "It's not just that marriage makes you give things up," she told me.[7] "*Life* makes you give things up." It's sort of depressing and sort of consoling: *Everything* is a trade-off, not just marriage.

William Doherty, professor of family social science at the University of Minnesota and the author of *Take Back Your Marriage,* says Generation X women are facing some new as well as old challenges of marriage.

"This was a generation of women who could take for granted the gains of feminism. My wife had to fight for insurance in her job because she was told that she had a husband, why would she need insurance? And you say that to a Gen X woman and they would think that you're from another century or another planet."[8]

The Gen X woman has higher expectations of marriage, too. She wants her partner to be: "her best friend, her soul mate, and the sex should always be great," says Doherty, "which of course doesn't happen.

And then the inevitable disappointments come.

"A lot of times women who are considering divorce are not able to or don't let themselves look around the bend after the divorce," says Doherty. "They see their unhappiness and they see a fix for that in getting out of the marriage. They don't realize the ways in which life is going to get much more complicated."

How many divorced friends do I have, I think, who had a glorious six months after their split, full of sex with people they met online and new haircuts and hobbies and so much time to themselves to do all the things they'd always wanted to do, with no one to hold them back?

"Why is divorce so expensive?" goes the classic joke.

"Because it's worth it."

Then these divorced friends made it around the bend in the road. A few of these women stayed happy and carefree. But many, even if they didn't regret the choice to divorce, hit a wall a few months later. Some discovered on dating apps that fifty-year-old men who still wear *Star Wars* T-shirts were hunting for twenty-eight-year-old women.[9] It's not all in our heads, either: A 2018 study found that on one online dating site, a woman's desirability peaks at eighteen and falls from there. A man's peak? Fifty.[10]

Soon after her divorce, one friend of mine had a heavy flirtation going with a colleague. When he came to pick her up for a date, his two young kids' car seats were in the back. The sight of them depressed her. They were a symbol of the stakes involved and proof that even if things went well, nothing would ever be simple.

Once remarriage is on the table, new difficulties arise.

"If [divorced women] aspire to having another mate," Doherty continued, "then they are looking at a stepfamily, which is the most complex family system we have. The children are not going to welcome this new person with the same enthusiasm."

Or they will welcome your ex's new partner with so much enthusiasm that it will make you jealous. My heart bleeds for friends of mine who look at Instagram and see pictures of their children smiling with an ex's new partner, or learning to ride a bike without them, or frolicking at the beach with people who used to be their friends, too.

Divorce, says Doherty, means "surrendering one set of problems for another set of problems. Now obviously sometimes it's the necessary solution. But there are a lot of unnecessary divorces. Many of these marriages could be salvaged and made better. Too many women make the mistake of not engaging their husband by saying they are despairing. You don't need to say, 'I'm thinking of divorcing you.' You can say, 'I'm finding my commitment shaken. I'm scared we won't be together in five years or ten years.' You can say it in a vulnerable way, but get his attention."

He says women may instead conduct the whole conversation in their own minds, grappling with whether to stay or go, while their men are unaware that there are even problems. "Sometimes she has actually given up. She's nicer to him because she's not trying to change him." But she hasn't become more accepting. She seems less miserable and less critical "because she's plotting her exit. And then she springs it on him and he is completely beside himself. A lot of times the guy then kicks into gear, but she has already exited in her mind and her heart. At the very time when her husband would sign up for change, she's out."

Troubles with sex are a significant cause of divorce. And sex is another thing that gets more complicated for women in midlife. Stacy Tessler Lindau, director of the Program in Integrative Sexual Medicine (PRISM) at the University of Chicago, told me that men's libido goes down around this age, and those of us with male partners might react to a lack of perceived desire with a lack of desire ourselves.[11] "There's not a lot of science," Dr. Lindau said, "around the morning erection," which is not a sentence I had heard spoken before. But she believes that the morning erection is important to a couple's sex life and it stops occurring for many men in middle age. "It's a subconscious reminder of his sexuality," she said. "Without that regular stimulus, a woman might lose that morning stimulation that gets the libido going."

Then there are the hormonal and physical changes. Between the ages of twenty and forty-five, women's levels of testosterone, the hormone most linked to libido, go down by about half. Changes in estrogen levels can cause the vagina to become dry; diminished blood flow can make arousal much slower; the risk of urinary incontinence increases.[12] Even without that, the emotional and mental pressures of midlife (not to mention the associated sleep deprivation) could be enough to kill a woman's sex drive. If you are exhausted, mad, or resentful, sex can become one more annoying item on your to-do list.

A Colorado woman who excelled in the military but has found marriage far more difficult said: "I don't really like my husband very much. Seeing other women's situations, I don't really have it 'that bad' with him. But my body is not all that eager for sex. With anyone. I guess now that I've got my kids, maybe I don't feel as much of a need for it? Or maybe my hormones are all shot to hell?"

More than one unhappily married woman I spoke with said a variation on: "I do it all. What is he even here for?"

One married woman told me that her husband had come to her after their second child was born and said, "I'm unsatisfied. I want more sex. I'm not going to masturbate anymore. I'm not going to watch porn anymore. I don't want to fantasize about or be aroused by anything other than you. And you need to help me with this."

They decided they would have sex every other night at least. And they've kept this plan going for a few months now. Her husband has been thrilled by the arrangement, but she's begun to feel oppressed by what she calls the schedule:

"If there's one night when we're supposed

to and I'm like, 'I just want to go to sleep,' then there is no getting out of the next night. There are some times when if I'm leaving town or if he's leaving town he'll say, 'We need to have sex every night this week since we're not going to have any sex next week.'

"I'll say, 'That is so unattractive. Really killing the whole mood.' But he says, 'If I don't say anything, we won't do it at all.' And it's true. There are maybe three or four nights a month where I really do want to put the effort in, and that's my authentic libido right there. The rest of the time, it's a job."

A few years ago, a study by the Kinsey Institute found that heterosexual women and men appeared to be cheating at the same rate.[13] A number of married women confessed to me that they'd had affairs or at least had vivid fantasies about going to bars and randomly hooking up with people. "I'd never do it, *of course,*" said one mother of two. "But I do think about it. A lot."

One reason you hear cited most often for the rise in married women cheating is opportunity — with more women in the workplace and with phones in their pockets. Thanks to social media, we know more than we used to how much we're missing by staying home.

"One of the things we see in the last five years is couples struggling with extra options," said psychotherapist Kelly Roberts.[14] "In the privacy of your cell phone, you have other worlds to explore. When you have these other worlds, you start kicking in the fantasies of what you don't have versus what you do. All of a sudden that plays into the what-ifs that couples didn't necessarily use to have at their disposal. The electronic idealizations spill out into unrealistic expectations of relationships they've had for ten or fifteen years. When you're flooded with something for so long, that can't help affecting the marriage."

Perhaps because of the negative examples we witnessed as children, Gen X seems focused on healthy divorcing, as advised in Constance Ahrons's book *The Good Divorce* or Wendy Paris's *Splitopia,* and our generation does seem to be doing it better than our parents did, with far more involvement from divorced fathers. But there is also, among many women of this generation, a huge sense of shame associated with divorce. That was supposed to be something our parents did. We waited to get married until we were sure, and we did all the sober vow writing. How could we have failed?

One woman who felt she had done everything right only to see it crumble anyway is
a forty-five-year-old Vassar grad. A few years
ago, she was living in the Northwest with
her three kids, ranging from age four to
fifteen, and working part-time. She thought
everything was great, but then her breadwinner husband had what she describes as "a
good old-fashioned nervous breakdown."

Like so many women, she'd run the
household money day to day but left all the
savings and investments up to him. One
thing experts have told me is especially valuable for Gen X women is to make sure you
have an updated will; know where your
money is; and maintain life, health, renter's,
home, car, and whatever other insurance
you can afford.

"He lost his job," she says. "And unbe-
knownst to me, he had siphoned off my
retirement account." She came home to
locked doors because the house had been
reclaimed by the bank. "We talked to some
financial planners, and it was so far gone,
they were like, 'Really, the only way to solve
this is to do bankruptcy and foreclosure.' "[15]

The divorce, though perhaps inevitable by
that point, was a nightmare both emotionally and financially, but she is much happier

these days, and the kids seem to have adjusted.

When I saw my housewarming-party friend Hannah again recently, she, too, was doing well. She had a new haircut and was wearing a flattering red dress. She'd been meditating and doing yoga. It had helped her stay calm at work and made traveling less stressful. The kids were thriving. She had some good dating prospects. She was decorating the new apartment. And the kittens, now cats?

"You know what?" she said. "They are surprisingly good company."

9
PERIMENOPAUSE

"It was pouring out of me. I couldn't control it. I looked down at my sundress and I was drenched."

"You are infantilizing women!" I heard my mother yell one day when I was a teenager. Alarmed, I went into the kitchen to find her slamming the phone receiver down on its wall cradle.

"What was that about?" I said.

"Have you *seen* this?" she said, holding up a roll of paper towels. Rather than the usual white, this roll had colorful images of teddy bears and blocks.

I stared at her for a second.

"Mom," I said. "Did you just call the Bounty paper-towel company to complain about these teddy bears?"

"Yes," she said, eyes flashing. "They should be *ashamed.*"

In retrospect, I think that my then middle-aged mother — dealing with a grouchy teenage daughter, dying parents, marriage problems, and an acting career ending because she was no longer young — might have been finding a way to express her feelings without bothering anyone except a supervisor at that paper-towel company.

She wasn't going to throw me out of the house, or deny my grandparents the care they needed, or get divorced, or tell the entertainment industry to go to hell. And so, instead, she focused her rage on a paper-towel motif.

Twenty-five years later, struggling with a career that felt over, facing various physical problems, and trying to get my son into a good public middle school, I found myself paying a lot of attention to my son's pet turtle.

"Jenny looks bored," I said, gazing into the tank as she swam or sat on her dock. "I think Jenny needs more space. When was the last time Jenny had some fun?"

"She's a turtle," my husband said. "Turtles don't have hobbies. They swim and eat and bask."

"Maybe they want more!" I snapped.

And that was the moment I realized that Jenny the turtle had become my very own paper-towel teddy bear.

■ ■ ■ ■

Menopause, defined as a full year with no period, still hits around age fifty-one, as it did when the last word on the subject was Gail Sheehy's 1992 book *The Silent Passage.* Our mothers and grandmothers weathered the same symptoms. But the years before that cessation — also called premenopause or perimenopause — can be more emotionally and physically fraught than we anticipate.[1]

We change a lot during these years. And, as we may remember from puberty, transitions can be awkward. Our bodies and our moods frequently betray us.

"The first time [I had a hot flash], I didn't know," one woman told me. "I just thought, 'I'm in Jamaica. It's warm, there's humidity. I'm just really sweating a lot.' But it was just *profusely* coming out of me. Pretend you have a balloon with water and somebody took a couple of stick pins. It was pouring out. I couldn't control it. I just felt like I was on fire. My sister knew what it was. She said, 'You're having a flash.'"

A friend in corporate America tells me about the first time she saw a woman executive have a hot flash in the boardroom: "She just started dripping sweat. It looked as if she'd just stepped out of a pool. And she was trying to keep giving her presentation as if nothing was happening. But something was happening!"

At the time, my friend, then in her thirties, was startled by the sight. Now that she's in her late forties, she has hot flashes of her own. "I have been sweating through my clothes at night," she said. "Every night. Sweating, especially right before my period. My knees even sweat. Seriously, my entire body, head to toe, is completely soaked. And that's the most gross and uncomfortable thing. And no one tells you that it's coming. I thought I was dying."

She's embarrassed in retrospect by her failure to reach out to that other woman, to turn up the A/C or at least to hand her a box of tissues. But how could she have known? One of the worst parts of menopause is that no one talks about it.

I'd never even heard the term "perimenopause" before this year, though now I seem to hear it every day.[2] (A transgender man I know who's been experiencing hot flashes jokes that he's going to take Perry Menopause as his DJ name. And then I suppose I'll take the stripper name Party Menopause, which is how someone at my transcription service heard the word.)

Perimenopause and menopause are as dramatic as puberty but far less discussed, to the point of being taboo. It's something we go through at a stage in life when we aren't the kids being driven to swim class but the one whose job it is to get them there.

If you're on the outside of menopause, too, it can seem very strange. Partners might perceive the women in their lives undergoing Jekyll-and-Hyde transformations or oddly manifesting anxiety. Recently I stocked the house with food before leaving town on a work trip. I maybe got a little carried away — a lasagna, a casserole, chili, tuna salad. My husband and son are only two people and it was just a few days and they are both capable of making or ordering their own food. My husband took one look in the fridge and texted me: "I love you girl but you gotta calm down."

Sometimes my perimenopausal moods are more rage than anxiety. I woke up the other day and felt that the walls were closing in. My apartment felt too small, my clothes too tight. I noticed that my husband had placed a couple of champagne corks on top of a picture frame. It made me want to start breaking things. *What is this, a goddamned dorm room?* I muttered while I made coffee. In this state, I noticed things I had missed before: bags spilling out of the closet, stacks of receipts and change on a table, my son's Magic the Gathering cards everywhere. "It's like living in *Hoarders!*" I ranted before leaving the house. By nature I am usually relaxed, even cheerful, but on this particular morning I felt that if I'd had a pack of matches and some kindling I could have burned the place down.

When I open 1955's *How to Face the Change of Life with Confidence,* I see a question from a thirty-seven-year-old woman who has wild mood swings before she gets her period. The expert male gynecologist author tells her: "Man reaches physical maturity at twenty-five years of age, and emotional maturity at thirty-five years. Unfortunately, you seem to have missed the boat somewhere along the line, and you are still in your childish stage of emotional reactions."[3]

Decades of that sort of condescension have kept us from asking certain questions twice.

"Almost every woman I know of my age is feeling confused and in a state of transition even as most of us are at the top of our game in our careers, financially stable, and pretty comfortable with being parents," said

Yvette, a forty-three-year-old California woman who is the COO of a major video game company. "It's a strange state of vacillating between having our shit together and feeling less and less like we give a damn about what the rest of the world thinks. I spend a lot of time with other friends of my age. We talk about what's really going on — the worry that we're self-medicating too much with wine or Xanax, the anger that seems to creep up more and more. *Is it hormones? Perimenopause?*

"The fact that we are widening and softening where we don't want to and don't know if it makes us shallow or not feminists to do something about it; the fear that we don't know how to monitor our children's screen time; the fact that we don't really like or need sex very often anymore; our worry that we are losing time to try our 'dream' job . . .

"I just had breakfast with a friend last week who runs a very successful law firm. One of the things we were talking about is rage. We're getting frustrated and overwhelmed. You are literally seeing red, and you want to throw your phone against the wall. So now, on top of everything else, it's also like, 'Did you meditate?' "

I can't even count how many women have confessed to me that they've flung something against a wall — their phone, a book, a plate — though it seems telling that in nearly every case, once the fit was over, the woman who threw the object then cleaned it up.

There are well-publicized tricks, of course, for handling such moments of rage. Deep breathing. Downers. One popular mantra is HALT, meaning that when you're about to start flipping tables, you should ask yourself if you are hungry, angry, lonely, or tired and take appropriate action (eat a sandwich, go to therapy, call a friend, take a nap; *then* flip the table). Still, in midlife these feelings can assume a primal character: not moodiness but despair, not irritability but something deeper and more dangerous.

Sometimes the only thing that helps is screaming. On a particularly rough work trip, her marriage foundering, a friend of mine rented herself a private karaoke room that had a three-person minimum. She lied to the staff, saying friends were coming to join her, then spent two hours alone singing as loud as she could. She ordered enough food for several people so the waiters would stop asking her when her friends were arriving. She felt the freedom to scream at the top of her lungs for two hours was worth the cost of twenty-four mozzarella sticks.

In *The Change,* her book about menopause, feminist scholar Germaine Greer says that women's midlife suffering comes in two forms: "One I have called misery, which has no useful function and should be avoided, and the other grief, which is wholesome, though painful, and must be recognized."[4] According to Greer, misery is "a grey and hopeless thing, born of having nothing to live for, of disappointment and resentment at having been gypped by consumer society, and surviving merely to be the butt of its unthinking scorn." But grief is something else. It's the natural mourning period for our fertility, something that a woman can emerge from "stronger and calmer, aware that death having brushed her with its wing has retreated to its accustomed place, and all will be well."

The experts in gynecology who spoke with me said that hormone replacement therapy (HRT) remains the single most effective scientifically proved treatment for the symptoms of menopause. And yet, fearing the increased risk of cancer, stroke, and blood clots that we've long heard comes with a hormone therapy regimen, we've gone rogue. And that, perhaps, is why Gwyneth Paltrow's online community Goop can get away with selling us $66 jade eggs to stick up our yonis.[5]

It's also, I believe, one reason why women around the country are looking into treatments like the use of LSD or psilocybin mushrooms as antidepressants or mind-expanders.[6] In her book *A Really Good Day,* Ayelet Waldman describes how minuscule doses of LSD produced in her a feeling of contentment.[7]

Those for whom hallucinogens feel too extreme may seek an altered state of consciousness by drinking wine. A downside of this indulgence is that alcohol is a known sleep disrupter. Comedian Bridget Everett describes the curse of the "chardonnay shocker" — when you're woken up by the booze wearing off at four in the morning. In my experience, this is often followed by what a *New Yorker* cartoon depicts as your own private movie theater hell: "Now playing . . . *Everything You Said at the Party.*"[8]

When Kristi Coulter quit drinking, she had an epiphany: "I realize that everyone around me is tanked. But it also dawns on me that the women are *super double* tanked. I see that booze is the oil in our motors, the thing that keeps us purring when we should be making other kinds of noise."[9]

Or we may try health-food crazes. One friend of mine told me she'd started taking a high-dosage vitamin called Optivite P.M.T., even though so far the only thing it's apparently done is turn her pee neon yellow. Middle-aged drug experimentation might be even more reckless than the teen kind. "It's funny, right?" my friend said. "How in college maybe we'd be trying pot or whippets, but now it's Optivite and collagen smoothies? 'It's made of some weird gland oil or poisonous plant? Who cares! Gimme that! I heard it gets rid of belly fat!' "

Gynecologists I spoke with said they weren't surprised that women were casting around for exotic or illicit fixes to their perimenopausal woes.

Jacqueline Thielen, who has been working at the Women's Health Clinic at the Mayo Clinic in Minnesota for twenty-three years, said that life for a Gen X woman today is "just much more complicated." She sees many women in their forties and fifties who tell her they're scared of hormone therapy but they're also made miserable by symptoms and swamped with responsibilities. "You used to go to the store," she said, "and you could buy either Crest or Colgate. Now you go to the store: Is it whitening? Is it brightening? Is it tarter control? Is it sensitive teeth? There are so many other choices and influences now that I think it's harder for women to just figure out what they should do."

This makes them vulnerable, Dr. Thielen said, to controversial things like subcutaneous hormone pellet therapy, inappropriate ovary removal, or pricey "vaginal rejuvenation," which can cost several thousand dollars and may involve labial surgery or shooting lasers into your vagina[10] — one more thing I guarantee you our mothers did not have on their to-do lists. She notes that the so-called compounded hormones promoted by certain celebrities are not FDA-approved.

"Women will say, 'Why do I feel like crying?' or 'Why do I feel like screaming if I'm still having my periods?' " said JoAnn Pinkerton, executive director of the North American Menopause Society and professor of obstetrics and gynecology at the University of Virginia Health System.[11] "If your levels of both estrogen and progesterone are fluctuating, in any given cycle you might have too much or too little of either or both of them."

Perimenopausal women often complain of sleeplessness, painful intercourse, breast pain and cysts, changes in appetite and energy level, mood swings, bulging midriff, trouble concentrating, and so on and so forth — all symptoms connected in one way or another to hormones.[12]

For some women, it's not a big deal. For others, it can be crushing. In a survey by AARP, 84 percent of participating women said that menopausal symptoms interfered with their lives.[13]

"You know," Dr. Pinkerton told me, "we tell people who are grieving not to make major changes for a year. I don't think anybody's ever said, 'Don't make a major decision when you're perimenopausal.' "

Good idea, I think. We can just take it easy until perimenopause ends.

"How long is that, anyway?" I asked Dr. Pinkerton. A year, I thought she'd say. Maybe two.

"Anywhere from a few months to ten to thirteen years," Dr. Pinkerton said.

"Oh my goodness," I said.

"On average, they call it four years," she said. But she added that what's important for women to know is that menopause "is actually a lot easier than the perimenopausal transition." Why? Because perimenopause "is unpredictable. It's based on ovarian fluctuations. You might have six months of severe hot flashes, skipping periods, and then your cycles come back for three to five

258

years before it happens again.

"How well your ovaries function depends on your cycle and your mental and emotional state," said Dr. Pinkerton. "It's all tied together. Women need to recognize that it's a time of vulnerability, and there are some things that they can do to help."

Dr. Pinkerton gave me an example: "A woman came into my office and said, 'I hate my husband. I hate my marriage. I need to get out of this.' The husband had called me earlier and said, 'I've noticed that my wife is really having exaggerated responses to things around the time of her periods.'

"We ended up getting her into counseling as well as on oral contraceptives. The oral contraceptives calmed the hormones down, and then doing some counseling let her start to see some of the stressors that were hidden. I just saw her and she said her marriage could not be better. She recognized that the perimenopausal hormonal fluctuations were making the problems seem incapable of being solved. Once we were able to calm down the hormonal fluctuations, which for her involved suppression with oral contraceptives, and she did counseling, she could start to see some of the stressors that were coming from his work and her work and their family issues. I guess

259

what I would just say is if you're in peri-menopause, recognize that hormonal fluctuations may make the problems at work or at home seem larger. Maybe you need to calm down the hormonal fluctuations so that you can see the problems in perspective."

Women also benefit exponentially from sleeping more, Dr. Pinkerton said. "How many women get seven hours of sleep a night? How many women keep their exercise going when they're mentally or physically stressed? It's often the first thing to go, but it's absolutely one of the things that can help you navigate this time. Then, stress reduction.[14]

"In my clinic, we draw a circle, and I turn it into a wheel. As I listen to perimenopausal women I put a dot in the center, and I draw a line, and I say, 'Okay, now, let's give a percentage to how much time you're spending at work.' And then I'll say, 'Okay, how about caretaking for children? You get extra credit if it's teenagers.' 'How about your parents and your in-laws? How much caregiving are you providing?' "

Dr. Pinkerton said that looking at that wheel helps women understand why they might be feeling the way they are. If she hears a woman say, "Why am I irritable at work?" she says, "Well, you don't just have

260

work. You have work at work and work at home and work in the family and work in the community."

Race may be a factor in the duration or intensity of menopausal symptoms. The Study of Women's Health Across the Nation, an observational study, found that the median white woman's experience of perimenopausal symptoms, including hot flashes and night sweats, is nearly seven years; for Japanese and Chinese women, about five years; African American women, about ten; and Hispanic women, nine.[15]

Other research has shown that women in Japan have far fewer hot flashes and night sweats than women in the United States and Canada. There could be both biological and cultural factors.[16] One theory as to why Japanese women seem to experience far fewer hot flashes than other women is all the soy in their diet.[17] It makes sense: hormones are affected by diet, stress, exercise, and sleep. While it's not easy for all of us to maintain a healthy weight, sleep eight hours a night, or go back in time and spend our whole lives eating a soy-rich diet, it's nice to know that at least *theoretically* some of that might help.

But here's what I want to know: why are American Gen X women arriving in their forties knowing *something* is going to happen, but without a clear idea of exactly what that is?

One answer is: denial. We have had incentives for a long time to pretend we are the same as men in every way. For decades, women have had to argue that they could still work and function through those messy period-, pregnancy-, and menopause-related symptoms, and as a result we've minimized them, both to others and to ourselves. So as not to call attention to ourselves as women, we pretend it's not happening.

Boomer women arguably started this, entering the work world in shoulder-pad armor. It makes sense that they felt they had to hide the inconvenient fact of their womanhood, particularly in middle age. In 1970, Representative Patsy T. Mink of Hawaii, who was pushing for women's rights, fell into a battle with Edgar F. Berman, a retired surgeon from Maryland and member of the Democratic Party's Committee on National Priorities, over what menopause meant for women's competence in the workplace.[18]

"As far as national priorities," Dr. Berman said, "women's rights are not high on the list," because "their hormonal states could endanger the world." Just think, he said, of a menopausal woman president who had to make the decision on the Bay of Pigs, a bank president "making a loan under these raging hormonal influences," or a pregnant female pilot making a tough landing. Female hormones are powerful enough, in other words, that they could tank the economy, kill hundreds in a ball of fire, or start a nuclear war.

Even the dissenting voices quoted in the *New York Times* didn't seem particularly reassuring. One expert quoted said nuclear war was going a little far: "A woman might be bitchy as hell, but not make serious errors in judgment."

After taking our children to see the latest *Star Wars* movie, a friend and I sat at her dining room table while the kids ran around her house.

"It's just too hard," she said about her menopause. "I thought it was best to do it naturally, so I've just been riding it out. But it's been two years and finally I thought, *This has ruined my life!* Two years without sleeping through the night! Two years with hot flashes! Two years with no energy."

I'd had no idea. I asked why she hadn't told me before.

"I hate talking about menopause," she said. "It's like saying you've closed up shop

263

as a sexual being. It's embarrassing."

Behind us, the kids raced up and down stairs — laughing, oblivious.

Ultimately, her doctor put her on antidepressants, which she said helped her.

They do not help everyone. A TV news producer in the Midwest told me that she felt numb when taking them, and her weight shot up: "I struggled with some depression and some anxiety in my late thirties, early forties," she said. "You're dealing with these feelings, and then you hear, 'Oh, you're a forty-year-old woman, you seem depressed. I'm going to give you medication that will make you gain weight.'"

Johann Hari's 2018 book *Lost Connections* argues that our culture has come to medicate depression first and ask questions later, without recognizing that some discomforts are not medical emergencies. He tells the story of how when he begged for antinausea medication in a jungle hospital in Vietnam, the doctors said, "You need your nausea. It is a message, and we must listen to the message. It will tell us what is wrong with you."[19]

When I felt depressed in my thirties, I was prescribed an antidepressant. I wish that I had also done more to explore why I was depressed. Now I can see it more clearly: I

264

was working more than full-time for people whose values I didn't share. I had a young child at home whom I missed horribly when I was at work. I had the pressure of being the breadwinner. Dreams of doing something meaningful with my life felt out of reach.

One of my oldest friends, Asia Wong, now a clinical social worker in New Orleans, told me: "When I, as a clinician, talk to people about depression, we talk about how three things contribute: your biology; your inner landscape or psychology, which we can work on in therapy; and then your life circumstances. If your life circumstances really suck, you are going to be sad most of the time. You're going to feel anxious and overwhelmed. If you say, 'I'm taking care of my aging parents, and I'm working full-time, and I have these little kids, and my husband still has some traditional gender-role stuff,' you're going to be sad. Not because you 'have depression,' but because your life is debilitatingly difficult. And what I think has changed is that we used to think this was true for poor people. And now it feels true for all of us."[20]

In her 2015 book *Moody Bitches,* psychiatrist Julie Holland says our moods are "our body's own amazing feedback system" and that we are using "comfort foods, lattes, alcohol, and an expanding array of neuro-modulators like antidepressants, painkillers, energy drinks, and amphetamines in an effort to maintain our unnatural pace."[21]

"I'm sure men are in the same boat as far as having to be on antidepressants because of outside circumstances," said a midwestern woman I talked to. "But looking at it from a woman's perspective, it makes me even more angry. We give so much of our bodies to others already." So much of womanhood just *hurts:* cramps, childbirth, mammograms, Pap smears, breastfeeding — not to mention eyebrow threading. "There's so much wear and tear on us, yet we're all expected to look younger than we are. Now we're also fucking with our brains so that we can live in this world. It's just so much."

Many of us are getting less help than we should be from our doctors. A 2013 Johns Hopkins survey found that only one in five obstetrics and gynecology residents had received formal training in menopause medicine.[22] That's 20 percent of *gynecologists.* Forget about general practitioners. Forty-two percent of menopausal women in one survey had never discussed menopause with a health provider; only one in five had received a referral to a menopause specialist.[23] The North American Menopause Society (NAMS) and other groups are fighting to change that. You can go to the NAMS website and plug in your zip code to find NAMS-certified menopause-trained gynecologists near you.[24]

One practitioner who will pop up if you live in New York City is the *Menopause Confidential* author and gynecologist Tara Allmen, who also happens to be a menopausal woman.[25] Dr. Allmen told me that there's good news for Gen X: "Your generation will be the generation that is the most educated. Now everyone has taken a collective deep breath and really does understand who can benefit from hormone therapy. You are the hopeful generation. You should be thinking, 'Lucky us!' even though plenty of misinformation still persists on the internet and among the older generation of physicians or the younger ones who haven't had the training."

As it turns out, the reason Generation X women have grown up believing that hormone replacement therapy — again, one of the only proven treatments for menopausal symptoms — is dangerous is something that happened in the medical community in 2002.

In the 1990s, menopause was becoming a hot topic. Many Boomer women were getting treatment for their symptoms. It was in the news and on the talk shows, especially because in 1991, for the first time, the head of the NIH was a woman: Bernadine Healy. Two years later, she launched Women's Health Initiative (WHI), a national, long-term study on the possible benefits of hormone treatment for postmenopausal women. But in July 2002, the NIH announced the premature termination of the estrogen-progesterone part of the study. The reason given was an apparent rise in the risk of coronary heart disease, stroke, blood clots, and breast cancer. There was a hitch in this: WHI had been looking at what the hormones did in women ages fifty to seventy-nine. The aim was to figure out if this type of hormone treatment could help protect these women from heart disease and other illnesses. It was not about short-term hormone therapy for treatment of symptoms in women in their forties and fifties. But many midlife women heard only "cancer" and went off HRT immediately.

Dr. Wulf Utian, founder of the North American Menopause Society, wrote an editorial calling the manner in which the study was ended "poorly planned, abrupt and inhumane."[26] In 2017, Professor Robert D. Langer, one of the original WHI investigators, said that errors in the 2002 report led to a lot of unnecessary suffering for women.[27] That same year, the North American Menopause Society's official policy position called hormone therapy "the most effective treatment" for symptoms like hot flashes, adding: "For women aged younger than 60 years or who are within 10 years of menopause onset and have no contraindications, the benefit-risk ratio is most favorable for treatment of bothersome VMS [vasomotor symptoms like hot flashes] and for those at elevated risk for bone loss or fracture."[28]

However, this has done little to calm the fears of hormone therapy among women — and even doctors — that the misleading news stories about the WHI study instilled.[29]

"July 9, 2002, was the day the music died for menopausal women," said Mary Jane Minkin of Yale, one of the nation's leading experts on gynecological health.[30] "One of the things that were very bad about it is that no OB/GYNs were given advance notice this report was coming out. There was also a journalistic snafu. A WHI investigator gave the story to the *Detroit Free Press* on the grounds that it was an embargoed study due to appear the following week in the *Journal of the American Medical Association.* The *Detroit Free Press* broke the embargo.

"Which is how *Good Morning America* got the story. It aired on a Tuesday morning. Everybody went insane. None of the OB/GYNs were prepared for this. And the *JAMA* article did not come out until July 17.

"In that week, every American woman went to her cabinet and took out her hormone prescription and flushed it down the toilet. Which of course was ridiculous, because the WHI Part One was the only study that was stopped at that point. That was the estrogen plus progesterone. The estrogen-only went on for another two years. It eventually showed a decreased risk of breast cancer, not an increased risk of breast cancer. But the minute you say 'breast cancer' to an American woman, she panics, goes to the toilet, and flushes everything down.

"As much as I love estrogen, and I love estrogen, I would not want to have been a fish in the United States on July 10, 2002. It'd have been awful."

In response to the panic, the North American Menopause Society started changing guidelines for estrogen use. The FDA issued warnings. American medical schools largely stopped teaching hormone therapy.

"Now what do you have in the equation? You have Gen X ladies who are hitting perimenopause," says Dr. Minkin. "People of this generation tend to be a bit demanding, and they're having all these things happening to them. *Why are they happening? What's going on?* Their OB/GYNs aren't talking to them about it. They're being told: 'Just ignore it; it's going to get better,' or 'You can take an SSRI [the class of antidepressants that block the reabsorption of serotonin], which will help your hot flashes — though, yeah, it's going to make you love sex less and get fat.' Your options are not too fabulous, but they don't know how to handle hormonal therapy, because they think it's going to give you breast cancer, and you're going to die.

"Then you have all the internal medicine people convinced that estrogen is bad for you, so even if I start somebody on something I have a young internist who's telling you, 'Minkin's trying to kill you. Cut it out.' This is the perfect storm, and the other part is the insurance companies are making it a real pain in the ass to treat people, because I have to get a preauthorization, and a lot of the products are expensive.

"The other part of the problem is you have such authoritative spokespeople as Dr. Kim Kardashian, Dr. Suzanne Sommers, Dr. Oprah Winfrey, Dr. Gwyneth Paltrow."

Dr. Minkin took my notebook and carefully drew a jagged descending line. She labeled it, "Dow Jones Industrial Average, September 2008."

This, she says, is almost identical to the graph you could draw tracing a woman's ovarian function fluctuation during perimenopause: "It's going down, but it's not a smooth line." That up and down illustrates the erratic mood swings so many of us experience.

She does not believe that women should grin and bear it. Here is some of her advice for us:

Get daily exercise, especially weight-bearing exercise; a good diet; and plenty of sleep.

For hot flashes, she advises layering clothes and keeping a dry set of nightclothes next to the bed so you can change quickly if you wake up in the middle of the night. She recommends keeping the bedroom cool and getting your partner an electric blanket if he or she complains.

Other nonpill things can make life easier, like absorbent "period-proof underwear" and period tracker apps.

She advises many women to consider estrogen-and-progesterone hormone therapy (or just estrogen, if you've had a hysterectomy), in the form of pills, patches, gels, or sprays, though it's important to do so only under the direction of a doctor because there are risks, just as with birth control pills. (Both Dr. Minkin and Dr. Allmen told me that a low-dose birth control pill could help me with my perimenopausal symptoms.)

Low doses of an SSRI or SNRI antidepressant can combat hot flashes, as can gabapentin (Neurontin). For heavy or irregular periods, Dr. Minkin says you can take a birth control pill or get a progesterone IUD called Mirena. When it comes to herbs and supplements like evening primrose oil or bee pollen, there's no proven benefit, though some women say that those things make them feel better. There's been some encouraging research on the effect of black cohosh, a member of the buttercup family, on hot flashes, though as with anything there are potential side effects.[31]

Sifting through all the advice is hard, especially because it can seem to change with every new headline. In her history of hormones, *Aroused,* Randi Epstein writes:

"Those of us old enough to be in menopause can't help but wonder if the experts are going to change their minds again."[32]

The writer Darcey Steinke's 2019 book *Flash Count Diary* is a search for meaning in a physically grueling menopause that had her flashing multiple times a day. She discovers that menopausal killer whales — yes, killer whales go through it, too — are the ones that lead others in their pods to food.[33] She finds comfort in identifying a reason behind the emotional and physical changes of middle age: some sign that it's not for nothing.

For better or worse, we are undergoing a transformation.

In her 2019 memoir, *Deep Creek,* Pam Houston gives a younger woman this advice: "I'm just saying, I guess, there's another version, after this version, to look forward to. Because of wisdom or hormones or just enough years going by. If you live long enough you quit chasing the things that hurt you; you eventually learn to hear the sound of your own voice."[34]

Perimenopause may last months or years; it may be more or less drastic; but one day it will be over. On the other side, we'll be different — perhaps more focused on what's most important to us and almost certainly

274

calmer. Psychotherapist Amy Jordan Jones told me,[35] "This is the time of life when we learn that we don't have to be pleasing; the work now is just to become more ourselves."

10
THE VERY FILTERED PROFILE PICTURE

"We're told: 'It's okay to be you!' But enter Instagram. I don't put up crappy pictures of myself. I use filters. We put a lot of filters on ourselves."

On my way to a party, I took out my phone, opened the camera, and tapped the reverse button. I was greeted with a sagging, weary face, so crone-like it made me gasp. I put on powder and lipstick. I changed filters and looked again. Still house of horrors. I put my phone away.

In our mothers' and grandmothers' eras, phones and mirrors sensibly sat on tables or hung on walls. But Generation X women noticed their first wrinkles in a zoomable smartphone camera. It's easy to obsess over that image.

"Are you insane, man?" a middle-aged friend of mine said when a young man went to take our picture at an unflattering angle.

"We aren't teenagers. Shoot us from above. Here, stand on this chair."

Boomer friends of mine have profile photos that could double as their work ID badges. Millennials change out their avatars all the time. But few are the Gen X women with a social media photo that hasn't been carefully planned, judiciously framed, and filtered. At school pickup recently, I looked around and realized that I could not recognize any of my fellow parents from their Facebook profile pictures.

Seeing airbrushed faces all day has brainwashed many of us into believing that we should not have lined faces in our forties.

"I will be the first person to tell you I am grasping," a Silicon Valley executive told me. "I work out every day. I eat super-clean. I have had Botox. Because I don't want to get old, right? I don't want to be dismissed. And regardless of what anyone says, man or woman, when you walk into a room and meet someone for the first time professionally, there is an assessment of what you look like. I don't want to lose that edge. And that's part of the crisis: am I going to lose my edge because, 'Oh look, here comes the dowdy middle-aged woman'?"

This fear of looking old is not new, of course. The other night, I watched *Sunset*

Boulevard for the first time in years. In the movie, the former silent film star Norma Desmond is holed up in her house, refusing to admit that time has passed and the world has moved on. She is a pathetic figure, mourning her lost youth and sex appeal. Do you know how old Norma Desmond is in that movie? *Fifty.*

The average age for a facelift has historically been over fifty, but the age at which women get plastic surgery has been dropping. According to the American Society of Plastic Surgeons, in 2015, more than 7.6 million cosmetic procedures were performed on people aged forty to fifty-four. Between the years 2000 and 2016 procedures for soft-tissue fillers like collagen went up about 300 percent, usage of Botox and comparable brands by more than 800 percent, and upper-arm lifts by *5,184 percent.*[1] This means that if you're not getting anything done, you could look older not only than your younger colleagues but also than a lot of people your own age.

"I was young for so long," said a woman standing near me around a firepit at a backyard party. "It feels like I was young until five minutes ago."

Her Facebook profile is a photo of herself as a little girl.

278

■ ■ ■ ■

Gen X straddles the pre- and post-internet worlds. The youngest Gen Xers belonged to the last graduating class to finish college pre–social media.[2] Facebook was invented in 2004. The iPhone came out in 2007. How fitting that many younger Gen Xers and older Millennials were introduced to computing by the bleak *Oregon Trail* — which frequently ended with you and all your friends dying from dysentery.[3] Personally, I loved the game. *Again, again! Maybe this time we'll get cholera!*

In *Zero Hour for Gen X: How the Last Adult Generation Can Save America from Millennials,* Matthew Hennessey delivers a tone poem of sorts about our precomputer world: "We were raised on analog technology — pencils, pens, notepads, books, index cards, the Dewey decimal system, newspapers, magazines, back issues, posters, mail order (sorry, no COD), records and record players, cassette tapes and boom boxes, video stores, landline telephones, answering machines . . ."[4] As nonnatives to the internet world, we have no natural immunity to the internet. Our poor 1970s and '80s brains, formed in the primordial ooze of the

279

Sony Walkman, Columbia House Record and Tape Club, pay phones, and typewriters, must now contend with Instagram Stories.

Hold on. Just one sec.

On Instagram, Jenny C. is now following me. Who is she again? Oh, right. She had a baby? Wow, that is a cute baby! I sort of wish I'd had another kid. Too late. Oh well. Good meme about the video game Fortnite! Heh. Alana's baby is getting big. So many babies. Sigh. Why is Waylon in Paris? Jami is in Italy. Liesl is in India. I want to go to Paris and India and Italy. Why do I suddenly feel lousy?

Social media doesn't just make us feel bad about our looks. It also — as we hear so often — makes us ashamed of our imperfect lives. Facebook does this,[5] experts say, "by showcasing the most witty, joyful, bullet-pointed versions of people's lives, and inviting constant comparisons in which we tend to see ourselves as the losers."[6]

"As we know more now than ever before," writes psychoanalyst Adam Phillips in *Missing Out,*[7] "about the kinds of lives it is possible to live — and affluence has allowed more people than ever before to think of their lives in terms of choices and options — we are always haunted by the myth of our potential, of what we might have it in ourselves to be or do."

Social media rewards us for adopting the self-congratulatory tone of holiday letters, all chipper spin-doctoring. If only someone would write an honest one of those: "We're disappointed the kids aren't doing better in school. We haven't had sex in a year. We fought with Brad's sister at Thanksgiving and haven't spoken to that side of the family since. I hate my job, but money is tight. Happy holidays!" If only there were some way to be genuine online and unaffected, too.

A Gen X friend of mine told me she had a question the other day for some of the Millennials she works with: "You send each other memes all day. Aren't you worried that the people who get them won't find them funny?" She says they looked at her as though she was insane.

That was when she realized that we are the only generation to overthink communication. "Our parents and grandparents have always sent newspaper clippings without worrying that people would find them annoying. Now kids send memes without a second thought. And you know why? Because they're not joyless. They aren't subjecting themselves to constant self-scrutiny. Meanwhile, we would agonize over a mixtape for weeks and then hand it over saying, 'It's nothing. It's fine if you hate it.' "

One North Carolina woman told me that social media, for her, has been an opportunity to perform a perfect life — a life she does not actually live: "No one knows you might be on your third shirt of the day at eight a.m., because the first one your toddler used as a napkin and the second one got splattered with coffee because you forgot to tighten the lid on your travel mug. No one knows that the perfect family beach photo you posted on Facebook was preceded by a dozen reject photos of your kids throwing sand at each other's faces and your baby trying to eat seagull poop."

Psychotherapist Deborah Luepnitz told me her Gen X clients suffer greatly from comparing themselves with others. When she tells them that everyone struggles, they tell her: " 'But you don't know the couple next door.' Everyone has an example. 'The couple across the street, they have a beautiful house. It's always clean. They both are at the top of their professions. The children are award-winning gymnasts. They never seem stressed out, and they don't have to cry to a therapist, and they never complain. They just entertain, and they seem so comfortable and low-key!' My advice is:

Don't ever compare your insides with their outsides. There are people, I guarantee you, who think *you* have the perfect life because they don't know what you're struggling with."

Maybe we should refuse to play the #winning social media game. It's exhausting to maintain the facade, and bragging all the time alienates others. There's another, perhaps even more destructive, drawback to telling our stories in short bursts on social media: it could be keeping us from contemplating our lives' broader plotlines.

Even if we opt out of posting, though, we're stuck with phones. Our mothers and our grandmothers never spent the busiest phase of life carrying around smartphones — little machines that demand charging and updating and that punch every emotional button. On our phone, we can see how much money we have, how much fun everyone else is having, what everyone's thinking politically, who isn't writing back to us. This steady drip of distractions is happening at just the stage of life when it's arguably most important for us to focus.

Even though I know I'll see something upsetting, I still want to look at social media. I don't really *like* looking at it. I almost never learn anything useful.[8] I don't feel my heart warmed. But I'm curious, and social media is like a mystery box. Every time you open it, there's something new in there — A kitten! A newborn baby! An ex's wedding pictures! Never mind that, intellectually, you can conceive no point in seeing another kitten or another baby, much less your rapturous ex. I find myself staring at my phone, opening one app and then another. The time just goes away.[9]

Before bed, I used a banking app to deposit a check. I emailed with someone about a potential work project and with various friends. I played a dozen games of Scrabble. I checked and rechecked a transit app. I looked at social media and breaking news, heard about global threats, and felt envious of my friend enjoying a sunset on the beach. (Why is there always a friend on a beach?)

Then, in the middle of the night, I wake up feeling warm, so I open the window and pull my hair back into a ponytail and drink some water. I glance at my phone, delete a few things, and see some spam. Unthinkingly, I hit unsubscribe and go back to bed. Then I lie there thinking, *What if by opening that spam email I got myself hacked? What if I just sent everyone in my contacts a Burger King ad at two in the morning?* Screen time, as we all know, correlates with poor sleep.[10] Generation X is more addicted to social media than either Millennials or Boomers. According to a 2017 Nielsen study, we spend almost seven hours a week on it, about forty minutes more than those ages eighteen to thirty-four.[11] A 2017 national report found that perimenopausal women were least likely to sleep more than seven hours a night, followed by postmenopausal women.[12]

A frequent topic of conversation when women gather is how to fall asleep and stay asleep. Some swear by a white noise machine, herbal tea, or melatonin. My friend Sheri buys something called the Meg-Rhythm Gentle Steam Eye Mask at Asian grocery stores. It's a disposable eye mask that gets hot and exudes a smell like lavender. "It looks like you're wearing a maxi pad on your face," Sheri said, "but otherwise it's awesome."

"In our forties, we're in the throes of everything — in the middle of our careers, in the middle of parenting, in the middle of whatever's happening with our own parents, all the big financial stuff," said Janet K. Kennedy, clinical psychologist and founder of NYC Sleep Doctor. "There is so much stress. And sleep is very sensitive to hormonal shifts. When your hormones start shifting in wild ways, there might be insomnia, changes to bedtime, night waking. It can come in any of those forms or all of them. The hardest part is that it's unpredictable."

Laura Vanderkam, the author of *Off the Clock: Feel Less Busy While Getting More Done,* says our phones do more than just rob us of sleep. They contribute to our moods of panic and the sensation of never having enough time.[13] If we keep a time diary, she says, we can see that the necessary time is there. She had nine hundred people track their time for a day and she compared people who felt they had plenty of time with people who felt rushed and harried and unhappy.

"I found that people who felt more relaxed checked their phones less often," she said. "It feels less like free time when you chop it up. And you're most of the time not dealing with a work problem . . . You're waiting at a red light. You're bored at a kids' game. You're sitting around waiting for everyone to get their shoes on to get in the car . . . Put the stupid thing in airplane mode."

I should. I know. I talked to a small army of therapists for this book, and not one of them said to look at screens more.

"Overwhelmed by the volume and velocity of our lives," writes Sherry Turkle in *Alone Together,*[14] "we turn to technology to help us find time. But technology makes us busier than ever and ever more in search of retreat . . . Technology reshapes the landscape of our emotional lives, but is it offering us the lives we want to lead?"

I think about this as I fall asleep. I resolve to wait in the morning, at least until I've had coffee, to go online.

The alarm goes off on my iPhone and when I go to turn it off I see a bunch of notifications. Before I'm out of bed, I'm scrolling.

On Twitter, a bunch of literary prizes got announced. I didn't get one. I wasn't eligible this year, but for some reason I still feel hurt. There's a walkout today to protest sexual assault. Oh God, look at all these sexual assault stories. Oof. Oof. Oof. Oh, now I see battles over "diversionary propaganda" and ah! Please don't get in a fight, friends! And they are fighting.

In middle age, past generations of American women faced a world that could be seen, objectively, in many ways, as more stressful than ours. As babies of World War II or the Great Depression, our mothers and grandmothers had less power to determine

287

their own lives. Their worlds were beset not only by economic downturns. They dealt with the effects of assassinations and wars. There may just be something about the way we live now that makes things *feel* worse. That may have something to do with the world being too much with us.

We know, but somehow it doesn't help to know, that companies and political machines use social media to spread anger, misinformation, and especially arouse fear. During the 2016 election, it was hard to avoid the churn of the news cycle — much of which we now know came to us via channels that were not, to put it mildly, concerned with the pursuit of truth or an informed electorate.[15] Every day, there was more drama and more ugliness and yet another shocking allegation; there were ever more stories about rape and terrorism and gun violence.[16]

Whenever the news is particularly bleak, therapists say they see in patients a rise in anxiety. One doctor coined the term "headline stress disorder."[17] Gallup surveys reported that the 2016 election served as a "significant source of stress" for many Americans. While Democrats have worried more since the election, Independents and Republicans haven't been far behind. The most worried groups were women, black people, those earning more than $90,000 a year, and people aged thirty to forty-five.[18] Gallup found that Americans' overall well-being declined significantly in 2017, with emotional and psychological metrics showing the worst effect and women among the groups suffering the most.[19]

One Gen X woman told me that since the election she'd been at "Defcon One every day. I feel like my head is going to explode."

According to the American Psychological Association's Stress in America survey, more than half of Americans believe this is the lowest point in our nation's history — and that holds true not only for Generation X but among elders who lived through Pearl Harbor and juniors whose earliest memory may be of September 11.[20]

I called the APA and asked if the researchers were surprised by the immense number of Americans in despair.

"Yes, I think we were," says Vaile Wright, who was on the research team. "Particularly that it seemed to be across all four generations. There was a sense that younger generations that have less perspective may say that this is the worst time in America. But we saw older adults — Baby Boomers, everybody — reporting a lot of stress. That was surprising."[21]

Of the four generations polled, Gen X was the most distraught.

The internet exacerbates anxiety that was already there, and it heightens the already trying physical self-consciousness of midlife, too.

One afternoon a colleague of mine sat down across from me looking ashen. "Someone in the elevator just congratulated me," she said. "She thought I was pregnant. I said, 'No, just fat!' and tried to laugh it off, but everyone was mortified."

And *that* is why you should never congratulate someone on being pregnant *unless you see the baby coming out of her.* Only then, at the crowning, may you say, "Oh! Are you having a baby?"

Among middle-aged women in the United States, 38 percent are obese, according to a comprehensive study by age group done in 2011.[22] The world's toilet stalls, airplane seats, and restaurant chairs are not built to cope with this reality. The fashion industry caters to the thin, though the average American woman now wears size 16–18.[23] In the *Washington Post, Project Runway* host Tim Gunn writes,[24] "Many designers — dripping with disdain, lacking imagination or simply too cowardly to take a risk — still refuse to make clothes for [plus-size women]."

Gen X women often try to exert control over their bodies at midlife only to find that the middle-aged body is remarkably resistant. "The illusion that each person can have the body that he or she wants is especially painful for women," writes Barry Schwartz in *The Paradox of Choice: Why More Is Less,*[25] "and especially in societies, like ours, in which the 'ideal' body is extremely thin."

Professor Judith A. Houck, author of the history of menopause *Hot and Bothered,*[26] tells me that a woman's wish to control her body frequently shades into a sense that she has an *obligation* to do so. Houck cites the old-timey childbirth strategy known as "twilight sleep," a kind of anesthesia that didn't take away any of the pain of childbirth but that erased women's memory of it.

"This typifies one of the ironies of asking for more medical intervention," says Houck. "Middle-class women wanted more control over their childbirth. They wanted less pain, less trauma." They asked for twilight sleep, but when they got it, they realized it had huge drawbacks. "This is a perfect example of the messiness that's always going to be with us. You want more medical attention, because you have significant problems. But once we start attracting medical attention, we get more than we asked for. The unintended consequences of medical attention are always complex."

The last thing women of this generation need to hear is that we have to work harder to get our bodies into line. Step counters like the Fitbit, which so many women of our generation have strapped to their wrists, monitor every move we make. When we were young women, our bodies often inspired admiring comments. Now, they attract a different kind of attention: concerned scrutiny. Our bodies are under constant surveillance — and we are both the guard in the watchtower and the prisoner.

"I'm not looking for inner peace," a friend quipped when I asked her about why she skipped the resting stage of Savasana at the end of a yoga class. "I'm looking for outer hotness." She is far from alone. In the past two decades, there's been an increasing focus on self-perfection.

So much of the advice older women receive when we express dissatisfaction involves bringing our bodies in line. I look at the women my age on treadmills at the gym — so determined, grinding away. From morning television to the evening news, experts tell us to make chore charts, to save a certain percent of our income, to clean out our closets, to get our BMI under twenty-five. Nothing seems to stimulate the economy like women feeling bad about themselves. And yet: "The effort to try to feel happy is often precisely the thing that makes us miserable," as Oliver Burkeman writes in *The Antidote: Happiness for People Who Can't Stand Positive Thinking.*[27]

Put another way: "Those who try to refuse suffering," wrote W. H. Auden in an essay about characters in Shakespeare, "not only fail to avoid it but are plunged deeper into sin and suffering." Everyone suffers in Shakespeare's plays, according to Auden. The difference is that in tragedies, suffering leads to "self-blindness, defiance, hatred"; in comedies, it leads to "self-knowledge, repentance, forgiveness, love."[28]

The barrage of advice we receive about how to avoid suffering reinforces an idea that Gen X women don't need emphasized: that we have to do more, work harder, try ever more classes and cleanses and programs. But the truth is that the most blameless lifestyle won't necessarily get anywhere near where the trouble is.

"I remember after my second kid was born," said one friend of mine, "and putting on three pounds every year, and thinking, *Huh, this isn't that great . . . Okay, these are the things I'm going to do to work out and blah, blah, blah,* and then at some point being like, *Can I actually just be a mom? Can I not have to be a MILF?* I'm just about to hit forty, so I'm solid MILF material, but also could I just be a squishy mom? Do we ever get permission to look forty rather than twenty, to just be old? And not even old, but 'Yeah, I popped a couple out, give me a break.' I don't want to have to go to Pilates. I don't remember all our moms looking that good at forty."

Second-wave feminist, activist, and writer Carol Hanisch, best known for popularizing the adage "The personal is political," told me that in some ways life for women in the 1970s had advantages: "Whether women have it better now is debatable. Certainly, there are more women in professional jobs, but on the other hand, we weren't pressured to shave our genital area and wear spike heels."[29]

A woman in Michigan told me that it's only in midlife that she's finally able to let go of her body shame. "In my twenties, I was a bartender," she told me. "I had a boob-job fund. And people would tip me extra money because I had really little tits. I raised thousands of dollars, setting aside this money because I was going to buy boobs, and thank God I had some little voice in my head that was like, 'No.' I spent it on a couch and a refrigerator. And I'm so glad. I remember this lady saying, 'Oh, honey, don't do it. As soon as you hit forty, they'll get bigger.' And she was right. I'm a little chubbier now, but she was right."

Judith Houck thinks that women should cut themselves slack during this phase of life. Self-denial is not inherently a virtue, she told me: "This idea that you get some sort of points for saying no to chocolate — where does that come from?"

Until Houck asked the question, though, I hadn't really thought much about it. Why can't we be pudgy, grouchy, or uncontained? I think about my heroes, whether teachers who were encouraging, writers I've tried to emulate, or relatives who were good to me when I was little. Not one could be mistaken for a supermodel.

"It's not the worst thing in the world," Houck said, "to be living with a body that's a little bit out of control."

One solution to the insecurity nurtured by

social media: replacing virtual connections with real ones. Middle-aged women tell me that one of the great gifts of midlife is connecting to other women.

I've begun to find camaraderie nearly everywhere a few women my age are gathered together.

"I *hate* this," a weary-looking woman in a hospital gown said out loud to me and everyone else in the waiting room at a New York medical clinic. We were sitting there together among the old *InStyle* magazines, traces of ultrasound gunk lingering on our breasts, making our blue "open to the front!" gowns stick to us.

Everyone made sympathetic noises.

She received her results before the rest of us got ours and she was fine. She looked surprised. "Well, that's a relief," she said. We cheered her good news as if we'd known her forever.

You can happen upon spontaneous support groups like that, or you can plan them. There used to be a culture of socializing around shared interests. In Robert Putnam's famous book *Bowling Alone,* published in the year 2000, he noted that we've moved away from that custom. Fifteen years later, he revisited the question in *Our Kids: The American Dream in Crisis.* Putnam reported that "both kin and nonkin networks have shrunk in the past two decades," with nonfamily connections decreasing even more rapidly. "Americans' social networks are collapsing inward, and now consist of fewer, denser, more homogeneous, more familial (and less nonkin) ties."[30]

Since turning forty, I've decided I need more support and more camaraderie than I happen upon in the course of most days, so I've started to schedule both.

"It's like at forty you decided you wanted more women in your life and you just manifested them," my husband said.

I was inspired by my son. Last year, when he was eleven, he and a twelve-year-old girl at his school formed a British Club, and it has continued ever since. The two of them meet each Friday at lunchtime. There, they pin a Union Jack to the wall, drink tea, eat British snacks, and speak in British accents. They even have a secret handshake, which involves pretending to clink teacups, pinkies out, and yelling, "To London!"

Hoping to capture the bonkers magic of British Club, I've formed as many of my own groups as possible. I'm in a monthly low-stakes poker game that rotates from one player's apartment to another's, and I sit in on a friend's trivia team that competes weekly during the summer. I have a Scrabble nemesis, Lisa, whom I meet for games a few times a year, and a regular Anagrams night with my friend Emily.

Most ambitiously, this year, two author girlfriends and I started a bar night for women nonfiction writers to talk shop, play the arcade game Big Buck Hunter, and engage — in the words of the classic *Onion* article about what really happens when girls go wild — in "validating the living shit out of each other."[31] It's a two-hour meeting every month or so at a dive bar with drinks and snacks cheap enough that showing up isn't prohibitive for anyone. We've named it Sob Sisters, after the old-fashioned, dismissive term for women reporters. The first meeting, we thought we'd get maybe ten fellow journalists. Fifty showed up. A few came in from out of town. *I guess maybe we need this,* I thought, as the women gossiped about editors and bought one another drinks.

It is notoriously hard to make new friends in middle age. As one writer puts it: "As people approach midlife, the days of youthful exploration, when life felt like one big blind date, are fading. Schedules compress, priorities change and people often become pickier in what they want in their friends."[32]

I've found that one route to fixing this is to find companionship in drudgery. My friend Tara and I check in with each other a few times a week, when we have a couple of minutes, waiting or walking, to kill. "I only have friends who will go to CVS with me," she tells me.

One piece of advice I feel comfortable giving women of this age, besides to visit a compassionate NAMS-certified gynecologist the second you start having perimenopause symptoms: start a club. A book club gives you a reason to read and to get together with friends. But you can make a club around anything. A stitch and bitch. A going-out-dancing club. Margarita Mondays. A try-every-pizza-place-in-town club. A New Midlife Crisis Initiation Club,™ perhaps!

If you're having trouble finding women to go out with you, you can join one of the many networks springing up around the country, from meet-ups for middle-aged and older women to paid professional societies like Tiffany Dufu's the Cru.[33] It may seem counterintuitive to add one more thing to a full calendar when the problem is feeling too busy — like putting on a scarf when you feel overheated — but it's worthwhile. "Middle age, especially for women of a generation that stayed young for a long time, is a weird place," one friend of mine said. She calls the midlife club "a menstruation hut of your choosing."

I've found it helps to pick two hours every month or two, like the third Monday of each month, 7:00 to 9:00 p.m., at a spot like happy hour at a bar or potluck in a church basement. Not everyone will make every meeting, but with luck there will be a gang every time and all the members will show up at least a few times a year. My friend Biz, who has hosted many regular events, including a rollicking annual Kentucky Derby party with mint juleps and absurd hats, told me: "You have to find ways to make adulthood fun."

At my club nights, when we smile at one another, the room is full of lined faces — and, for a minute, no one cares.

11
NEW NARRATIVES

"There's this idea that women have to be superpowers, basically. On the one hand: 'Of course we can do that.' On the other: 'Why? It's ridiculous.' "

Her fancy was running riot along those days ahead of her. Spring days, and summer days, and all sorts of days that would be her own. She breathed a quick prayer that life might be long. It was only yesterday that she had thought with a shudder that life might be long.

— Kate Chopin,
"The Story of an Hour," 1894[1]

I woke up at 4:00 a.m. last night as usual. Then — not so much later — I fell back asleep. I did not fill the space in between by cursing my sleeping husband. I did not dwell on my finances or job prospects — or on national politics. I did not dread the day to come. I just rolled over, and the next thing I knew my alarm was going off and it was time to make breakfast.

Writing this book cured my midlife crisis. I've given up on a magic bullet that will make this age easy, but I've learned that there are many things that make it harder or easier, and I've made changes accordingly.

I've assembled a team of helpers worthy of *Ocean's Eleven.* I know a good therapist I can call on when I need her. I found an accountant who understands the vicissitudes of freelancing. My mother and I talked to an estate-planning attorney to ensure that everyone's wills, health care proxies, and other papers were in order. I have a tailor to fix hems, an urgent care clinic for strep tests, and a teenage turtle-sitter for when we're out of town. I started and joined clubs so I would be guaranteed regular contact with people in my field and community whom I enjoy.

On the micro level, I've figured out what makes me feel worse (drinking too much, looking at social media) and what makes me feel better (eating three meals a day, walking around in fresh air), and try to behave accordingly — or at least not to be blindsided if I feel despair the morning after

302

a party or the evening after a day in front of the computer.

I began taking synthetic estrogen and progesterone — the same hormones involved in HRT — in the form of a low-dose birth control pill. I found the adjustment phase, which is said to take three to four months, rough. My periods became even more unpredictable. I retained water and became convinced I was gaining weight permanently. Then those issues went away and I found myself on a more even keel.

Then, all of a sudden, my periods stopped. I wondered if it could be early menopause, but no, not yet. My new doctor — I left the one who prescribed bee pollen — explained that the pill suppresses ovulation. This means that nothing may build up in the uterus that needs to be expelled, so either there's just spotting or there's no period at all. I don't miss it.

With my body presenting less of a distraction, I've been able to think more clearly about my place in the world — not as the ingenue but as a mother, mentor, neighbor, or (dare to dream it) MILF. "Look at you walking!" I recently shouted to a newly mobile baby who lives on my block. Before, when I was engulfed in a haze of worry or self-criticism, that baby might have flown

303

down the sidewalk on a skateboard without my noticing.

My expectations are way lower. I no longer believe that at this age I should have rock-hard abs, a perfectly calm disposition, or a million dollars in the bank. It helps to surround myself with women my age who speak honestly about their lives.

I'm more patient, too. I know that perimenopause is tough on many women and also that it ends. In less than a decade, no matter what I do or don't do, things will be different. I've made friends with some older women who remind me by their example that a more serene future is possible.

Note: none of what I'm saying falls under the umbrella of what's commonly called "self-care." Short-term perks like spa days or facials are like putting a Band-Aid on a broken bone. Our problems are beyond the reach of "me-time." The last thing we need at this stage of life is self-help. Everyone keeps telling us what to do, as if there is a quick fix for the human condition. What we need at this stage isn't more advice, but solace.

One of the biggest midlife problems I had to confront was anxiety paired with an abiding belief that I *should not be anxious.* That's unreasonable. It would be weird, frankly, if

I weren't anxious. Human beings are wired to see situations as being unfair to us.[2] As comedian Tim Minchin said in a 2013 commencement speech in Australia: "We didn't evolve to be constantly content. Contented *Homo erectus* got eaten before passing on their genes."[3] Oddly, knowing that I have every reason in the world to be freaking out has made me much more relaxed.

For me, the first step to peace in middle age has been learning that the game is rigged. If we feel that things are tougher now, it could mean only that we're paying more attention. This is a bumpy stretch in life. We should not expect to feel fine.

"Women are not prepared to have 'everything,' not success-type 'everything,'" writes Eve Babitz in *Slow Days, Fast Company*.[4] "I mean, not when the 'everything' isn't about living happily ever after with the prince (where even if it falls through and the prince runs off with the baby-sitter, there's at least a *precedent*). There's no precedent for women getting their own 'everything' and learning that it's not the answer."

I know too well that it's easy to turn these facts against women and to declare that feminism has made us unhappy. *Ah, you do not like these possibilities?* says the villain's voice. *No problem! We vill take them away!*

I'm not knocking choices, just saying that having so many of them with so little support has led to a great deal of shame. Being a full and equal partner both at work and at home, having a rich social life, contributing to society, staying in shape — doing all that is exponentially harder than doing any one thing. We asked for more, and did we ever get it. I firmly believe it's fairer. Easier? No.

One night in December 2018, the Tony-winning actress and singer Tonya Pinkins talked onstage about her experience of menopause, adding: "Things are so much better than they were decades ago, but they can be bad and better at the same time."[5] "Bad and better" is one way to think about our prospects at this stage of life, too.

Listening to other women's stories this year has given me confirmation, finally, that our expectations have been absurd. So many women I spoke with — objectively successful women — felt ashamed of their perceived failures.

What if we're not failures? What if what we've done is good? At any rate, maybe it's good enough.

"It used to be, you rated yourself on maybe three or four things," says Jennifer J. Deal, senior research scientist at the Center for Creative Leadership[6] — "your looks, your house, your husband, and your kids. Now it's all that, *plus* your career, your finances, how eco-conscious you are, how healthy you are, and on and on and on."

So many Gen X women have told me that they were raised believing that if you don't care about everything, you're squandering opportunity. They felt pressure to take advantage of all the chances their mothers and grandmothers didn't have. And they've worn themselves out in the process.

"The people I know who are happy realize they can't care about everything," says Deal. "You have to decide what you care about. If everything matters to you, you're going to go nuts."

That's what's happening. And the message we've heard is that with enough ingenuity or willpower we can fix it.

Again and again, I've heard women say that they were depressed or exhausted but were meditating, going to yoga, going to therapy, or going to church three times a week. Their higher power was Oprah. They were doing a cleanse. They were doing a retreat. They were going to spas, getting makeovers, getting plastic surgery. Soon, they knew, they would figure out which of their many missteps had brought them to this age without the life they'd envisioned, and they could get back on track.

"The minute the phrase 'having it all' lost favor among women, wellness came in to pick up the pieces," wrote Taffy Brodesser-Akner in a story about Gwyneth Paltrow's Goop.[7] "Before we knew it, the wellness point of view had invaded everything in our lives: Summer-solstice sales are wellness. Yoga in the park is wellness . . . SoulCycle, açaí, antioxidants, the phrase 'mind-body,' meditation, the mindfulness jar my son brought home from school, kombucha, chai, juice bars, oat milk, almond milk, all the milks from substances that can't technically be milked."

After spending months steeped in Goopiana, Brodesser-Akner had an epiphany: "We are doomed to aspire for the rest of our lives. Aspiration is suffering. Wellness is suffering. As soon as you level up, you greet how infinite the possibilities are, and it all becomes too awful to live without."

I eat reasonably well and try to get out in nature occasionally, but I am under no illusion that these things will fix the existential crunch that is middle age. The only thing for that is a new story.

Here's a real-world parable that has helped me:

In the midst of a hectic day, a woman called a car. When she hopped into her Uber, she found it was messy. Of course: another annoyance! Could this day get any worse? She started cleaning up the back seat and handing the trash to the driver.

He stared back at her without saying anything.

She grew madder and madder. *Here she was helping! All day, she's been doing things for other people! He wasn't even saying thank you!*

Then she looked out the window and saw a woman waiting to get in the car. And she realized this was not her Uber. She saw the woman and the driver making eye contact and raising their eyebrows at each other. This wasn't an Uber at all. She had hopped into the back seat of a random car and huffily handed a man his own back seat trash.

She explained her mistake and apologized.

At this point, the situation could have gone in various directions. The man could have yelled at her. He could have mocked her. The woman waiting outside the car — the man's wife, it turned out — could have been angry or suspicious. The woman having the bad day could have become abjectly embarrassed.

Instead, something else happened: the

man laughed. He got out of the car and told his wife what had occurred. She laughed. And then the woman herself laughed, too. The three of them could not stop laughing. Here they were, strangers laughing together in the middle of the day, on a city sidewalk. The woman went off to find her real Uber, still giggling. She found herself not only relieved of her earlier gloom but also delighted for the rest of the day. What made the difference? The driver reacted to her error with glee rather than judgment. She could accept her mistake.

I asked my friend Asia, a therapist in New Orleans, to tell me why I like this story so much. She said it's a good one for middle age, because it shows how helpful it can be to reframe a situation. So often, she says, we see the task of living well in a negative, self-punishing way: "I should be exercising more!" "I have to be the most mindful yogi ever!" "I have to eat perfectly vegan every second of the day!"

"We take basically good ideas and turn them into something with which to self-flagellate," said Asia. But the driver and the woman in the Uber story "both showed this ability to take that moment when you could have both been embarrassed or grumpy or angry and instead find it hilarious and lovable and adorable."

You could say this attitude comes down to the old cliché about "looking on the bright side," but I think it's more profound than that. It's about telling the story of our mistakes, our life, in a new way, in which we're heroines worth rooting for.

When teaching memoir classes, I've talked about making meaning in the process of structuring a story. What's the beginning, middle, and end? What are the key plot points? What are the most moving scenes?

Deliverance from suffering in midlife could come from some outside force, but it could also come from reframing your life as being about something unexpected.[8] Many of the inspirational authors that women I talked to recommended to me, including Barbara Bradley Hagerty, Brené Brown, Elizabeth Gilbert, and Cheryl Strayed, speak of recasting and rethinking our lives. In a recent op-ed about midlife, Ann Voskamp wrote, "Life doesn't have to get easier to be good."[9]

Maybe the Generation X story need not be: *We're broke. We're unstable. We're alone.* Maybe it can be: *We've had a hard row to hoe. We've been one big experiment. And yet, look at us: we've accomplished so much.*

Generation X women, who as children

lacked cell phones and helicopter parents, came up relying on our own wits. To keep ourselves safe, we took control. We worked hard and made lists and tried to do everything all at once for a very long time and without much help. We took responsibility for ourselves — and later we also took responsibility for our work or partners or children or parents. We should be proud of ourselves.

I keep thinking about the 1980s–90s TV show *Double Dare*,[10] in which child contestants had to find orange flags among obstacles such as mountains of slime. That, I think, is an excellent analogy for our generation in midlife: we've been glopped with slime, but somewhere in the mess there's that little orange flag.

One of my favorite studies is about how children benefit from hearing an "oscillating family narrative."[11] The researchers found that what helps build resilience in children is a story like this: "Dear, let me tell you, we've had ups and downs in our family. We built a family business. Your grandfather was a pillar of the community. Your mother was on the board of the hospital. But we also had setbacks. You had an uncle who was once arrested. We had a house burn down. Your father lost a job.

But no matter what happened, we always stuck together as a family." That kind of tale fosters self-confidence — more, even, than one in which the family has been on a steady upward climb.

Gen X might not live on an economic up-slope, but perhaps we can make meaning out of our dip in prosperity, and say: We will be okay. If we don't fix it all, maybe our kids will. Post-Millennials, also known as Gen Z, are likely to be the most diverse and best-educated generation in American history.[12] There will be ups and downs in the future just as there have been in the past. Whatever comes, we know we can handle it.

A woman I know who does a lot for other people told me she doesn't mind that her husband is selfish while she is generous, because: "Look who has a richer life . . . I may do so much more, he may get away with sitting alone all day never doing anything for other people, but look what I get out of it. I have all these friends. I have the best life."

This past spring, I had dinner at a restaurant with a friend who lives in Florida. We stayed up late, so late the staff put chairs on tables around us but told us we could stay as long as we wanted (she knew the owner). She'd been through a divorce and a career change, but seemed happy. She'd found meaning in her work. She was proud of her sons.

She knew she could feel bad. She had less money than she'd like. She was trying to make herself go to the gym more often. Still, she found herself feeling strangely hopeful.

"I'm kind of *interested,*" she told me. "Interested in what my life is and how it's evolving. Because it's kind of like a weird little adventure. What could possibly happen next, you know? It's been kind of weirdly . . . terribly . . . *fun.* It's like, *terrible fun,* you know?"

To me, this is a transformative way of thinking about life, every day, all day — as a story in which the bad things are part of the plot and not random disasters.

When I had a job writing copy for a home decorating magazine, I grew resentful of all the edits I would get: "What *kind* of wicker chair was it?" One day, though, I realized I needed the job for the money and so I had to find a way to like it. I started to think of my editor as a writing class teacher. I was taking a course in descriptive writing, and her notes were my assignments. "What kind of wicker? How about 'sky blue, distressed, wide-binding cane'?" Once I started to think of it as a class I was getting paid to take, I could enjoy it and learn from it — at least until I was able to get out of there into a job that was a better fit.

I have friends who will say things like "I'm just a contracts analyst." But the world needs contracts analysts. The world needs administration. The world needs organization. The world needs money moved around. The world needs teachers and bankers and lawyers and doctors and firefighters and someone to analyze all those people's contracts.

Displaying "generativity" means caring about people besides just yourself and your family. That leads to helping guide the next generation, which often leads to a positive legacy. Maybe our legacy is our children. Maybe it's our work. Maybe it's our friendships or the house we fixed up.

Some psychologists are exploring the connection between being generative and telling our personal narratives in certain ways.[13] The professor Dan McAdams looks at how people recount their lives. The script that "highly generative" adults follow often includes turning points — "redemption sequences" — where negative experiences somehow became meaningful.[14] People in

315

midlife who see redemption sequences in their life show more overall well-being.[15] Could that be our recourse? To look back and around and say this means that and this thing is over and this other thing is beginning? Writing our stories in midlife calls for identifying the characters in them. Who are our heroes, who are our villains?

Almost every story I've heard of a Gen X woman pulling herself out of a midlife crisis has involved, in one way or another, the letting go of expectations. That's been the most important part of my own reckoning: When I start criticizing myself for not having saved enough money or for not having written enough of value or for my son's bad handwriting, or for not working out or for any other failures small and large, I try to put my finger on the expectation that any of these things would be different.

I also try to remind myself that if I were in better shape or my son did calligraphy or I had $30,000 in an emergency fund as I'm supposed to, life would not necessarily be any better. Even padded with achievement or glamour or cash, midlife is very likely going to be challenging. Even if you don't subscribe to the belief in a crisis point, you cannot deny the onset of new physical limitations and stressors.

Therefore, if the first piece of a solution is getting support and the second is reframing the way we see our life to remove unrealistic expectations, the third might be . . . waiting. One day, midlife will end. Kids will grow up; relationships will evolve. Women in their fifties and sixties tell me that after menopause they felt so much better — less nervous, more confident, no longer afraid of looking stupid.[16]

One said that menopause gave her clarity, about her life and about her own feelings: "Now I cut to the chase. I say no when I mean no. My husband is like, 'Who the hell are you?' " And not in a bad way. He's just getting to know this new, decisive woman he finds himself married to now — the same way she had to get used to being married to someone bald.

"It cannot be too soon realized that in the lives of women there is capacity for a *second youth,*" Anna Garlin Spencer wrote long ago, in 1913.[17] My friend Barbara, who grew up in Mexico, said something similar: "The thirties are the adolescence of your adulthood, and when you reach fifty, it's a restart — *empieza de nuevo* — a second chance."

Middle-aged women have perspective enough to see what's important and what isn't. "If you are young and you are reading this," says writer Mary Ruefle, "perhaps you will understand the gleam in the eye of any woman who is sixty, seventy, eighty, or ninety: they cannot take you seriously (sorry) for you are just a girl to them, despite your babies and shoes and lovemaking and all of that. You are just a girl playing at life."[18]

Older people tend to be happier, and someday we will be those people.

Just in the course of writing this book, I saw the lives of many of the women I spoke with change, mostly for the better. They found new jobs or new towns or new partners or figured out how to better enjoy the ones they had. They got on hormones or got off hormones or started exercising or stopped exercising. Time passed. Things were different.

In their 1991 book *Generations,* William Strauss and Neil Howe made some predictions about our generation, which they called 13ers, because we are the thirteenth generation since the founding of the United States — and also because, like the number thirteen, we seem unlucky. In the years 2004–2025, they wrote, the Gen X demographic would be "entering midlife in a crisis era." Gen X would look at the graying

Boomers in charge and "appreciate that whatever bad hand history dealt them, they at least grew up with clear heads."[19]

Eerily, Strauss and Howe predicted a 2020 crisis brought about by Boomers, one for which Gen X will "provide able on-site managers and behind-the-scenes facilitators, the ones whose quick decisions could spell the difference between triumph and tragedy . . . In an age of rising social intolerance, the very incorrigibility of midlife 13ers will at times be a national blessing."

One CEO I know, a Gen X woman who grew up in southern Illinois and now oversees huge swaths of American farmland, said she hires Gen X women to do the hardest jobs at her company because they show tremendous resilience.[20]

"They are the best," she said. "They can have six screens open at once and not miss a thing. They're not crybabies. They're capable. They will work long and hard for you. They have zero sense of entitlement. They hold people accountable and they speak up." She pays her most cherished Gen X women managers six figures and lets them work from anywhere. "I'll do a lot to keep them," she said. "They're that valuable."

Could we see even our newfound midlife

invisibility as a source of power? In Harry Potter's world, one of the most prized magical tools is an invisibility cloak. There are great advantages to being underestimated. Two of the best reporters I know are women in their fifties. They look so friendly and nonthreatening, if you notice them at all. They can lurk in any room without usually wary people remembering to keep their guard up. Then they write devastating whistle-blowing articles. The world ignores middle-aged women at its peril.[21]

When we're driving through East Texas to visit my in-laws, my husband and son and I like to play a car game called School or Prison. Thanks to the region's austere architecture, it can be hard to tell from afar which is which. So, spotting a massive, institutional-looking building on the horizon, we call out, "Time to play . . . *School or Prison!*" Then we each guess. Only when we get close enough to see if there's barbed wire do we know who's won.

When the tough things happen — parents get sick, relationships go sour, careers stall — we might ask ourselves if the situation is a prison or a school: a place to escape or one in which to learn.

This past summer, I broke my big toe slipping on some steps. The doctor looked at the X-ray and said, "Wow, you did a good job breaking that!" (I've had this same feeling when researching Gen X's timing in history: "Wow, it's really quite impressively bad!") I wound up on crutches and had to cancel a work trip that was scheduled for the following week.

Breaking my toe seemed like prison. Then, slowly, it became school. For the weeks I was recovering, I did no weeding of gardens, no cleaning of cabinets, no vacuuming, no errands. My mother brought me groceries and my son gave me his rolling desk chair to scoot around the house on and my husband did all the cooking and cleaning. And I let them.

My friend Nola came over to keep me company and we got to joking about the incredibly boring book I could write: *The Wisdom of the Crutches.* It was a gift, in the end. When I sat on the couch all day, the world didn't spin off its axis. If it weren't for my accident, I never would have known it.

On my forty-second birthday, I woke to the sound of my husband and son whispering and the smell of brewing coffee. When I went into the next room, I found it had been decorated with streamers and a "Happy Birthday!" banner. On the table sat presents and a cake. Later, friends — many of whom I've now known for decades — came over and laughed and talked at a table full of platters of food and bottles of wine, our kids running into and out of the room.

That afternoon, I went to the Price Chopper and, standing there in the parking lot, I looked up at the clear, blue sky and had a strange, unfamiliar feeling: joy.

My choices may have brought me debt and uncertainty and a lot of people depending on me. But they've also brought me a family that will wake up early to decorate the house and friends coming over to eat and drink and make jokes and the capacity to appreciate a clear sky on a cold day.

Assuming we keep living, there will be a next year and another year after that. There will be tears and money stress and caregiving pressure, but also moments when we might walk through a supermarket parking lot and feel the sun on our face and think, out of nowhere, *What a lovely day.*

APPENDIX:
A MIDLIFE CRISIS MIXTAPE

"19 Somethin' " — Mark Wills
"1979" — Smashing Pumpkins
"1985" — Bowling for Soup
"Better Days" — Bruce Springsteen
"Changes" — David Bowie
"Constant Craving" — k. d. lang
"Divorce Song" — Liz Phair
"Emotional Rollercoaster" — Vivian Green
"Fade Away" — Oasis
"Ghost!" — Kid Cudi
"Girl of 100 Lists" — Go-Go's
"Good Feeling" — Violent Femmes
"Gypsy" — Fleetwood Mac
"Heads Carolina, Tails California" — Jo Dee Messina
"Here" — Pavement
"Hey Cinderella" — Suzy Bogguss
"I Did It All" — Tracy Chapman
"I'm a Woman" — Peggy Lee
"Just for You" — Lionel Richie (feat. Billy Currington)

323

"Let the Mystery Be" — Iris DeMent

"Life Begins at Forty" — Sophie Tucker

"Losing My Edge" — LCD Soundsystem

"(Love Is Like a) Heat Wave" — Martha and the Vandellas

"Montezuma" — Fleet Foxes

"Old College Try" — Mountain Goats

"PMS Blues" — Dolly Parton

"Revival" — Me Phi Me (*Reality Bites*)

"Rich" — Maren Morris

"Save Me" — Aimee Mann

"She Let Herself Go" — George Strait

"Strawberry Wine" — Deana Carter

"Suddenly I See" — KT Tunstall

"Teenage Talk" — St. Vincent

"Too Much on My Mind" — Kinks

"Tossin' and Turnin' " — Bobby Lewis

"Unsatisfied" — Replacements

"Waiting for Somebody" — Paul Westerberg (*Singles*)

"We Are Not Alone" — Karla DeVito (*The Breakfast Club*)

"When We Were Young" — Adele

"Work in Progress (Growing Pains)" — Mary J. Blige

"You Don't Know How It Feels" — Tom Petty

"Your Generation" — Generation X

"Yo Vivré" — Celia Cruz

BIBLIOGRAPHY

Albertine, Viv. *To Throw Away Unopened: A Memoir.* London: Faber and Faber, 2018.

Allmen, Tara, MD. *Menopause Confidential: A Doctor Reveals the Secrets to Thriving Through Midlife.* New York: HarperOne, reprint edition, 2017.

Altonji, Joseph G., Lisa B. Kahn, and Jamin D. Speer. "Cashier or Consultant? Entry Labor Market Conditions, Field of Study, and Career Success." *Journal of Labor Economics* 34, no. S1 (2016): S361–401.

Apter, Terri. *Secret Paths: Women in the New Midlife.* New York: W. W. Norton and Co., 1995.

Barnes, Kim, and Claire Davis. *Kiss Tomorrow Hello: Notes from the Midlife Underground by Twenty-Five Women over Forty.* New York: Doubleday, 2006.

Beaudoin, Tom. *Virtual Faith: The Irreverent*

Spiritual Quest of Generation X. San Francisco: Jossey-Bass, 1998.

Benjamin, Marina. *The Middlepause: On Life After Youth.* New York: Catapult, 2016.

Block, Jennifer. *Everything Below the Waist: Why Health Care Needs a Feminist Revolution.* New York: St. Martin's Press, 2019.

Boushey, Heather. *Finding Time: The Economics of Work-Life Conflict.* Cambridge, MA: Harvard University Press, 2016.

Chamberlain, Lisa. *Slackonomics: Generation X in the Age of Creative Destruction.* Cambridge, MA: Da Capo Press, 2008.

Cohen, Patricia. *In Our Prime: The Invention of Middle Age.* New York: Scribner, 2012.

Collins, Whitney. "Generation X's Journey from Jaded to Sated." Salon.com, October 1, 2013.

Conley, Dalton. *Elsewhere, U.S.A.: How We Got from the Company Man, Family Dinners, and the Affluent Society to the Home Office, BlackBerry Moms, and Economic Anxiety.* New York: Pantheon Books, 2009.

Conway, Jim. *Men in Midlife Crisis.* Colorado Springs, CO: Life Journey, 1997. Original publication: 1978.

Coontz, Stephanie. *Marriage, a History: How Love Conquered Marriage.* New York: Penguin, 2005.

Currier, Andrew F. *The Menopause; A Consideration of the Phenomena Which Occur to Women at the Close of the Child-Bearing Period.* New York: D. Appleton and Company, 1897.

Davis, Lisa Selin. "Opinion: Puberty for the Middle-Aged." *New York Times,* November 19, 2018.

de Marneffe, Daphne, PhD. *Maternal Desire: On Children, Love, and the Inner Life.* New York: Back Bay Books, 2004.

————. *The Rough Patch: Midlife and the Art of Living Together.* New York: Scribner, 2018.

Duffy, Brooke Erin. *(Not) Getting Paid to Do What You Love: Gender, Social Media, and Aspirational Work.* New Haven: Yale University Press, 2017.

Edelstein, Linda N. *The Art of Midlife: Courage and Creative Living for Women.* Westport, CT: Bergin and Garvey, 1999.

Epstein, Eve, and Leonora Epstein. *X vs. Y: A Culture War, a Love Story.* New York: Abrams Image, 2014.

Epstein, Randi Hutter, MD. *Aroused: The History of Hormones and How They Control Just About Everything.* New York: W. W. Norton, 2018.

Foster, Brooke Lea. "I Married a Millen-

nial. I Married a Gen Xer. Now What?"
New York Times, June 7, 2018.

Friedan, Betty. *The Fountain of Age.* New
York: Simon and Schuster, 1993. Paper-
back edition, 2006.

Gibson, Jules Lewis. "Gen X Takeover."
Gravitas, December 2015.

Gordinier, Jeff. *X Saves the World: How
Generation X Got the Shaft but Can Still
Keep Everything from Sucking.* New York:
Viking Penguin, 2008.

Greer, Germaine. *The Change: Women, Aging and the Menopause.* London: Hamish
Hamilton, 1991.

Gregg, Melissa. *Work's Intimacy.* Malden,
MA: Polity Press, 2011.

Gurwitch, Annabelle. *I See You Made an Effort: Older, Wiser, and (Getting) Happier.*
New York: Blue Rider Press, 2014.

Hanauer, Cathi, ed. *The Bitch Is Back.* New
York: William Morrow, 2016.

Hari, Johann. *Lost Connections: Uncovering
the Real Causes of Depression — and the
Unexpected Solutions.* New York: Bloomsbury, 2018.

Heilbrun, Carolyn. *Writing a Woman's Life.*
New York: Ballantine Books, 1988.

Hennessey, Matthew. *Zero Hour for Gen X:
How the Last Adult Generation Can Save*

America from Millennials. New York: Encounter Books, 2018.

Heti, Sheila. *Motherhood.* New York: Henry Holt and Co., 2018.

Hochschild, Arlie Russell, with Anne Machung. *The Second Shift: Working Families and the Revolution at Home.* New York: Penguin, 2012. Original publication: 1989.

Holland, Julie, MD. *Moody Bitches: The Truth About the Drugs You're Taking, the Sleep You're Missing, the Sex You're Not Having, and What's Really Making You Crazy.* New York: Penguin, 2015.

Hornblower, Margot. "Great Xpectations of So-Called Slackers." *Time,* June 9, 1997.

Houck, Judith A., PhD. *Hot and Bothered: Women, Medicine, and Menopause in Modern America.* Cambridge, MA: Harvard University Press, 2006.

Jaques, Elliott. *Creativity and Work.* Madison, CT: International Universities Press, Inc., Emotion and Behavior Monograph: Monograph No. 9, ed. George H. Pollock, 1990.

Jong, Erica. *Fear of Fifty: A Midlife Memoir.* New York: HarperCollins, 1994.

Kahn, Lisa B. "The Long-Term Market Consequences of Graduating from College in a Bad Economy." *Labour Econom-*

ics 17, no. 2 (2010): 303–16.

Katz, Donald. *Home Fires: An Intimate Portrait of One Middle-Class Family in Postwar America.* Unabridged Audible audiobook. Narrated by Joe Barrett. Release date: May 27, 2014.

Kihn, Martin. "The Gen X Hucksters." *New York,* August 29, 1994.

Kramer, Peter D. *Should You Leave? A Psychiatrist Explores Intimacy and Autonomy — and the Nature of Advice.* New York: Scribner, 1997.

Levinson, Daniel J. *The Seasons of a Man's Life.* New York: Knopf, 1978.

———. *The Seasons of a Woman's Life.* New York: Knopf, 1996.

Lipsky, David, and Alexander Abrams. *Late Bloomers: Coming of Age in Today's America: The Right Place at the Wrong Time.* New York: Crown, 1994.

Lock, Margaret. *Encounters with Aging: Mythologies of Menopause in Japan and North America.* Berkeley: University of California Press, 1993.

Luepnitz, Deborah Anna, PhD. *The Family Interpreted: Psychoanalysis, Feminism, and Family Therapy.* New York: Basic Books, 2002.

———. *Schopenhauer's Porcupines: Intimacy*

and Its Dilemmas — Five Stories of Psychotherapy. New York: Basic Books, 2003.

MacNicol, Glynnis. *No One Tells You This: A Memoir.* New York: Simon and Schuster, 2018.

Magai, Carol, and Susan H. McFadden, eds. *Handbook of Emotion, Adult Development, and Aging.* San Diego, CA: Academic Press, 1996.

Maran, Meredith. *The New Old Me: My Late-Life Reinvention.* New York: Blue Rider Press, 2017.

Miller, Marilyn Suzanne. *How to Be a Middle-Aged Babe.* New York: Scribner, 2007.

Moses, Barbara, PhD. *Women Confidential: Midlife Women Explode the Myths of Having It All.* New York: Marlowe and Company, 2006.

Oreopoulos, Philip, Till von Wachter, and Andrew Heisz. "The Short- and Long-Term Career Effects of Graduating in a Recession." *American Economic Journal: Applied Economics* 4, no. 1 (2012): 1–29.

Phillips, Adam. *Missing Out: In Praise of the Unlived Life.* New York: Farrar, Straus and Giroux, 2012.

Pitkin, Walter B. *Life Begins at Forty.* New York: McGraw-Hill, 1932.

Primis, Ashley, "Whatever Happened to Generation X?" *Philadelphia,* January 27, 2018.

Putnam, Robert D. *Our Kids: The American Dream in Crisis.* New York: Simon and Schuster, 2015.

Rauch, Jonathan. *The Happiness Curve: Why Life Gets Better After 50.* New York: Thomas Dunne Books, 2018.

Richards, Lyn, Carmel Seibold, and Nicole Davis, eds. *Intermission: Women's Experience of Menopause and Midlife.* Melbourne: Oxford University Press, 1997.

Robbins, Alexandra, and Abby Wilner. *Quarterlife Crisis: The Unique Challenges of Life in Your Twenties.* New York: Putnam/Tarcher, 2001.

Sawhill, Isabel V. *Generation Unbound: Drifting into Sex and Parenthood Without Marriage.* Washington, DC: Brookings Institution Press, 2014.

Schmidt, Susanne. "The Anti-Feminist Reconstruction of the Midlife Crisis: Popular Psychology, Journalism and Social Science in 1970s USA." *Gender and History* 30, no. 1 (March 2018):153–76.

Schwartz, Barry. *The Paradox of Choice: Why More Is Less.* New York: Ecco, 2004.

Scribner, Sara. "Generation X Gets Really

Old: How Do Slackers Have a Midlife Crisis?" Salon.com, August 11, 2013.

Senior, Jennifer. *All Joy and No Fun: The Paradox of Modern Parenthood.* New York: HarperCollins, 2014.

Sheehy, Gail. *Passages: Predictable Crises of Adult Life.* New York: Ballantine, 2006. Original publication: 1974.

————. *The Silent Passage: Menopause.* New York: Random House, 1992.

Shellenbarger, Sue. *The Breaking Point: How Female Midlife Crisis Is Transforming Today's Women.* New York: Henry Holt and Co., 2004.

Spencer, Anna Garlin. *Woman's Share in Social Culture.* New York and London: Mitchell Kennerley, 1913.

Steinke, Darcey. *Flash Count Diary: Menopause and the Vindication of Natural Life.* New York: Sarah Crichton Books, 2019.

Strauss, William, and Neil Howe. *Generations: The History of America's Future, 1584 to 2069.* New York: William Morrow and Co., 1991.

Thomas, Susan Gregory. *In Spite of Everything: A Memoir.* New York: Random House, 2011.

Traister, Rebecca. *All the Single Ladies: Unmarried Women and the Rise of an*

Independent Nation. New York: Simon and Schuster, 2016.

Twenge, Jean M., PhD. *iGen: Why Today's Super-Connected Kids Are Growing Up Less Rebellious, More Tolerant, Less Happy — and Completely Unprepared for Adulthood.* New York: Atria, 2017.

Utian, Wulf, MD. *Change Your Menopause: Why One Size Does Not Fit All.* Beachwood, OH: Utian Press, 2011.

Watkins, Elizabeth Siegel. *The Estrogen Elixir: A History of Hormone Replacement Therapy in America.* Baltimore, MD: Johns Hopkins University Press, 2007.

Williams-Ellis, Amabel. *The Art of Being a Woman.* London: Bodley Head, 1951.

Wilk, Katarina. *Perimenopower: The Ultimate Guide Through the Change.* Jönköping, Sweden: Ehrlin Publishing, 2018.

Wilson, Robert A., MD. *Feminine Forever.* New York: Pocket Books, 1968.

Yarrow, Allison. *90s Bitch: Media, Culture, and the Failed Promise of Gender Equality.* New York: Harper Perennial, 2018.

ACKNOWLEDGMENTS

I saw *Working Girl* when it came out in 1988. I was twelve, so most of the sex stuff went over my head, but I loved the part where Melanie Griffith's Tess McGill has a career-making idea for Trask Industries while reading tabloids on the Staten Island Ferry.

In 2017, I received an email from the editor Mamie Healey, then of Oprah.com, that read: "We came across something you wrote recently. And in one of those *Working Girl* /Trask Industries moments, we thought you might be great for a piece we're looking to assign." The proposed story was about why Generation X women seemed to be floundering in midlife.

I was dubious. Sure, I was having a hard time that summer. Yes, many of my friends were. But I wasn't bold enough to assume that this meant our whole *generation* was in trouble. A few weeks into the research,

335

though, I became convinced, then obsessed.

When the story came out that fall, the link was shared hundreds of thousands of times on Facebook in a matter of days. It seemed there was more to say on the topic than those six thousand words, so my heaven-sent agent Daniel Greenberg, in his usual graceful fashion, began looking for a publisher for a book-length version.

With the help of his colleague, the delightful Tim Wojcik, Dan found the project a dream home — one that would even let the book incorporate audio from the interviews. I heard Tess McGill's voice in my head: "And then I thought Trask . . . radio . . . Trask . . . radio!"

How lucky I am to have landed at Audible. All praise to Laura Gachko, David Blum, Kristin Lang, Don Katz, Jess Kessler, and Esther Bochner. Thanks especially to my editors Katie Salisbury — she of on-target Track Change bubbles like: "Damn. This is dark" — and wise and wonderful Jessica Almon Galland. Audible even put at my disposal the services of meticulous fact-checkers Susan Banta and Mary Marge Locker.

Thanks to Morgan Entrekin and his incredible team at Grove Atlantic, for publishing this book. Everyone I've encountered there — Kaitlin Astrella, Justina Batchelor, Julia Berner-Tobin, Sal Destro, Ian Dreiblatt, Chad Felix, Becca Fox, Susan Gamer, Jazmine Goguen, Judy Hottensen, Amy Hundley, Gretchen Mergenthaler, Erica Nunez, Deb Seager, Andrew Unger — has made me feel welcome and in good hands. The deservedly famous duo, editorial director Elisabeth Schmitz and editor Katie Raissian, worked wonders on this manuscript, as did their exquisite copyeditor Paula Cooper Hughes.

On a personal note, thank you, Asia Wong, Carlene Bauer, Tim Gunn, Tara McKelvey, Jason Zinoman, Sarah Hepola, Kathleen Hanna, Adam Horovitz, Murray Hill, Bridget Everett, Jim Andralis, Larry Krone, my pen pals, my godchildren, my poker buddies, plus everyone with the Invisible Institute. I'm especially grateful these days for Sob Sisters, the journalists' bar night I started last year with two women who vastly enhance my experience of midlife: Susannah Cahalan and Karen Abbott.

My parents, Brooke Alderson and Peter Schjeldahl, give Boomers a good name (and my father gave this book a very good proofread). My Millennial stepson, Andrew Blake; and Gen Z son, Oliver, give me hope for the future.

My husband, Neal Medlyn, whom I've been with since the year 2000, has been extra charming and helpful lately. I don't even care if it was because I was writing this book and he didn't want to look bad in it.

So many busy experts took my questions with equanimity — among them, Isabel Sawhill, Jillian Bashore, Jessica Smock, Amy Jordan Jones, Dan P. McAdams, Kelly Maxwell Haer, Elizabeth Earnshaw, Chip Rose, Janet Kennedy, Amy Goyer, Bruce Bergman, Catherine Coccia, Aaron Lohr, Faith Popcorn, Eric Young, Jacqueline Thielen, Randi Epstein, Mary Jane Minkin, Brooke Erin Duffy, William Doherty, Brad Wilcox, Deborah Luepnitz, Virginia T. Ladd, Tom Smith, Stacy Lindau, Jennifer Deal, Tom Smith, JoAnn Pinkerton, Bryn Chafin, Tara Allmen, Rebecca Henderson, Margie Lachman, Judith A. Houck, Laura Vanderkam, Joanne Ciulla, Linda Waite, Debby Carr, Robert Fluegge, Vaile Wright, and Kelly Roberts.

Finally, thanks most of all to the women who opened up to me about their lives with bravery, honesty, and dark humor. Tess McGill landed her dream job and Jack Trainer, played by in-his-prime Harrison Ford. Getting to spend time with so many smart and funny women, for me, has been that good.

ENDNOTES

Author's Note

1 In the 1970s, the number one girls' name, with a bullet, was Jennifer. "Popular Baby Names by Decade," SSA.gov. I interviewed six Jennys. The rest of the top ten names of the decade were: Amy, Melissa, Michelle, Kimberly, Lisa, Angela, Heather, Stephanie, and Nicole. Looking in my transcript folder, I see every one of these names.

Introduction

1 There are many opinions about what counts as Generation X. The Harvard Center's years are 1965–1984. So, from the year *Doctor Zhivago* came out to the year *Ghostbusters* did. George Masnick Fellow, "Defining the Generations," Housing Perspectives, Harvard Joint Center for

Housing Studies, November 28, 2012. I've also heard 1961 as a starting year — though in my experience people born in the early 1960s tend to identify more strongly with the Baby Boom — and either 1981 or 1985 as the Gen X end year. I tend to put most stock in the Pew Research Center: Silent Generation 1928–1945, Boomers 1946–1964, Gen X 1965–1980, Millennials 1981–1996, Generation Z 1997–2012. Michael Dimock, "Defining Generations: Where Millennials End and Generation X Begins," Pew Research Center, January 17, 2019. I'm also well aware of the fact that plenty of people think the whole business of describing a generational experience or ethos is a fool's errand. For this argument see, for example: David Costanza, "Can We Please Stop Talking About Generations as If They Are a Thing?" Slate.com, April 13, 2018. No, we can't. Next question.

2 Neil Howe and William Strauss, *13th Gen: Abort, Retry, Ignore, Fail?* (New York: Vintage, 1993). And in their 1991 book *Generations,* the same authors called us "Gen 13ers."

3 Paul Taylor and George Gao, "Generation X: America's Neglected 'Middle Child,' " Pew Research Center, June 5, 2014.

4 You can run these numbers a few different ways. By another measure, the breakdown is: Generation X at 66 million, Boomers at 74 million, and Millennials at 71 million. Kimberly Lankford, "Generation X: Time Is on Your Side for Retirement," *Kiplinger's Personal Finance,* January 3, 2019.

5 Richard Fry, "Millennials Projected to Overtake Baby Boomers as America's Largest Generation," Pew Research Center, March 1, 2018. (Also, note: some people count Gen X as just 1965–1977, in which case we're 45 million versus 75 million Millennials and 78 million Boomers.) Some demographers push for another category: Generation Y, which is generally thought to overlap a bit with both Gen X and Millennials. When people go with the Gen X years 1965 to 1979, the Gen Y birth years are typically given as 1980 to 1994. This category has always felt extra forced to me, though, so in this book I just stick with the bigger umbrellas of Boomer, Gen X, and Millennial.

6 Ed Mazza, "Generation Xers Have the Most Gen X Response to Being Left Off the List," *Huffington Post,* January 21, 2019.

7 Faith Popcorn, interview with the author,

August 30, 2017.

8 Jennifer Szalai, "The Complicated Origins of 'Having It All," *New York Times Magazine,* January 2, 2015.

9 It's worth noting that Helen Gurley Brown, who popularized the term with her 1982 bestseller, did not have children. Helen Gurley Brown, *Having It All: Love, Success, Sex, Money — Even If You're Starting with Nothing* (New York: Simon and Schuster, 1982).

10 *Generation Unbound* author Isabel V. Sawhill sees three issues that could make a real difference in the lives of women: birth control, so women can decide "if, when, and with whom to have children"; wage equality; and measures in aid of work-family balance (child care, flexible hours, paid family leave). Isabel V. Sawhill, "Improving Women's Lives: Purposeful Parenthood, Decent Wages, and Paid Family Leave," Talk for Bucks County Women's Advocacy Coalition, May 23, 2018. Provided to the author via email May 30, 2018.

11 Betsey Stevenson and Justin Wolfers, "The Paradox of Declining Female Happiness," *American Economic Journal: Economic Policy* 1, no. 2 (August 2009): 190–225.

12 In December 2017, Gallup reported that eight in ten Americans say they frequently or sometimes encounter stress in their daily lives, with women and people between the ages of thirty and forty-nine more likely than men or people of other ages to report frequent stress. The poll showed 49 percent of women reporting frequent stress, compared with 40 percent of men; and 56 percent of those aged fifty to sixty-four claimed frequent stress compared with, for example, 24 percent of those sixty-five and older. "Eight in 10 Americans Afflicted by Stress," Gallup .com, December 20, 2017.

13 Roni Caryn Rabin, "A Glut of Anti-depressants," *New York Times,* August 12, 2013. Also: Daniel Smith, "It's Still the 'Age of Anxiety.' Or Is It?" *New York Times,* January 14, 2012.

14 AARP Snapshots: Generation X Health. Retrieved August 5, 2018.

15 "Gen X Women: Flirting with Forty," J. Walter Thompson Intelligence, Slide-share.net, May 19, 2010. Retrieved August 5, 2018.

16 Margie E. Lachman, "Mind the Gap in the Middle: A Call to Study Midlife," *Research in Human Development* 12 (2015): 327–34.

17 There are *some* books about women going through crises in midlife. The cover of *A Woman's Worth* (1993) by Marianne Williamson (the presidential candidate) shows a sepia-tone, topless woman hunched over. I opened to a random page and read: "Most women today are borderline hysterical."

18 One interesting history of the concept of a midlife crisis is Susanne Schmidt's "The Anti-Feminist Reconstruction of the Midlife Crisis: Popular Psychology, Journalism and Social Science in 1970s USA," *Gender and History* 30, no. 1 (March 2018): 153–76. She argues that the usual way the "midlife crisis" idea is understood — as discovered by male social scientists and then popularized by Gail Sheehy's bestseller *Passages* (New York: Ballantine, 2006) — is wrong. She says, "the midlife crisis has historical roots in debate about gender roles and work and family values, and the shape these took in the United States in the 1970s." In other words, it was a conversation people were having; Sheehy reported on it; then a bunch of male social scientists whose work she had discussed along with her reporting and feminist critique said she had "popularized" their "discoveries."

19 Elliott Jaques, "Death and the Midlife Crisis," in *Creativity and Work* (Madison, CT: International Universities Press, 1990), 306.

20 Daniel J. Levinson, *The Seasons of a Man's Life* (New York: Knopf, 1978), 199.

21 Susan Krauss Whitbourne, "The Top 10 Myths About the Midlife Crisis," Psychology Today.com, July 21, 2012.

22 Someone could write a dissertation on women insisting they don't deserve to feel bad. In 1975's *The Romantic Englishwoman,* the wife (played by Glenda Jackson) is asked in bed by her husband (played by Michael Caine): "Are you discontented?" Her reply: "I would be, but I don't feel I have the right." The husband steals the line for a screenplay he's writing.

23 The song was also covered in 1998 by Ace of Base. After I broke up with him, my boyfriend when I was fourteen left many notes in my locker that sometimes included Ace of Base and Wilson Phillips lyrics. This did not rekindle the passion.

24 Richard Eisenberg, "Boomers and Gen Xers Skipping Health Care Due to Cost," Forbes.com, March 27, 2018.

25 Viv Albertine, *To Throw Away Unopened* (London: Faber and Faber, 2018), 21.

26 Jim Tankersley, "Jobless Recoveries Are Here to Stay, Economists Say, But It's a Mystery Why," *Washington Post,* September 19, 2013.

27 Lynnette Khalfani-Cox, "5 Interesting Facts About Generation X," AARP.org. Retrieved May 18, 2018. According to research by Experian, Millennials average $52,120 in debt (including mortgages, credit cards, and student and car loans); Boomers and the Silent Generation $87,438; Generation X, $125,000. Also see: Chris Matthews, "America's Most Indebted Generation? Gen X," Fortune .com, August 27, 2014.

28 Khalfani-Cox, "5 Interesting Facts About Generation X." Retrieved August 5, 2018.

29 Jeffry Bartash, "Higher Rents and Home Prices Drive Increase in Consumer Prices in December, CPI Finds," *MarketWatch,* January 12, 2018.

30 The average age of a college-educated first-time mother in big cities like San Francisco or New York City is now thirty-three. Quoctrung Bui and Claire Cain Miller, "The Age That Women Have Babies: How a Gap Divides America," *New York Times,* August 4, 2018.

31 Clive Thompson, "You Know Who's

Really Addicted to Their Phones? The Olds," *Wired,* March 27, 2018.

32 Sheehy, *Passages,* 345.

33 Ibid., xviii.

1: Possibilities Create Pressure

1 Details of Title IX are on the US Department of Education's website, www2.ed.gov. Retrieved July 5, 2018.

2 Enjoli commercial, YouTube.com. Retrieved August 30, 2018. I recently ordered some Enjoli off eBay. It smells like musk, jasmine, peach, and unrealistic expectations.

3 "I'm a Woman" was written by Jerry Leiber and Mike Stoller and recorded in 1962 first by Christine Kittrell and then by Peggy Lee. The song has since been covered by Bette Midler, Reba McEntire, Wynonna Judd, cast members of *Ally McBeal;* and, in duets, Raquel Welch with Cher, in 1975 on *The Cher Show* and in 1978 with Miss Piggy on *The Muppet Show.*

4 *Working Girl* (1988), YouTube.com. Retrieved July 11, 2018.

5 Matthew Hennessey, *Zero Hour for Gen X* (New York: Encounter, 2018), 45.

6 Caryn James, "Television View; 'Murphy

Brown' Meets 'Life with Father,' " *New York Times,* November 15, 1992.

7 Kathryn Chetkovich's "Envy," *Granta 82: Life's Like That,* July 1, 2003, is a revealing essay about what it's like to be Jonathan Franzen's girlfriend and a writer with her own ambitions.

8 Jay D. Teachman and Kathleen M. Paasch, "Financial Impact of Divorce on Children and Their Families," *Future of Children* 4, no. 1: Children and Divorce (Spring 1994): 63–83.

9 Mary E. Corcoran and Ajay Chaudry, "The Dynamics of Childhood Poverty," *Future of Children* 7, no. 2 (1997): 40–54. And P. O. Corcoran, unpublished paper, Survey Research Center, University of Michigan at Ann Arbor, May 1994.

10 According to one study done when many Gen Xers were teenagers, even when combined, the asset base of a divorced couple was just half that of married couples. Joseph P. Lupton and James P. Smith, "Marriage, Assets, and Savings," Labor and Population Program, Working Paper Series 99-12, Rand Corporation, 1999. This disparity tended to be even greater for black children: according to one study, 87 percent of those with continuously married parents exceeded their parents'

income in adulthood, whereas only 53 percent with divorced parents did. "Family Structure and the Economic Mobility of Children," Economic Mobility Project, PewTrusts.org, May 18, 2010.

11 Ted Halstead, "A Politics for Generation X," *Atlantic,* August 1999.

12 The average child in 1979 scored lower in confidence assessments than 81 percent of kids in the mid-1960s. Jean M. Twenge, *Generation Me* (New York: Free Press, 2006), 69.

13 James Poniewozik, "All-TIME 100 TV Shows: *The Day After,*" *Time,* August 11, 2014.

14 S. J. Kiraly, "Psychological Effects of the Threat of Nuclear War," *Canada Family Physician* 32 (January 1986): 170–74.

15 Tom McBride, "The Mindset List of Generation X," Mindsetlist.com, May 15, 2017.

16 Daniel Burstein, "How Much Millennials, Gen X, and Other Age Groups Trust TV Ads When Making a Purchase Decision," MarketingSherpa.com, August 22, 2017.

17 "Slinky — It's a Wonderful Toy — It's Fun for a Girl and a Boy," YouTube.com. Retrieved August 16, 2018.

18 Kevin Gilbert, "Goodness Gracious,"

from the album *Thud,* 1995. Posted on YouTube December 1, 2008. Retrieved August 28, 2018.

19 "Nature of President Clinton's Relationship with Monica Lewinsky," Section I.A.5, *Washington Post* online. Retrieved July 7, 2018.

20 *MTV Video Music Awards,* September 14, 1984.

21 Cynthia Heimel, *Sex Tips for Girls* (New York: Simon and Schuster, 1983), 123.

22 Tad Friend, "Do-Me Feminism," *Esquire,* February 1994.

23 Katherine Rosman, "At the College That Pioneered the Rules on Consent, Some Students Want More," *New York Times,* February 24, 2018.

24 "Patience," Guns N' Roses, 1989. Retrieved from YouTube May 29, 2018.

25 Erin Blakemore, "Big Bird Narrowly Escaped Death on the *Challenger* Mission," History.com, January 26, 2018.

26 "*Challenger* Disaster Live on CNN," 1986. Retrieved from YouTube May 29, 2018.

27 Beatings in public schools were explicitly permitted by a 1977 US Supreme Court ruling. Corporal punishment is still legal in many states but has declined since Gen X was in school. Melinda D. Anderson,

"Where Teachers Are Still Allowed to Spank Students," *Atlantic*, December 15, 2015.

28 Joe Keohane, "The Crime Wave in Our Heads," *Dallas News*, March 23, 2010.

29 The Crimes Against Children Research Center has identified this decline as one of the most significant data points in recent years. Lisa Jones and David Finkelhor, "The Decline in Child Sexual Abuse Cases," *Juvenile Justice Bulletin*, Office of Juvenile Justice and Delinquency Prevention, January 2001.

30 Since 1990, sexual abuse has declined by 63 percent and physical abuse by 56 percent. And that is a nationwide trend, appearing in many studies and from many sources. Institute of Medicine and National Research Council. *Child Maltreatment Research, Policy, and Practice for the Next Decade: Workshop Summary* (Washington, DC: National Academies Press, 2012).

31 Halstead, "A Politics for Generation X."

32 Jeff Shesol, "Fun in Politics? As If," *Washington Post*, March 2, 1997.

33 Third Millennium (Douglas Kennedy et al.), "Third Millennium Declaration," in John Williamson et al., eds, *The Generational Equity Debate* (New York: Columbia

University Press, 1993).

34 Michele Mitchell, "Lead or Leave Has Left," NPR.org, March 14, 1996.

35 "Billionaires for Bush . . . or Gore," De mocracyNow.com, July 31, 2000.

36 George Packer, "Decline and Fall: How American Society Unraveled," *Guardian,* June 19, 2013.

37 V.J. Felitti, R.F. Anda, et al., "Relationship of Childhood Abuse and Household Dysfunction to Many of the Leading Causes of Death in Adults: The Adverse Childhood Experiences (ACE) Study," *American Journal of Preventive Medicine* 14 (1998): 245–58.

38 Jane Stevens, email to the author, July 10, 2018. Stevens, founder and publisher of ACEsConnection.com, said she didn't know of any studies comparing ACEs through generations, but she encouraged me to reach out to the ACEs Connection community of twenty-four thousand members, which I did.

39 Kimberly Konkel, a member of ACEs Connection, email to the author, July 17, 2018.

40 "Suicide Rates for Males and Females by Age in the United States (2016)," National Institute of Mental Health website. Data Courtesy of CDC.

41 "Leading Causes of Death (LCOD) by Age Group, All Females — United States, 2015," Centers for Disease Control and Prevention.

42 Felitti, Anda, et al., "Relationship of Childhood Abuse and Household Dysfunction to Many of the Leading Causes of Death in Adults."

43 On women and high ACE scores see, for example: Donna Jackson Nakaza, *Childhood Disrupted: How Your Biography Becomes Your Biology, and How You Can Heal* (New York: Atria Books, 2015). You can check your own ACE score at Aces TooHigh.com.

44 William Mahedy and Janet Bernardi, *A Generation Alone* (Downers Grove, IL: InterVarsity Press, 1994), 32.

45 "Selling to Gen X Parents" slide in "Generation X" PowerPoint, Scouting .com. Retrieved July 12, 2018.

46 "Fred Rogers: Look for the Helpers." Retrieved from YouTube, February 12, 2019.

47 "*Mister Rogers' Neighborhood:* 1969 Senate Hearing." Retrieved from YouTube, September 19, 2018.

48 "Fred Rogers Talks About Tragic Events in the News." Retrieved from YouTube, July 7, 2018.

49 David Sedaris has written that in middle age everyone goes crazy over one of two things: our diet or our dogs. David Sedaris, "Leviathan," *New Yorker,* January 5, 2015.

50 Brené Brown says women do one of three things: move away from the shame (shrinking), move toward the shame (overfunctioning), or move against the shame (try to make the other person feel shame). Brené Brown, "Listening to Shame," TED2012, Ted.com, minute 15.

51 Bryn Chafin LMSW, interview with the author, June 12, 2018.

2: The Doldrums

1 Lauren E. Corona et al., "Use of Other Treatments Before Hysterectomy for Benign Conditions in a Statewide Hospital Collaborative," *American Journal of Obstetrics and Gynecology* 212, no. 3 (March 2015): 304e1–304e7.

2 Boomers had an average of eleven sexual partners. J. M. Twenge, R. A. Sherman, and B. E. Wells, "Changes in American Adults' Sexual Behavior and Attitudes, 1972–2012," *Archives of Sexual Behavior* 44, no. 8 (November 2015): 2273–85.

3: The Caregiving Rack

1 Dorothy A. Miller, "The 'Sandwich' Generation: Adult Children of the Aging," *Social Work* 26, no. 5 (September 1981), pp. 419–23.

2 A 2018 Pew study found that 12 percent of US parents are also caring for an adult. Gretchen Livingston, "More Than One-in-Ten U.S. Parents Are Also Caring for an Adult," Pew Research Center, November 29, 2018.

3 Jennifer Senior, *All Joy and No Fun* (New York: HarperCollins, 2014), 9.

4 Claire Cain Miller, "The Relentlessness of Modern Parenting," *New York Times,* December 25, 2018.

5 More fun stats: Today, 70 percent of mothers with children under the age of eighteen are in the workforce, with both parents employed full-time in close to half of households with a mother and a father. Twenty-four percent are raising children alone. Gretchen Livingston, "7 Facts About U.S. Moms," Pew Research Center, May 10, 2018.

6 Lyman Stone, "One Way to Boost Fertility: Babysit Other People's Kids," Institute for Family Studies, January 24, 2018.

7 Katrina Leupp, "Depression, Work and

Family Roles, and the Gendered Life Course," *Journal of Health and Social Behavior,* October 20, 2017. This study makes use of the National Longitudinal Survey of Youth.

8 M. Lino, K. Kuczynski, N. Rodriguez, and T. Schap, *Expenditures on Children by Families,* 2015. Miscellaneous Publication no. 1528-2015, US Department of Agriculture, Center for Nutritional Policy and Promotion, 2017.

9 Melissa Korn, "Schools Post Record-Low Acceptance Rates," *Wall Street Journal,* March 30–31, 2019.

10 Lydia Saad, "Children a Key Factor in Women's Desire to Work Outside the Home," Gallup.com, October 7, 2015.

11 Barkley and FutureCast, *Millennials as New Parents: The Rise of a New American Pragmatism,* September 2013.

12 Gretchen Livingston, "More Than a Million Millennials Are Becoming Moms Each Year," Pew Research Center, May 4, 2018.

13 Eli J. Finkel, *The All-or-Nothing Marriage* (New York: Dutton, 2017), 137–38.

14 This is, for example, how Ethan Hawke's character describes his marriage in *Before Sunset* (2004).

15 Stephanie Pappas, "Why Supermoms Should Chill," *Live Science,* August 20, 2011.

16 Anna Pallai, interview with the author, March 14, 2017.

17 John Mulaney, *The Comeback Kid,* Netflix, 2015. Text is here: scrapsfromtheloft.com.

18 Richard Schlesinger, "*Sesame Street . . .* for Adults Only?" CBSNews.com, January 17, 2008.

19 This cartoon explaining the mental load went viral: "You Should Have Asked," emmaclit.com, May 20, 2017.

20 *American Time Use Survey Summary — 2017 Results,* Bureau of Labor Statistics, June 28, 2018.

21 Kim Parker and Gretchen Livingston, "7 Facts About American Dads," Pew Research Center, June 13, 2018.

22 "Raising Kids and Running a Household: How Working Partners Share the Load," Pew Research Center, November 11, 2015.

23 Claire Cain Miller, "Men Do More at Home, but Not as Much as They Think," *New York Times,* November 12, 2015.

24 Marta Murray-Close and Misty L. Heggeness, "Manning Up and Womaning Down: How Husbands and Wives Report

Their Earnings When She Earns More," Social, Economic, and Housing Statistics Division, US Census Bureau, June 6, 2018.

25 Richard V. Reeves and Isabel V. Shill, "Men's Lib!" *New York Times,* November 14, 2015.

26 "I Don't Want to Be the Breadwinner in My Marriage Anymore!" *Dear Sugars,* NPR, December 3, 2016.

27 *Caregiving in the U.S. 2015,* National Alliance for Caregiving and the AARP Public Policy Institute, June 2015. The report also found that 62 percent of what are called higher-hour caregivers (meaning more than twenty hours a week) are women. Fifty-nine percent of these caregivers felt they had "no choice in taking on their caregiving role."

28 "Gen X Women: Flirting with Forty," J. Walter Thompson Intelligence, Slide share.net, May 19, 2010. Retrieved August 5, 2018.

29 Donald Redfoot, Lynn Feinberg, and Ari Houser, "The Aging of the Baby Boom and the Growing Care Gap: A Look at Future Declines in the Availability of Family Caregivers," *Insight on the Issues* 85 (August 2013), AARP Public Policy Institute. Also worth noting: some 28

percent of caregivers also have a child under the age of eighteen living in their household. And 60 percent are employed. The average duration of caregiving is four years, though 24 percent of caregivers wind up in the role for five years or more. *Caregiving in the U.S. 2015,* National Alliance for Caregiving and the AARP Public Policy Institute, June 2015.

30 "Caregiving Costs to Working Caregivers," MetLife Research, June 2011.

31 *Caregiving in the U.S. 2015,* National Alliance for Caregiving and the AARP Public Policy Institute, June 2015.

32 Chuck Rainville, Laura Skufca, and Laura Mehegan, "Family Caregiving and Out-of-Pocket Costs: 2016 Report," AARP Research.

33 Amy Goyer, interview with the author, August 8, 2017.

34 Brendan Finn, *Millennials: The Emerging Generation of Family Caregivers,* AARP Public Policy Institute, May 2018.

35 "FMLA Is Working," Department of Labor, 2013 factsheet.

36 Katy Hall and Chris Spurlock, "Paid Parental Leave: U.S. vs. the World," HuffingtonPost.com, February 4, 2013.

37 "Stress in America: Uncertainty About Health Care," American Psychological As-

sociation, January 24, 2018.

38 Emily Cooke, "In the Middle Class, and Barely Getting By," *New York Times,* July 9, 2018.

39 Michael Shermer, "The Number of Americans with No Religious Affiliation Is Rising," *Scientific American,* April 1, 2018.

40 Emma Green, "It's Hard to Go to Church," *Atlantic,* August 23, 2016.

41 Tom Beaudoin, *Virtual Faith* (San Francisco: Jossey-Bass, 1998), 25.

42 Chris Mooney, "More and More Americans Think Astrology Is Science," *Mother Jones,* February 11, 2014. According to General Social Survey data compiled by the National Science Foundation, around 40 percent of Generation X sees astrology as "very" or "sort of" scientific.

43 Text to the author from Mira Ptacin, May 27, 2018.

44 According to the US Department of Health and Human Services, in the United States the percentage of need being met is less than a third. *Designated Health Professional Shortage Areas Statistics,* Bureau of Health Workforce, Health Resources and Services Administration (HRSA), US Department of Health and Human Services, as of December 31,

2017. Retrieved from KFF.org August 9, 2018.

45 Min Jin Lee also discusses this in the introduction to the new reissue of her novel *Free Food for Millionaires* (New York: Grand Central Publishing, 2018).

4: Job Instability

1 The truck should clearly be called Wheels of Cheese.

2 Nikki Graf, Anna Brown, and Eileen Patten, "The Narrowing, but Persistent, Gender Gap in Pay," Pew Research Center, April 9, 2018.

3 Bureau of Labor Statistics reports that women's median weekly earnings are highest for women thirty-five to forty-four and slightly less for women forty-five to fifty-four. Men's earnings, not surprisingly, are higher than women's in all age groups, including these Gen X–heavy cohorts, but it's notable that earnings are higher for men forty-five to fifty-four than for men thirty-five to forty-four; there's no plateau for men. *Women's and Men's Earnings by Age in 2016,* BLS.gov, August 25, 2017.

4 Claudia Goldin, "How to Win the Battle of the Sexes over Pay (Hint: It Isn't

Simple)," *New York Times,* November 10, 2017.

5 Stephen J. Rose and Heidi Hartmann, *Still a Man's Labor Market: The Slowly Narrowing Gender Wage Gap,* Institute for Women's Policy Research, November 26, 2018.

6 Claire Cain Miller, "When Wives Earn More Than Their Husbands, Neither Partner Likes to Admit It," *New York Times,* July 17, 2018.

7 "America's Highest Paying Jobs See Women Underrepresented," LinkedIn.com, March 29, 2017.

8 *The State of the Gender Pay Gap 2018,* PayScale.com, 2018.

9 Faith Guvenen, Greg Kaplan, Jae Song, and Justin Weidner, "Lifetime Incomes in the United States over Six Decades," NBER working paper no. 23371, April 2017.

10 Julia Pimsleur, CEO of the children's language-learning company Little Pim, founded the Double-Digit Academy in 2013. Through lectures, workshops, and her book, she seeks to help female entrepreneurs raise money for their companies and get to a million dollars in revenues. As of research from 2011 to 2014, only 2 percent of women-owned firms reach a million in revenues. Pimsleur is trying to

get the proportion of venture capital going to women to at least 10 percent. Elaine Pofeldt, "How Women Can Build Million-Dollar Businesses," Money.com, September 30, 2015.

11 "List: Women CEOs of the S&P 500," Catalyst.org, January 24, 2019.

12 Justin Wolfers, "Fewer Women Run Big Companies Than Men Named John," *New York Times,* March 2, 2015.

13 Nationally 37 percent: Lydia Dishman, "The Overlooked Benefit Gen X Workers Need," *Fast Company,* May 7, 2018. Globally 51 percent: The *Global Leadership Forecast 2018.* Stephanie Neal and Richard Wellins, "Generation X — Not Millennials — Is Changing the Nature of Work," CNBC.com, April 11, 2018.

14 Andrew Balls, "The Flattening of Corporate Management," in "The Flattening of the Firm: Evidence from Panel Data on the Changing Nature of Corporate Hierarchies," National Bureau of Economic Research working paper no. 9633. Retrieved from NBER.org June 20, 2018.

15 Lauren Sherman, "Hudson's Bay Company Announces 2,000 Job Cuts, Including Senior Management," BusinessofFashion.com, June 8, 2017.

16 Gen X leaders had an average of only

1.2 promotions in the past five years, compared with 1.6 for Millennials and 1.4 for Boomers. *Global Leadership Forecast 2018*. Neal and Wellins, "Generation X — Not Millennials — Is Changing the Nature of Work."

17 "MetLife's 17th Annual U.S. Employee Benefit Trends Study: Thriving in the New Work-Life World," March 2019, 20.

18 Stella Fayer, Alan Lacey, and Audrey Watson, *STEM Occupations: Past, Present, and Future,* BLS.gov, January 2017.

19 Alexis Krivkovich et al., "Women in the Workplace 2018," McKinsey.com, October 2018.

20 Liana Christin Landivar, "Disparities in STEM Employment by Sex, Race, and Hispanic Origin," Census.gov, September 2013.

21 Eileen Appelbaum, email to the author, June 10, 2018.

22 Eileen Appelbaum, *What's Behind the Increase in Inequality?* Center for Economic and Policy Research, September 2017.

23 *Women and Work in the Fourth Industrial Revolution,* World Economic Forum, 2016. Retrieved from reports.weforum.org November 3, 2018.

24 Lauren Stiller Rikleen, "Older Women Are Being Forced Out of the Workforce," *Harvard Business Review,* March 10, 2016.

25 Teresa Ghilarducci, "Why Women over 50 Can't Find Jobs," *PBS NewsHour,* January 4, 2016.

26 Dionne Searcey, "For Women in Midlife, Career Gains Slip Away," *New York Times,* June 23, 2014.

27 Natalie Kitroeff, "Unemployment Rate Hits 3.9%, a Rare Low, as Job Market Becomes More Competitive," *New York Times,* May 4, 2018.

28 Julia Angwin, Noam Scheiber, and Ariana Tobin, "Facebook Job Ads Raise Concerns About Age Discrimination," *New York Times,* December 20, 2017. In March 2019, Facebook announced that it would stop letting employment advertisers target specific age groups. Noam Scheiber and Mike Isaac, "Facebook Halts Ad Targeting Cited in Bias Complaints," *New York Times,* March 19, 2019.

29 Steve Cavendish, "The Fight to Be a Middle-Aged Female News Anchor," *New York Times,* March 11, 2019.

30 William Safire, "On Language: Downsized," *New York Times,* May 26, 1996.

31 Margot Hornblower, "Great Xpectations

of So-Called Slackers," *Time,* June 9, 1997.

32 "Generation X: Overlooked and Hugely Important," Center for Work-Life Policy press release for: *The X Factor: Tapping into the Strengths of the 33-to-46-Year-Old Generation,* Center for Work-Life Policy, September 16, 2011.

33 Ann Sterzinger, "Hey Generation X: Stop Apologizing," Medium.com, March 28, 2018. She adds: "And now we're supposed to be checking our privilege? I would rather you check my asshole."

34 Amy Adkins, "Millennials: The Job-Hopping Generation," Gallup.com, May 12, 2016.

35 According to one study, "intergenerational cohesion" was named one of the most significant challenges their companies faced. Tania Lennon, "Managing a Multi-Generational Workforce," Hay Group, thought paper, 2015.

36 Rebecca Henderson, interview with the author, August 3, 2017.

37 The 2018 Catalyst Awards Conference: Carla Harris Keynote, New York Hilton Midtown, March 20, 2018, YouTube.com, minute 45.

38 Theodore Caplow, Louis Hicks, and

Ben J. Wattenberg, Companion website to PBS special *The First Measured Century,* PBS.org/fmc. Retrieved March 21, 2018. Statistics sourced from sites including *Statistical Abstract of the United States* (Washington, DC: US Census Bureau, annual).

39 Claudia Goldin, "The Quiet Revolution That Transformed Women's Employment, Education, and Family," National Bureau of Economic Research, working paper no. 11953, January 2006.

40 Claudia Goldin, "A Grand Gender Convergence: Its Last Chapter," *American Economic Review* 104, no. 4 (2014): 1091–1119.

41 Grainne Fitzsimons, Aaron Kay, and Jae Yun Kim, " 'Lean In' Messages and the Illusion of Control," *Harvard Business Review,* July 30, 2018.

42 Ellen Pao, *Reset* (New York: Random House, 2017), 78–79.

43 Opheli Garcia Lawler, "Michelle Obama Is Done with the Gospel of 'Lean In,' " The Cut, December 2, 2018.

44 Susan Chira, "Why Women Aren't C.E.O.s, According to Women Who Almost Were," *New York Times,* July 21, 2017.

45 "The Double-Bind Dilemma for Women in Leadership," Catalyst.org, 2007.

46 One woman sued Walmart because her boss said Demi Moore had done an acrobatic routine on *Late Night* while pregnant, and so the employee had no excuse not to lift heavy boxes. Never mind that Demi Moore was a rich, famous actress *and* that the flipping in question was done by a stunt double. Natalie Kitroeff and Jessica Silver-Greenberg, "Pregnancy Discrimination Is Rampant Inside America's Biggest Companies," *New York Times,* June 15, 2018.

47 "Gen X Women: Flirting with Forty."

48 Joanne B. Ciulla, *The Working Life: The Promise and Betrayal of Modern Work* (New York: Three Rivers Press, 2000), 234.

49 Joanne B. Ciulla, PhD, interview with the author, April 27, 2018.

50 If CEOs don't make diversity a priority, states could compel them to. In the fall of 2018, California became the first state to mandate female board directors, with noncompliance punishable by a fine. Vanessa Fuhrmans, "California Becomes First State to Mandate Female Board Directors," *Wall Street Journal,* September 30, 2018. Don't hold your breath, though. The Paycheck Fairness Act has failed repeatedly since being introduced in 2012.

Burgess Everett, "Senate Blocks Pay Equity Bill," Politico.com, September 15, 2014.

51 Sara Horowitz, "Why Are More Women Than Men Freelancing?" FastCompany .com, March 11, 2015.

52 A couple of years ago, a report by the National Bureau of Economic Research said that between 2005 and 2015, the proportion of workers engaged in "alternative work arrangements" rose from 10.7 to 15.8 percent. Lawrence F. Katz and Alan B. Krueger, "The Rise of and Nature of Alternative Work Arrangements in the United States, 1995–2015," NBER, working paper no. 22667, September 2016.

53 Robert McGuire, "Ultimate Guide to Gig Economy Data," Nation1099.com, July 16, 2018.

54 Micha Kaufman, "Five Reasons Half of You Will Be Freelancers in 2020," Forbes .com, February 28, 2014.

55 Brooke Erin Duffy, *(Not) Getting Paid to Do What You Love: Gender, Social Media, and Aspirational Work* (New Haven: Yale University Press, 2017), 4–5.

56 Brooke Erin Duffy, PhD, interview with the author, March 19, 2018.

5: Money Panic

1 Inequality.org has a roundup of eye-opening charts, culled from sources including the Congressional Budget Office and the Institute for Policy Studies.

2 C. Eugene Steuerle, Signe-Mary McKernan, Caroline Ratcliffe, and Sisi Zhang, "Lost Generations? Wealth Building Among Young Americans," Urban Institute, March 14, 2013.

3 "Retirement Reality Bites Unless Answers Are Implemented," Fifteenth Annual Transamerica Retirement Survey of Workers, August 2014.

4 Raj Chetty, David Grusky, et al., *The Fading American Dream: Trends in Absolute Income Mobility Since 1940,* Equality of Opportunity Project at Harvard, executive summary, December 2016. See also: Raj Chetty, Nathaniel Hendren, Maggie R. Jones, and Sonya R. Porter, "Race and Economic Opportunity in the United States: An Intergenerational Perspective," Equality of Opportunity Project, equality-of-opportunity.org. Retrieved June 27, 2018.

5 Robert Fluegge, interview with the author, May 3, 2018.

6 "Living Paycheck to Paycheck Is a Way of

Life for Majority of U.S. Workers, According to New CareerBuilder Survey," CareerBuilder.com, August 24, 2017.

7 Lisa Chamberlain, *Slackonomics* (Cambridge, MA: Da Capo Press, 2008), 4.

8 Daniel H. Pink, *When: The Scientific Secrets of Perfect Timing* (New York: Riverhead Books, 2018), 101.

9 Robert D. McFadden, "Scramble for Jobs: Graduating into a Recession — A Special Report," *New York Times,* April 22, 1991.

10 Carol Kleiman, "Bleak Job Market Awaits Class of '92," *Chicago Tribune,* December 13, 1991.

11 Carol Kleiman, "For '93 Graduates, Job-Hunting 101 Won't Be a Breeze," *Chicago Tribune,* December 11, 1992.

12 These summaries by Lipsky and Abrams are based on Lindquist-Endicott Survey data, and I removed some of their exposition within the quote. David Lipsky and Alexander Abrams, *Late Bloomers: Coming of Age in Today's America: The Right Place at the Wrong Time* (New York: Times Books, 1994), 64.

13 "Figure 5: Wages of Young College Grads Have Been Falling Since 2000," EPI analysis of Current Population Survey Outgoing Rotation Group microdata, Economic Policy Institute, epi.org. Re-

trieved August 9, 2018.

14 Lisa B. Kahn, "The Long-Term Labor Market Consequences of Graduating from College in a Bad Economy," *Labour Economics* 17, no. 2 (2010): 303–16. I found this study in Pink, *When: The Scientific Secrets of Perfect Timing,* 99.

15 Halstead, "A Politics for Generation X."

16 Joshua C. Pinkston and James R. Spletzer, "Annual Measures of Gross Job Gains and Gross Job Losses," *Monthly Labor Review,* November 2004.

17 "Why You Need to Know About Gen-X," Goldman Sachs, YouTube.com, August 19, 2016. Retrieved June 25, 2018.

18 "Retirement Reality Bites Unless Answers Are Implemented," Fifteenth Annual Transamerica Retirement Survey of Workers, August 2014.

19 Sarah O'Brien, "Majority of Young Workers Have Already Tapped Their Retirement Savings," CNBC.com, August 21, 2018.

20 "The MetLife Study of Gen X: The MTV Generation Moves into Mid-Life," April 2013.

21 D. H. Lawrence, *The Rocking-Horse Winner* (Mankato, MN: Creative Education, Inc., 1982), 10.

22 "Insights from Fiscal 50's Key Measures of State Fiscal Health," Pew Research Center, March 11, 2019.

23 For example: Matt Phillips, "What's the Yield Curve? 'A Powerful Signal of Recessions' Has Wall Street's Attention," *New York Times,* June 25, 2018.

24 Neil Irwin, "What Will Cause the Next Recession? A Look at the 3 Most Likely Possibilities," *New York Times,* August 2, 2018.

25 Steve Henderson, "Spending Habits by Generation," blog.dol.gov, November 3, 2016.

26 "The Allianz Generations Apart Study," Allianz Life, June 16, 2016.

27 Amrita Jayakumar, "Millennial Money: Playing Catch-Up with Credit Cards," *Washington Post,* December 18, 2018.

28 Catey Hill, "All the Ways Gen X Is Financially Wrecked," Market-Watch, March 11, 2019.

29 Bob Sullivan, "State of Credit: 2017," Experian.com, January 11, 2018. See also, on car loans, TransUnion: Steven Finlay, "Subprime Lending Decreases; Consumer Credit Scores Increase," WardsAuto.com, August 22, 2018. And, on overall debt: Amelia Josephson, "The Average Debt by Age," Smart Asset, August 20, 2018.

30 Brittney Mayer, "3 Studies Show the Average Credit Score by Age and Generation (2019)," BadCredit.org. Retrieved March 20, 2019.

31 "A New Financial Reality: The Balance Sheets and Economic Mobility of Generation X," Pew Charitable Trusts, September 2014.

32 Richard Fry, "Gen X Rebounds as the Only Generation to Recover the Wealth Lost After the Housing Crash," Pew Research Center, July 23, 2018.

33 Guvenen et al., "Lifetime Incomes in the United States over Six Decades."

34 "By 2016, as middle-aged Americans, they were 12 percent less likely to say they were satisfied financially, and 18 percent more likely to say they were unhappy." Robert Gebeloff, "Generation Grumpy: Why You May Be Unhappy If You're Around 50," New York Times, November 30, 2017.

35 Judi Ketteler, "Drowning at Midlife? Start Swimming," New York Times, May 17, 2018.

36 "BLS Spotlight on Statistics: The Recession of 2007–2009," Bureau of Labor Statistics, BLS.gov, February 2012.

37 Les Christie, "Home Prices Post Record 18% Drop," CNNMoney.com, December

30, 2008.

38 "The State of the Nation's Housing," Joint Center for Housing Studies of Harvard University, 2015.

39 Ryan McMaken, "U.S. Home Prices Are Rising Twice as Fast as Inflation," Busi nessInsider.com, May 2, 2016.

40 "Census of Housing," Census.gov. Retrieved August 6, 2018.

41 Chris Kirkham, "Housing Bust Lingers for Generation X," *Wall Street Journal,* April 8, 2016.

42 For a terrifying interactive graphic, see: "Mapping America's Rental Housing Crisis," urban.org, April 27, 2017.

43 Emily Badger, "Why Don't People Who Can't Afford Housing Just Move Where It's Cheaper?" *New York Times,* May 15, 2018.

44 Ben Casselman, "Housing Market Slows, as Rising Prices Outpace Wages," *New York Times,* September 29, 2018.

45 Lisa Chamberlain, interview with the author, March 26, 2018.

46 Abby Jackson, "This Chart Shows How Quickly College Tuition Has Skyrocketed Since 1980," BusinessInsider.com, July 20, 2015.

47 College Board, "Tuition and Fee and Room and Board Changes over Time,"

collegeboard.com. Accessed November 9, 2017 for a chart by ProCon.org.

48 Andrew Atkinson, "Millennials Buck the Wealth Trend," *Bloomberg Businessweek,* February 20, 2018.

49 M. H. Miller, "Been Down So Long It Looks Like Debt to Me," *Baffler,* no. 40 (July 5, 2018).

50 North American Menopause Society, menopause.org. Retrieved August 9, 2018.

51 "Women's Health in Review," NIH.gov. Retrieved August 9, 2018.

52 "Breast Cancer Risk in American Women," National Cancer Institute, Cancer.gov, September 24, 2012.

53 Virginia T. Ladd, RT, interview with the author, July 24, 2017.

54 "A Summary of the 2018 Annual Reports: Status of the Social Security and Medicare Programs," ssa.gov. Retrieved March 20, 2019.

55 Per this study the proportion of Gen Xers who don't believe Social Security will provide them with full benefits when they retire is 70 percent: "The MetLife Study of Gen X: The MTV Generation Moves into Mid-Life," April 2013. According to Transamerica that number is 83 percent: "Retirement Reality Bites Unless Answers Are Implemented," Fifteenth

Annual Transamerica Retirement Survey of Workers, August 2014.

56 Jo Ann Jenkins, "Protect America's Bedrock Programs," *AARP Bulletin,* July/August 2015.

57 Helaine Olen, "Many Americans Think They'll Never Receive Social Security Benefits. They're Wrong," *Washington Post,* June 8, 2018.

58 Ron Lieber, "How to Win at Retirement Savings," *New York Times,* June 15, 2017.

59 Andrew Osterland, "Advisors Brace for the $30 Trillion 'Great Wealth Transfer,' " CNBC.com, June 16, 2016.

60 Mark Rovner, "The Next Generation of American Giving," Blackbaud Institute, April 2018.

61 "Costs of Care," LongTermCare.gov. National average costs in 2016. Retrieved December 24, 2018.

62 Rich Cohen, "Why Generation X Might Be Our Last, Best Hope," *Vanity Fair,* August 11, 2017.

63 Hennessey, *Zero Hour for Gen X,* x.

6: Decision Fatigue

1 David M. Gross and Sophfronia Scott, "Proceeding with Caution," *Time,* July 16, 1990.

2 Molly Ringwald, "What About 'The Breakfast Club'?" *New Yorker,* April 6, 2018.

3 Elizabeth Earnshaw, interview with the author, August 4, 2017.

4 The book was inspired by a popular 2014 article he wrote for the *Atlantic:* Jonathan Rauch, "The Real Roots of Midlife Crisis," *Atlantic,* December 2014.

5 Susan Krauss Whitbourne summarizes them in "That Midlife Happiness Curve? It's More Like a Line," PsychologyToday.com, September 15, 2018.

6 Tara Parker-Pope, "The Midlife Crisis Goes Global," *New York Times,* January 30, 2008.

7 Jonathan Rauch, *The Happiness Curve* (New York: Thomas Dunne Books, 2018), 70.

8 Laura Carstensen, "Older People Are Happier," TEDxWomen, 2011.

9 "Midlife Crisis?" Part of the series: Middle Adulthood, Learning Seed, 2000. Platform: Kanopy via the New York Public Library.

10 Erik German and Solana Pyne, *The Mommy Wars,* RetroReport.org and Quartz.com, June 28, 2016.

11 Judy (Syfers) Brady, " 'I Want a Wife': The Timeless '70s Feminist Manifesto,"

Reprinted in TheCut.com, November 22, 2017. Original publication: *New York,* December 20, 1971.

12 Heather Boushey, *Finding Time* (Cambridge, MA: Harvard University Press, 2016), x–5.

13 Heather Boushey, "Are Women Opting Out? Debunking the Myth," Center for Economic and Policy Research briefing paper, November 2005.

14 Beaudoin, *Virtual Faith,* xi.

15 Meredith Bagby, *Rational Exuberance: The Influence of Generation X on the New American Economy* (New York: Dutton, 1998), xi.

16 "The Whiny Generation," *Newsweek,* October 31, 1993.

17 Carl Wilson, "Riff My So-Called Adulthood," *New York Times Magazine,* August 4, 2011.

18 For the movie's ironic backstory, see Soraya Roberts, "*Reality Bites* Captured Gen X with Perfect Irony," *Atlantic,* March 6, 2019.

19 Something similar is argued by Camille S. Johnson, PhD, in "The Lloyd Dobler Effect," *Psychology Today,* January 31, 2014. She also says we may be unconsciously judging romantic prospects against idealized partners like Lloyd

Dobler and finding ourselves dissatisfied with reality as a result.

20 In his book about the heyday of Gen X indie bands, Michael Azerrad quotes a convincing, if cynical, theory about why the Seattle scene was so focused on community: extreme consumption of Ecstasy and beer. Michael Azerrad, *Our Band Could Be Your Life: Scenes from the American Indie Underground 1981–1991* (New York: Back Bay Books, 2002), 419.

21 Ginia Bellafante, " 'Risky Business' and Brett Kavanaugh, 35 Years Later," *New York Times,* September 27, 2018.

22 Alina Tugend, "Too Many Choices: A Problem That Can Paralyze," *New York Times,* February 26, 2010.

7: Single, Childless

1 Sarah Hepola, interview with the author, February 17, 2018.

2 "Current Population Survey, 2016 Annual Social and Economic Supplement," Census.gov, 2017.

3 Joyce A. Martin et al., "Births: Final Data for 2017," *National Vital Statistics Reports* 67, no. 8, US Department of Health and Human Services, November 7, 2018.

4 "Gallup Analysis: Millennials, Marriage

and Family," Gallup.com, May 19, 2016. The Bureau of Labor Statistics Current Population Survey that same year said the proportion of never-married Gen Xers was 19 percent, about 1 in 5.

5 Wendy Wang and Kim Parker, "Record Share of Americans Have Never Married," PewSocialTrends.org, September 24, 2014.

6 Marissa Hermanson, "How Millennials Are Redefining Marriage," Gottman.com, July 3, 2018.

7 U.S. Census Bureau, Decennial Censuses, 1890 to 1940, and Current Population Survey, Annual Social and Economic Supplements, 1947 to 2018.

8 Kay Hymowitz et al., "Knot Yet: The Benefits and Costs of Delayed Marriage in America," National Marriage Project at the University of Virginia, National Campaign to Prevent Teen and Unplanned Pregnancy, and the Relate Institute, 2013.

9 For more on the subject of good news, see: Rebecca Traister, *All the Single Ladies* (New York: Simon and Schuster, 2016).

10 Eleanor Barkhorn, "Getting Married Later Is Great for College-Educated Women," *Atlantic,* March 15, 2013.

11 Hymowitz et al., "Knot Yet: The Benefits

and Costs of Delayed Marriage in America."

12 "Women in the Housing Ecosystem Report," vol. 1: "The State of Women's Homeownership," Women in the Housing and Real Estate Ecosystem (NAWRB), 2018.

13 Joseph Stromberg, "Eric Klinenberg on *Going Solo*," *Smithsonian,* February 2012.

14 Jon Birger, *Date-onomics* (New York: Workman Publishing), 2015.

15 "Population Facts," NYC Department of City Planning. Retrieved March 15, 2019.

16 Wendy Wang and Kim Parker, "Ch. 3: Marriage Market for All Unmarried Adults," PewSocialTrends.org, September 24, 2014.

17 By age 33, among Boomers only 17 percent of men and 14 percent of women had graduated with a four-year degree. Among Gen X it's 18 percent of men and 20 percent of women. Erin Currier, "How Generation X Could Change the American Dream," Pew Research, January 26, 2018.

18 Lora E. Park, Ariana F. Young, and Paul W. Eastwick, "(Psychological) Distance Makes the Heart Grow Fonder: Effects of Psychological Distance and Rela-

tive Intelligence on Men's Attraction to Women," *Personality and Social Psychology Bulletin* 41, no. 11 (November 1, 2015): 1459–73.

19 Susan Patton, "A Little Valentine's Day Straight Talk," *Wall Street Journal,* February 13, 2014.

20 *UnREAL,* season 3, episode 1: "Oath," February 26, 2018.

21 David E. Bloom and Neil G. Bennett, "Marriage Patterns in the United States," National Bureau of Economic Research, working paper no. 1701, *Labor Studies,* September 1985.

22 Traister, *All the Single Ladies,* 272.

23 Vanessa Grigoriadis, "Baby Panic," *New York,* May 20, 2002.

24 *Saturday Night Live,* May 18, 2002.

25 "Committee Opinion Number 589," American College of Obstetricians and Gynecologists, March 2014. Reaffirmed 2018.

26 Megan Garber, "When Newsweek 'Struck Terror in the Hearts of Single Women,' " *Atlantic,* June 2, 2016.

27 Briallen Hopper, "How to Be Single," *Los Angeles Review of Books,* February 11, 2016.

28 Bella DePaulo, *Singled Out,* highlights document on BellaDePaulo.com. Re-

trieved on July 25, 2018.

29 Glynnis MacNicol, "I'm in My 40s, Child-Free and Happy. Why Won't Anyone Believe Me?" *New York Times,* July 5, 2018.

30 Lyman Stone, "American Women Are Having Fewer Children Than They'd Like," *New York Times,* February 13, 2018.

31 Claire Cain Miller, "Americans Are Having Fewer Babies. They Told Us Why," *New York Times,* July 5, 2018.

32 Briallen Hopper, *Hard to Love* (New York: Bloomsbury, 2019), 257.

33 Centers for Disease Control and Prevention, American Society for Reproductive Medicine, Society for Assisted Reproductive Technology, *2016 Assisted Reproductive Technology Fertility Clinic Success Rate Report* (Atlanta, GA: US Department of Health and Human Services, October 2018).

34 Ibid.

35 "Adoption Cost and Timing in 2016–2017," AdoptiveFamilies.com. Retrieved March 28, 2019.

36 "About Adoption from Foster Care," AdoptUSKids.org. Retrieved March 28, 2019.

8: After the Divorce

1 Abigail Abrams, "Divorce Rate in U.S. Drops to Nearly 40-Year Low," Time.com, December 5, 2016.

2 Susan Gregory Thomas, "The Good Divorce," *New York Times,* October 28, 2011.

3 Elizabeth Stabinski, MS, LMFT, interview with the author, August 29, 2017.

4 Rose McDermott et al, "Breaking Up Is Hard to Do, Unless Everyone Else Is Doing It Too: Social Network Effects on Divorce in a Longitudinal Sample," *Social Forces* 92, Issue 2 (December 2013): 491–519.

5 "One paradox of gender, marriage, and the life course," writes Stanford professor Michael J. Rosenfeld, "is that young single women appear to desire marriage and commitment more than men do, yet married women appear to be less satisfied by their marital experiences than married men are." Michael J. Rosenfeld, "Who Wants the Breakup? Gender and Breakup in Heterosexual Couples," in *Social Networks and the Life Course,* ed. Duane F. Alwin et al. (New York: Springer, 2018), 221–43.

6 Daphne de Marneffe, PhD, *The Rough*

Patch (New York: Simon and Schuster, 2018), 80.

7 Daphne de Marneffe, PhD, interview with the author, October 24, 2017.

8 William Doherty, PhD, interview with the author, July 27, 2018.

9 On the dating site OkCupid, "the older men get, the younger the women they message (relative to their age)." By the time they're fifty-five, men send more than half of their messages to women at least eight years younger than they are. Dale Markowitz, "Undressed: What's the Deal with the Age Gap in Relationships?" Ok Cupid.com, June 1, 2017.

10 Elizabeth E. Bruch and M. E. J. Newman, "Aspirational Pursuit of Mates in Online Dating Markets," *Science Advances* 4, no. 8 (August 8, 2018).

11 Stacy Tessler Lindau, MD, interview with the author, August 7, 2017.

12 Jane E. Brody, "A Dip in the Sex Drive, Tied to Menopause," *New York Times,* March 30, 2009.

13 Kristen P. Mark, Erick Janssen, and Robin R. Milhausen, "Infidelity in Heterosexual Couples: Demographic, Interpersonal, and Personality-Related Predictors of Extradyadic Sex," Center for Sexual Health Promotion, Department of Ap-

plied Health Science, Indiana University, published online at KinseyInstitute.org, June 11, 2011.

14 Kelly Roberts, PsyD, interview with the author, March 1, 2016.

15 More than half of divorcees and widows are in for financial surprises. Among the most common shocks: secret spending, debt, and outdated wills. Suzanne Woolley, "Rise of 'Gray' Divorce Forces Financial Reckoning After 50," Bloomberg.com, April 13, 2018.

9: Perimenopause

1 Bernice L. Neugarten, "The Awareness of Middle Age," in Bernice L. Neugarten, ed., *Middle Age and Aging: A Reader in Social Psychology* (Chicago: University of Chicago Press, 1968, fifth impression, 1975), 93.

2 "Perimenopause" is a term that almost no layperson used twenty years ago but that now is much more popular. The Google n-gram for the word "perimenopause" shows almost no instances of use in 1975 and then a pretty steady rise from 1990 until now.

3 The Rev. Fred B. Trevitt and Freda Dunlop White, *How to Face the Change of Life*

with Confidence (New York: Exposition Press, 1955), 44.

4 Germaine Greer, *The Change* (London: Hamish Hamilton, 1991), 7.

5 "Used by women to increase sexual energy and pleasure; this nephrite jade stone helps connect the second chakra (the heart) and yoni for optimal self-love and well-being." Retrieved June 27, 2018 from goop.com.

6 Michael Pollan, *How to Change Your Mind* (New York: Penguin, 2018).

7 Ayelet Waldman, *A Really Good Day* (New York: Knopf, 2017).

8 Cartoon by Hilary Fitzgerald Campbell, *The New Yorker,* January 14, 2019.

9 Kristi Coulter, "Giving Up Alcohol Opened My Eyes to the Infuriating Truth About Why Women Drink," Qz.com, August 21, 2016.

10 "The field of nonsurgical female genital rejuvenation is growing as the changes women experience receive greater attention," says PlasticSurgery.org in its description of the procedure. Retrieved June 27, 2018.

11 JoAnn Pinkerton, interview with the author, July 26, 2017.

12 M. de Kruif, A. T. Spijker, and M. L. Molendijk, "Depression During the

Perimenopause: A Meta-Analysis," *Journal of Affective Disorders* 206 (December 2016): 174–80.

13 Jennifer Wolff, "Doctors Don't Know How to Treat Menopause Symptoms," *AARP,* August/September 2018.

14 Janine A. Clayton, MD, NIH associate director for Women's Health, "Celebrating a Quarter Century in Women's Health Research," Office of Research on Women's Health, NIH, "Advisory Committee on Research on Women's Health," Forty-Second Meeting minutes, September 25, 2016.

15 Study of Women's Health Across the Nation et al., "Duration of Menopausal Vasomotor Symptoms over the Menopause Transition," *JAMA Internal Medicine* 175, no. 4 (April 2015): 531–39.

16 "Menopause Affects Japanese Women Less Than Westerners," Center for the Advancement of Health, ScienceDaily, July 27, 1998.

17 Chisato Nagata et al., "Soy Product Intake and Hot Flashes in Japanese Women: Results from a Community-Based Prospective Study," *American Journal of Epidemiology* 153, no. 8 (April 15, 2001): 790–93.

18 Marilyn Bender, "Doctors Deny Wom-

an's Hormones Affect Her as an Executive," *New York Times,* July 31, 1970.

19 Johann Hari, *Lost Connections* (New York: Bloomsbury, 2018), 3.

20 Asia Wong, interview with the author, December 26, 2018.

21 Julie Holland, MD, *Moody Bitches* (New York: Penguin, 2015), 290.

22 John Lazarou, "OB/GYNs Need Menopause Medicine Training," *Johns Hopkins University Gazette,* June 2013.

23 Wolff, "Doctors Don't Know How to Treat Menopause Symptoms."

24 The site is menopause.org. Note that in some parts of the country you will find there are none within a hundred miles. Finding one who takes your insurance presents another challenge.

25 Tara Allmen, MD, interview with the author, April 11, 2018.

26 Utian goes so far as to say that between 2002 and 2012, as many as 91,610 postmenopausal women may have died prematurely because of health problems that estrogen could have helped prevent. "Dr. Wulf Utian Speaks Out on Hormone Therapy," HealthyWomen.org. Retrieved August 9, 2018.

27 Robert D. Langer, "The Evidence Base for HRT: What Can We Believe?" *Climac-*

teric 2, (April 2017): 91–96.

28 *The 2017 Hormone Therapy Position Statement of the North American Menopause Society, NAMS,* 2018; 24(7):728–53.

29 Bootie Cosgrove-Mather, "New Methods Ease Menopause," AP for CBSNews.com, December 29, 2003.

30 Randi Hutter Epstein and Mary Jane Minkin, MD, interview with the author, March 1, 2018. You can also watch Dr. Minkin's great videos about menopause at madameovary.com.

31 The NIH provides a "Fact Sheet for Consumers" for each of the major supplements at nccih.nih.gov.

32 Randi Hutter Epstein, *Aroused: The History of Hormones and How They Control Just About Everything* (New York: W. W. Norton, 2018), 252.

33 Full disclosure: I was guest-editing The Cut at the time and had her do the story for the magazine. Darcey Steinke, "What Menopause Taught Me," TheCut.com, August 23, 2015. She expanded this into a book, *Flash Count Diary* (New York: Sarah Crichton Books, 2019).

34 Pam Houston, *Deep Creek: Finding Hope in the High Country* (New York: W.W. Norton & Co, 2019), 96.

35 Amy Jordan Jones, Ed.M, LCSW, interview with the author, October 31, 2018.

10: The Very Filtered Profile Picture

1 *2016 Cosmetic Plastic Surgery Statistics Report,* American Society of Plastic Surgeons, PlasticSurgery.org. Retrieved June 27, 2018.

2 Anna Garvey, "The Oregon Trail Generation: Life Before and After Mainstream Tech," SocialMediaWeek.org, April 21, 2015.

3 Some of us died from diphtheria, measles, and typhoid fever. It was a super-fun game. Laura Turner Garrison, "Where Are They Now? Diseases That Killed You in Oregon Trail," MentalFloss.com, May 28, 2014.

4 Hennessey, *Zero Hour for Gen X,* 9–10.

5 "The use of Facebook was negatively associated with well-being." Holly B. Shakya and Nicholas A. Christakis, "Association of Facebook Use with Compromised Well-Being: A Longitudinal Study," *American Journal of Epidemiology* 185, no. 3 (February 1, 2017): 203–211.

6 Libby Copeland, "The Anti-Social Network," Slate.com, January 26, 2011.

7 Adam Phillips, *Missing Out* (New York:

Farrar, Straus and Giroux, 2012), xii.

8 In his bestseller *The Shallows,* Nicholas Carr wrote that the internet has changed our brains and not so as to make us calmer or more reflective but rather in a way that's evaporating our ability to concentrate or think deeply. Nicholas Carr, *The Shallows* (New York: W. W. Norton and Co., 2010), 6–7.

9 A recent study suggested that just having a cell phone nearby distracts us enough to reduce our cognitive ability. Adrian F. Ward, Kristen Duke, Ayelet Gneezy, and Maarten W. Bos, "Brain Drain: The Mere Presence of One's Own Smartphone Reduces Available Cognitive Capacity," *Journal of the Association for Consumer Research* 2, no. 2 (April 2017): 140–54.

10 Matthew A. Christensen et al., "Direct Measurements of Smartphone Screen-Time: Relationships with Demographics and Sleep," *PLoS ONE,* November 9, 2016.

11 Jonah Engel Bromwich, "Generation X More Addicted to Social Media Than Millennials, Report Finds," *New York Times,* January 27, 2017. The research described here is from Nielsen.

12 Ashley Strickland, "Women in Midlife Aren't Sleeping Enough, Study Says,"

CNN.com, September 7, 2017.

13 Laura Vanderkam, interview with the author, April 9, 2018.

14 Sherry Turkle, *Alone Together: Why We Expect More from Technology and Less from Each Other,* third ed. (New York: Basic Books, 2017), 17.

15 Kevin Granville, "Facebook and Cambridge Analytica: What You Need to Know as the Fallout Widens," *New York Times,* March 19, 2018.

16 Allison Benedikt, "The Year in Push Alerts," Slate.com, November 6, 2017.

17 Nicole Spector, " 'Headline Stress Disorder': How to Cope with the Anxiety Caused by the 24/7 News Cycle," NBCNews.com, December 16, 2017. Updated June 20, 2018. Retrieved June 27, 2018.

18 Alyssa Davis and Diana Liu, "Daily Worry Up Sharply Since U.S. Presidential Election," Gallup.com, March 1, 2017.

19 Dan Witters, "Americans' Well-Being Declines in 2017," Gallup.com, November 8, 2017.

20 "Stress in America: Uncertainty About Health Care," American Psychological Association, January 24, 2018.

21 Interview by the author with Dr. Vaile Wright, one of the psychologists on the

team, April 9, 2018.

22 "Women in America: Indicators of Social and Economic Well-Being," prepared for the White House Council on Women and Girls, March 2011.

23 Deborah A. Christel and Susan C. Dunn, "Average American Women's Clothing size," *International Journal of Fashion Design, Technology and Education* 10, no. 2 (2017).

24 Tim Gunn, "Tim Gunn: Designers Refuse to Make Clothes to Fit American Women. It's a Disgrace," *Washington Post,* September 8, 2016.

25 Barry Schwartz, *The Paradox of Choice* (New York: Ecco, 2004), 213.

26 Judith A. Houck, PhD, interview with the author, April 23, 2018. See also: Judith A. Houck. *Hot and Bothered: Women, Medicine, and Menopause in Modern America* (Cambridge, MA: Harvard University Press, 2006).

27 Oliver Burkeman, *The Antidote: Happiness for People Who Can't Stand Positive Thinking* (New York: Farrar, Straus and Giroux, 2012), 7.

28 W. H. Auden, "The Globe" in *The Dyer's Hand* (New York: Vintage International, 1989), 175.

29 Carol Hanisch, interview with the author, March 10, 2017.

30 Robert D. Putnam, *Our Kids: The American Dream in Crisis* (New York: Simon and Schuster, 2015), 211.

31 "Female Friends Spend Raucous Night Validating the Living Shit Out of Each Other," *Onion,* February 23, 2012.

32 Alex Williams, "Why Is It Hard to Make Friends over 30?" *New York Times,* July 13, 2012.

33 Rozette Rago, "Finding Female Friends over 50 Can Be Hard. These Women Figured It Out," *New York Times,* December 31, 2018. And: FindYourCru.com.

11: New Narratives

1 Kate Chopin, "The Story of an Hour" (New York: Holt, Rinehart and Winston, 1894). Retrieved online, July 9, 2018.

2 Shai Davidai and Thomas Gilovich, "The Headwinds/Tailwinds Asymmetry: An Availability Bias in Assessments of Barriers and Blessings," *Journal of Personality and Social Psychology* 111, no. 6 (December 2016): 835–51.

3 Tim Minchin, commencement address, University of Western Australia, 2013 graduation ceremony.

4 Eve Babitz, *Slow Days, Fast Company* (New York: New York Review of Books reprint edition, 2016), 54–55.

5 Tonya Pinkins with Brad Simmons, "A Naughty and Nice Evening," *Green Room* 42 (December 16, 2018).

6 Jennifer J. Deal, PhD, interview with the author, April 16, 2018.

7 Taffy Brodesser-Akner, "The Big Business of Being Gwyneth Paltrow," *New York Times Magazine,* July 25, 2018.

8 Our attitude has the ability not only to make our life more tolerable but also to potentially change our circumstances. In one study, college students who reframed their struggles as an opportunity for growth got better grades. Tara Parker-Pope, "How to Build Resilience in Mid-life," *New York Times,* July 25, 2017.

9 Ann Voskamp, "When You're Struggling with Midlife and Another Year Older — Remember This," FoxNews.com, August 19, 2018.

10 Marah Eakin, " 'It Smelled Like Death': An Oral History of the *Double Dare* Obstacle Course," *AV Club,* November 12, 2016.

11 Bruce Feiler, "The Stories That Bind Us," *New York Times,* March 15, 2013.

12 Richard Fry and Kim Parker, "Early

Benchmarks Show 'Post-Millennials' on Track to Be Most Diverse, Best-Educated Generation Yet," Pew Research Center, November 15, 2018.

13 Among those who've done work around these ideas of generativity are Erik Erikson and Bertram Cohler. The Northwestern personality psychologist Dan P. McAdams, who also runs the Foley Center for the Study of Lives, arguably invented the field of narrative psychology. See his article: "The Life Narrative at Midlife," *New Directions for Child and Adolescent Development* 145 (2014): 57–69. This is from the abstract: "Contemporary research reveals that the most generative adults in American society tend to construe their lives as narratives of personal redemption. As such, life stories may serve as valuable psychological resources for midlife adults, even as they reflect and refract prevailing cultural themes."

14 Dan P. McAdams, "Caring Lives, Redemptive Life Stories," talk given at the Love and Human Agency Conference at Franklin and Marshall College, September 20, 2014. Viewed on YouTube March 29, 2018. He talks about the conflict between personal agency and societal structure. He identifies "care" as a major theme of

midlife. To avoid stagnation, you need to care for the next generation, either children or the future in some other way. See also: Dan P. McAdams, " 'I Am What Survives Me': Generativity and the Self," in J. A. Frey and C. Vogler, eds., *Self-Transcendence and Virtue: Perspectives from Philosophy, Psychology, and Theology* (London: Routledge, April 2018). Provided to the author via email.

15 Dan P. McAdams, PhD, interview with the author, April 9, 2018.

16 Margaret Renkl, "The Gift of Menopause," *New York Times,* August 5, 2018.

17 Anna Garlin Spencer, *Woman's Share in Social Culture* (New York and London: Mitchell Kennerley, 1913), 231.

18 Mary Ruefle, "Pause," *Granta 131: The Map Is Not the Territory* (London: Granta Publications, June 1, 2015).

19 William Strauss and Neil Howe, *Generations* (New York: William Morrow and Co., 1991), 414–16.

20 In 2006, researchers came up with a way to calculate your resilience score, a measure of the "protective factors" that could counterbalance a high "adverse childhood experience" score. You can check yours at acestoohigh.com.

21 "A red nose!" says Elsie Lindtner, the narrator of a 1910 Danish novel about a woman's midlife crisis. "It is the worst catastrophe that can befall a beautiful woman. I always suspected this was the reason why Adelaide Svanstroem took poison. Poor woman, unluckily she did not take a big enough dose!" Karin Michaëlis, *The Dangerous Age: Letters and Fragments from a Woman's Diary* (Evanston, IL: Northwestern University Press, 1991), 117–18. I think about Adelaide Svanstroem a lot. I have a feeling she turned out fine.

ABOUT THE AUTHOR

Award-winning journalist **Ada Calhoun** is the author of *Wedding Toasts I'll Never Give,* named one of Amazon's Best Books of the Month and one of *W* magazine's top ten memoirs of 2017; and *St. Marks Is Dead,* one of the best books of 2015, according to *Kirkus Reviews,* the *Village Voice,* and the *Boston Globe.* She has written for *O Magazine, National Geographic Traveler,* and the *New York Times.*